The Great Convergence VS. The Great Divergence

Zheng Yongnian

The Great Convergence VS. The Great Divergence

Chinese Modernization Under Momentous World Changes

浙江人民出版社
ZHEJIANG PEOPLE' S PUBLISHING HOUSE

palgrave
macmillan

Zheng Yongnian
School of Public Policy
The Chinese University of Hong Kong
Shenzhen, China

Translated by
Jin Ping
School of International Cultures
and Communications
Communication University of Zhejiang
Hangzhou, China

ISBN 978-981-96-7845-7 ISBN 978-981-96-7846-4 (eBook)
https://doi.org/10.1007/978-981-96-7846-4

The print edition is not for sale in China (Mainland). Customers from China (Mainland) please order the print book from: Zhejiang People's Publishing House
Jointly published with Zhejiang People's Publishing House
ISBN of the Copublisher's edition: 978-7-213-10994-2

Translation from the Chinese Simplified language edition: "大汇合与大分流：大变局下的中国现代化" by Zheng Yongnian, © Zhejiang People's Press 2023. Published by Zhejiang People's Press. All Rights Reserved.

This Palgrave Macmillan imprint is published by the registered company Springer Nature Singapore Pte Ltd.
The registered company address is: 152 Beach Road, #21-01/04 Gateway East, Singapore 189721, Singapore

Zheng Yongnian

The Great Convergence VS. The Great Divergence

Chinese Modernization Under Momentous World Changes

浙江人民出版社
ZHEJIANG PEOPLE' S PUBLISHING HOUSE

palgrave
macmillan

Zheng Yongnian
School of Public Policy
The Chinese University of Hong Kong
Shenzhen, China

Translated by
Jin Ping
School of International Cultures
and Communications
Communication University of Zhejiang
Hangzhou, China

ISBN 978-981-96-7845-7 ISBN 978-981-96-7846-4 (eBook)
https://doi.org/10.1007/978-981-96-7846-4

The print edition is not for sale in China (Mainland). Customers from China (Mainland) please order the print book from: Zhejiang People's Publishing House
Jointly published with Zhejiang People's Publishing House
ISBN of the Copublisher's edition: 978-7-213-10994-2

Translation from the Chinese Simplified language edition: "大汇合与大分流: 大变局下的中国现代化" by Zheng Yongnian, © Zhejiang People's Press 2023. Published by Zhejiang People's Press. All Rights Reserved.

This Palgrave Macmillan imprint is published by the registered company Springer Nature Singapore Pte Ltd.
The registered company address is: 152 Beach Road, #21-01/04 Gateway East, Singapore 189721, Singapore

Publication Notes and Acknowledgments

"At present, the momentous changes unseen in a century is accelerating its evolution across the world. Our world, our times and our history are changing with more obvious characteristics". This judgment by the Chinese leader accurately summarizes the overall development trend of the world today.

In recent years, our generation has witnessed the transition from rule to chaos in the world order. Over the past several decades, the international system with the United Nations at its core and the international order underpinned by international law have ensured the world peace and stability on the whole. In the state of globalization, the economic interdependence of all countries has reached an unprecedented degree, the logic of world economy operation has been formed, and what we call "a community with a shared future for mankind" has gradually taken shape among countries. However, since the Trump administration, the United States has been engaged in a big push for anti-globalization, with economic nationalism prevailing and trade protectionism making its way. With regard to China in particular, the United States, without mercy, has carried out all-around containment and crackdown through trade wars and other means. The trade war initiated by the United States has led to an imbalance in the order of globalization. Following this, the COVID-19 pandemic has further impacted the internal and external order of all countries and the momentous world changes have accelerated its evolving steps. Within countries, the gap between the poor and the rich has brought out the spread of social discontent, and further speeded up the rise of populism. The outbreak of Russia-Ukraine conflict and the extreme sanctions imposed by Western countries afterwards, disturbed the global supply chains, trigged the global energy and food crisis, further impelled the differentiation and combination of various strategic forces and quickened the pace of anti-globalization. The cornerstone of the existing international order has been severely damaged and the international order has become regionalized and fragmentized. At a time when geopolitics has become the dominant force, it is becoming dramatically harder to reformulate international rules and reshape international order.

The momentous world changes have thrown people into an era of uncertainty and insecurity. "Will this world ever be all right?" In the face of the current chaos and conflict in the world, especially the sharply intensifying confrontation among major powers and the trends of anti-globalization, people generally have a deep worry and anxiety about the prospect of the world order and their personal future lives.

It is obvious that the current momentous changes have exerted a profound influence over every country and every society. Among them, China not only has become an important force promoting momentous changes, but also has been deeply influenced by them. Objectively speaking, while providing China with opportunities to gain momentum and move forward, the momentous changes are also bringing us historic tests and pressures.

The change of situation is a process. At the moment, we are in the early stages of the changes. How the situation will evolve in future, whether technological innovation and reglobalization will really change the current international power structure, and whether China can win more space for its development, to a large extent, depends on how we judge the key issues we are facing and what strategic actions we should take. Past practical experiences have shown that if there is no precise judgment of the international situation, it will be difficult to formulate correct policies and seize strategic opportunities.

On many occasions, the Chinese leader has put forward the judgment "momentous changes unseen in a century". Quite a lot of domestic scholars in the ideological and theoretical circles have been setting off a discussion on the nature, characteristics, causes, and strategic measures that China should adopt concerning this judgment. I have long been concerned about China's domestic transformation and its external relations in the context of globalization. Books such as *Trade and Rationality* (2020), *Limited Globalization* (2021) and *Opportunities in Great Changes* (2021) include my articles and comments I have published in recent years about the world order changes and China's development strategies. On this basis, the present book is to make a further thinking, sorting out and systematic elaborating of Chinese modernization. In my opinion, no matter how the international situation changes, for China, the core of the new momentous changes it is facing today is still the worldwide anti-globalization or even deglobalization. In the past 40 years and over, Chinese modernization has gained unprecedented opportunities and great achievements due to its merging into the wave of economic globalization. Then with the intensifying momentum of anti-globalization and deglobalization today, where Chinese modernization is going has become the most challenging question raised by the momentous changes for China. Therefore, this book also puts the main focus on clarifying the relationship between Chinese path to modernization and economic globalization, exploring the deep-seated reasons for the momentous world changes and the significant challenges they posed to China's continued modernization, and more importantly, what China should do next. In my view, China's goal should be clear, that is, instead of moving with the tide of anti-globalization, China should continue to adhere to the concept of peace and development, further open up to the outside world and carry out the domestic reform, strive to get rid of the confrontation structure, innovate the development modes, do its best to lead a new wave of globalization, and become a participant, contributor, and leader of the new world changes.

This book has its origins in real-world problems, but its core ideas have been formed during the process of many academic exchanges. In several small seminars held by The Institute for International Affairs, Qianhai at the Chinese University of Hong Kong (Shenzhen), the Institute of Public Policy at South China University of Technology, the Guangzhou Institute of the Guangdong-Hong Kong-Macao Greater Bay Area, and the Institution of Politics and Economics at Shanghai Jiao Tong University, many of these viewpoints in the book have been exchanged with the researchers from these institutes. They also raised many questions which motivated and urged me to think more and deeply. Here I would like to thank many colleagues who participated in the discussions. At the same time, I would also like to thank Wang Libo, editor-in-chief and

Mo Yingping, responsible editor of Zhejiang People's Publishing House. They have provided strong support with their own professionalism and dedication for the publication of this book.

January 2023 Zheng Yongnian

Translation Notes and Acknowledgments

On May 9, 2023, Professor Zheng Yongnian's new Chinese book *The Great Convergence VS. The Great Divergence: Chinese Modernization Under Momentous World Changes* held a press conference and seminar in Hangzhou city. As the only English translator of this book, I was honored to participate in the whole activity. It was just during this activity that my knowledge and understanding of this new book has been further deepened. This book is considered to be one of the few works that seriously respond to the momentous changes unseen in a century from a global perspective, representing the highest level of research by Chinese scholars on this issue, and has great academic value and knowledge dissemination value. Meanwhile, the English translation of this book is of positive significance for the international community to understand the value implication and global meaning of Chinese modernization, enhance international understanding and promote the construction of a community with a shared future for human beings. So, how can this book be accurately and authentically delivered to readers in the Western world? This is a question that the translator of this book needs to consider at the beginning of translation. To sum up, the English translator mainly follows the following principles:

The first is to reproduce the content and spirit of the original work to the greatest extent. The content of the book is rich and informative. For example, there are some terms and concepts from the fields of politics, economics, philosophy, and so on. In this regard, the translator adopts the principle of uniformity in the process of translation by consulting the first-hand resources for these expressions.

The second is to be as close to the intention and expression of the original work as possible. In this book, Professor Zheng Yongnian mentions some unique Chinese governance ideas such as "this-worldly secularism", "level-stability economics", and "sustainable institutional support and leadership". In translating, the translator tries to use accurate, understandable, and fluent expressions, rather than hard and difficult terms.

The third is to be faithful to the style and language charm of the original work to the greatest extent. What runs through this book is Professor Zheng Yongnian's speculation logic, and his objective and plain language style. In this regard, the translator adopts the principle of literal translation, preserving the original style and avoiding any subjective and arbitrary play as much as possible.

In addition, the translator has also read a certain amount of knowledge resources in Chinese and foreign languages in order to understand and convey the original meaning more accurately. Here, I would like to thank all the authors of these knowledge resources for bringing rich nourishment for the translator's work. At the same time, I would also like to thank the relevant staff of Zhejiang People's Publishing House and Palgrave Macmillan (SPRINGER NATURE) for their help and support at different stages of this translation work.

Finally, I would like to thank Professor Zheng Yongnian for his affirmation and appreciation of my professional knowledge and accomplishment, providing me with this opportunity to translate his new book!

Translation is a never-ending process of pursuing perfection. For the translator, each translating strives to be as close to perfection as possible. So, it is inevitable that there will be inappropriateness for each translating. Readers and friends, please criticize and correct them! Thanks!

May 2024 Jin Ping

About This Book

At present, the world is undergoing "momentous changes unseen in a century". What is the essence and core of the momentous changes? Will the momentous changes bring another historical opportunity or another historical crisis to Chinese modernization? If it is an opportunity, how can we seize this opportunity? If it is a crisis, is it possible to turn "crisis" into "opportunity"? How do we actively create such opportunities? How can we reverse the trend of anti-globalization and lead a new wave of globalization? How do we bring about another great convergence of globalization and modernization? Thinking about these questions and trying to answer them form the theme of this book.

This book focuses on clarifying the relationship between Chinese path to modernization and globalization, exploring the deep-seated reasons for the momentous changes and the significant challenges they posed to China's continued modernization. In particular, it answers the question of "what is the next step for China", providing readers with profound insights and forward-looking thinking for understanding the world changes and mastering the future of China.

Contents

About the Author

Professor Zheng Yongnian is the Presidential Chair Professor and Dean in School of Public Policy, The Chinese University of Hong Kong, Shenzhen. He received his BA and MA in law from Peking University and his PhD in political science from Princeton University. Professor Zheng is Editor of *The Asian Review of Political Economy*, and the China Policy Series of Routledge. He is mainly engaged in the research of China's domestic transformation and its external relations, and has published and edited more than 100 books in both Chinese and English, including *Market in State: The Political Economy of Domination in China*, *Society Must Be Defended* and *The China Model: Experience and Challenges*.

About the Translator

Jin Ping is now working as an Associate Professor in the School of International Cultures and Communications at Communication University of Zhejiang. She received her BA in English education, MA in English language and literature, and PhD in education from Northwest Normal University in Lanzhou, Gansu Province, China. From 2013 to 2015 she completed her postdoctoral research in foreign languages and literature at the School of International Studies of Zhejiang University. From 2018 to 2019 she was a visiting scholar of the Institute of Advanced Studies at University College London. She is currently engaged in translation and cross-cultural research with a special focus on cultural interpretation and understanding between contemporary China and the world. Jin Ping is the author of a few books, including *Pathway to Translation Instruction: Based on an Exploratory-Empirical Study of Development of Translation Competence*, *An English-Chinese Bilingual Translation Coursebook: Comparative Transference and Case Analysis*, *Language and The Making of Cultural Meaning of Place: Configurating, Safeguarding and Use of Historic Space on Zou-Lu Region* and *Nations at War: A Scientific Study of International Conflict* (translated work). Her representative papers have been published in journals, including *Chinese Translators Journal* and *Foreign Literature Studies*.

CHAPTER 1

Formulation of Questions

Just as China has set about forging ahead into "basically realizing socialist modernization" in 2035 and "achieving socialist modernization in all respects" in 2050 from "building a moderately prosperous society in all respects", the world began the momentous changes unseen in a century. From the perspective of big history, people are not surprised that the momentous changes have happened, because history is open and always in a state of flux, and history has also gone through countless momentous changes. Once in a while, a momentous change will always come along. The momentous change itself is only an objective "social thing" (the concept of French sociologist Émile Durkheim). However, the profound impact of each momentous change is different for different countries and people who are also in the midst of the same momentous change: Some countries and individuals are more fortunate and have achieved the opportunities for progress and development, while other countries and individuals are less fortunate, and have been abandoned by the momentous change, or even become victims by the momentous change.

Today, the most challenging question that the momentous changes have posed to China is: where will Chinese modernization go under the momentous changes? Although modernization has been the pursuit for every generation of Chinese people since modern times, yet Chinese path to modernization has been interrupted several times, both by external

Z. Yongnian, *The Great Convergence VS. The Great Divergence*,
https://doi.org/10.1007/978-981-96-7846-4_1

factors and domestic factors. Today the core of the new momentous changes we are facing is the worldwide anti-globalization or even deglobalization. In the past few decades, or more precisely, from the early 1980s until the Trump administration launched its trade war with China, there has been what some economists call hyper-globalization in the world. During this time, capital, technology, and talents have gained unprecedented mobility across the world. In the language of economics, hyper-globalization has led to the efficient market-oriented allocation of production factors on a global scale, thus greatly improving labor productivity and creating huge wealth for mankind.

Hyper-globalization and China's reform and opening-up occurred at the same time, or in other words, China's reform and opening-up is an intrinsic part of hyper-globalization, which not only greatly promoted Chinese modernization, but also made Chinese modernization and the worldwide globalization meet with each other in the same direction. Chinese path to modernization since its reform and opening-up can only be effectively explained in the process of hyper-globalization.

Therefore, the question we are facing now is—what impact will anti-globalization and deglobalization have on Chinese modernization? Under such a big question, we can ask more questions, at least including the following:

1. Will the momentous changes bring another historical opportunity or another historical crisis to Chinese modernization?
2. If it is an opportunity, what kind of opportunity is it?
3. How can we seize this opportunity?
4. If it is a crisis, will Chinese modernization be interrupted again?
5. In what ways is Chinese modernization likely be interrupted?
6. How can we effectively avoid the interruption of Chinese modernization?
7. Is it possible to turn "crisis" into "opportunity"?

If these kinds of questions indicate that we are in a passive role, then we can also ask some positive questions like the following:

1. When the external environment no longer allows opportunities for our modernization, do we have the ability to actively create opportunities for our modernization?

2. What do such opportunities look like? How do we create such opportunities?
3. How can we reverse the trend of anti-globalization and lead a new wave of globalization?
4. How do we bring about another great convergence of globalization and modernization?
5. If so, what characteristics will our modernization show? Will it be different from the previous kind of modernization where we are relatively passive? What impact will this difference have on the future of Chinese modernization? What impact will it have on the outside world?

Thinking about these questions and trying to answer them form the theme of this book.

CHAPTER 2

Material, Institution, and People: Three Coordinates of Modernization

How do I answer these questions listed above? This is not an easy thing to do. In fact, people can ask more questions about modernization. In any case, since modern times, almost all the problems of human society have been related to "modernization".[1] After the concept "modernization" was coined, "modernization" has almost become synonymous with "future". No matter what things or societies are involved, they will touch on the future, so the concept of modernization is often generalized or abused. Therefore, we must qualify the "modernization" discussed here.

To put it in a nutshell, we are to discuss the three aspects of modernization here, including material modernization, institutional modernization, and human modernization. They are three interrelated and independent levels. If they are illustrated by a graph, we can call them the three coordinates of modernization. Among them, the material coordinate and the human coordinate can be used as the vertical axis and the horizontal axis

[1] In English, "近代化" and "现代化" are both translated into the same word, namely "modernization". In China's literature, the term "近代化" is used more in the early periods, while the term "现代化" is used more in the contemporary era. Here, it is sufficient to just notice that the two Chinese words are the same concept.

Z. Yongnian, *The Great Convergence VS. The Great Divergence*, https://doi.org/10.1007/978-981-96-7846-4_2

respectively, while the institutional coordinate is in between, because institutional modernization is the regulator or intermediary between material modernization and human modernization.

The first is the material coordinate of the objective world. The changes in the material world are often independent of human will, or the changes in the material world have their own objective laws. Many changes at this level are determined by the logic of things themselves, but there are also a lot of changes that have also been caused by superimposing human factors on it. In the case of human factors, people often use the concept "development" to replace the concept "change", because the former implies subjective initiative or purpose, while the latter is purposeless (at least for human beings). The biological evolution is also a change, but the biological evolution has no purpose. Although, as Darwin put it, the biological evolution follows the rule of "survival of the fittest", yet the "survival of the fittest" in the biological world is not an end in itself. However, "capitalism" as a "social thing" is different. It is a human behavior, so it has a purpose. Therefore, people often use the concept of "development" to describe the changes brought about by the operation of capitalism.

On the material aspect, it is much easier for people to reach a consensus on what modernization is. With the exception of a very small number of religions or belief groups, such as ascetics, people all accept and pursue material modernization. Here, modernization is manifested in the physical form of infrastructure, such as roads, bridges, airports, seaports, high-rise buildings, schools, stadiums, hospitals, etc. And it also includes what was considered the most advanced technology so far. Before the reform and opening-up, China put forward the "Four Modernizations", namely, the four modernizations in the fields of industry, agriculture, national defense, and science and technology, which basically belong to material modernization. The modernizations at the material level are pursued not just because they are in line with human nature, that is, they can improve and enhance the quality of human life. More importantly, at the international level, material modernization represents the hard power of a country. If a country does not have a strong enough hard power, then it will be bullied or defeated by other countries.

The second is the coordinate of the subjective world, that is, the coordinate of people. The Human coordinate includes subjective goals, morality, values, identity, and other aspects, which is also the difference between human society and the animal world. Since modern times, the core of modernization has been people. The modernization of people is manifested in different kinds of relationships with people, including the relationship between people and nature, between people and society, and between people and people. The significance of changes or development at the objective material level must be shown in the human coordinate. Although the changes and development in the objective material world are not subject to human will, yet the changes or development have different meanings for different people. People is not an abstract, but a concrete existence. Everyone has the characteristics of his own civilization, culture and country, so people's cognition of things is subject to the civilization, culture, and national conditions in which he lives. What is seen as a positive change by some is seen as a negative change by others. What is seen as an up-side change by some is seen as down-side change by others. What some see as a progressive change is regressive to others. It is not hard to understand that for all these changes, everyone and every social group will make judgments according to their own life experiences and practical knowledge.

If people's response to the changes in objective things can only be "survival of the fittest" in most cases, then their response to the changes in "social things" is manifested by emotion. For example, although economic development will inevitably have an impact on environment and lead to the widening gap between the rich and the poor, most people will still pursue economic development except for a very small number of people. However, when the economy develops to a certain stage, people no longer accept a wealthy but unjust society, and then the pursuit of equality has turned into the ideal of people. For another example, although a lot of problems have arisen after the spread of democracy from Western countries to non-Western countries and many people do not necessarily have positive experience of democracy, yet the people in non-Western countries still flock to democracy. This is simply because they have elevated democracy to a value, a value that must be pursued no matter how much it costs. In these years, the COVID-19 pandemic control policies of various countries have also been a good example. During the outbreak of COVID-19 pandemic, in the West where individual freedom is valued, many social groups have opposed any control measures imposed by the government, including wearing masks and banning public gatherings, but as they gradually experienced the novel coronavirus threatening their lives, or saw their relatives or friends die from the virus, they no longer refused to accept the government's control policies. But in the East where collectivism is valued, the process is almost the opposite. At the early stage, people were willing to accept the control measures imposed by the government, even some measures of excessive control. However, as time went on, people began to complain about the layers of excessive control from local governments, especially when they saw that other countries have relaxed their control and they were still under strict control, people's mood was quite different. Even though strict control for the government is for the sake of people's health and safety, when people begin to have their own choices about control and freedom, they have different evaluation systems for the government's control policies. In a word, if people identify with this social thing, the evaluations tend to be positive. If people cannot identity with this social thing, the evaluations tend to be negative.

The third is the coordinate of institution. There is also an institutional coordinate between the material coordinate and the human coordinate. The importance of institution is self-evident. Without institution, it is difficult for people to coexist with the material world, or even with others. Therefore, in any society, people put a high value on institution. In fact, human society, whether it is primitive society or modern complex society, is manifested as a set of institutional system, and the complexity of the institutional system is different in different societies. The functions of institution can be basically divided into the following three categories. First of all, adjusting the material coordinate and the human coordinate, that is, adjusting the relationship between material modernization and human modernization. Second, intervening in the changes in the material world. As discussed above, the material world has its own laws of change, but human beings have been intervening in changes in the material world since human beings came into being. In the process of human intervention in the material world, its science and technology have been developed, and the development of science and technology in turns enhances human ability to intervene in the material world. Economic development is a classic example. In academia, there has been a large amount of literature on what kinds of institutions promote economic development, what kinds of institutions hinder economic development, what kinds of institutions contribute to the success of a country, and what kinds of institutions lead to the failure of a country. Finally, intervening in the changes in the human world, that is, intervening in the relationship between people and people, between people and society, and between different social groups. The order of human society is basically divided into two categories: One is the natural order formed from the bottom up, just as the natural society advocated by the ancient Chinese Taoism; the other is the social order imposed from the top down, as the society advocated by the ancient Chinese Legalism. In reality, however, a completely bottom-up spontaneous order is not possible, nor is a completely top-down imposed order possible. The actual order is mostly a combination of the two, just as the order advocated by Confucianism.

Furthermore, accordingly, from the academic point of view, the institutional coordinate involves two levels of questions. The first level of question is the ought, that is, what kind of institution the institution should become through what kind of changes; the second level of question is the reality, that is, how the institution is actually changing and what kind of institution it will become. Those who answer questions in the first way may be called idealists. And those who answer questions in the second way may be called realists. However, the result of the actual change is neither ideal as idealist nor realistic as realists, but a mixture of the two. Idealists have an influence on changing reality and the influence of subjective intentions on the objective environment should not be ignored, otherwise it is difficult to explain the progress of history. Meanwhile, idealism is subject to realistic environment, so that the ideal will not be realized as originally envisioned. In this way, the outcome of the change will certainly not be happy for all the people, because it does not conform to idealism or realism.

With these three coordinates, we can answer the various questions raised here about Chinese modernization with a relative focus. The theme of the book can be simply expressed as follows: Over the past 40 years, under the environment of hyper-globalization, the three aspects of Chinese modernization—material modernization, institutional modernization and human modernization—all have shown the general trend of moving in the same direction, both at the international level and at the domestic level, thus manifesting themselves as a great convergence or a great integration. Then, under the environment of anti-globalization or deglobalization, will the modernization of these three aspects show a general trend of going in a different direction or even in the reverse direction, and thus will it be manifested as a great divergence with the outside world at the international level and as a different direction and unbalanced development at the domestic level? In the author's opinion, the answer to this question will not only determine whether Chinese modernization is sustainable, but also determine China's relevance to the world as well as China's "identity recognition" and the international role it can play in the future world.

It is obvious that China has realized the profound impact of changes in the international environment on its modernization process. Therefore, the 20th CPC National Congress has put forward the concept of "Chinese Modernization". This is not only the summary of China's past experience in pursuing its modernization, but also shows that China should consciously pursue its own modernization in its own way. At the same time, this concept also suggests that other countries need to find their own ways to modernize in accordance with their own civilization, culture, and national conditions. Moreover, from a deeper understanding, this concept also indicates that from inside, Chinese modernization will not be interrupted by changes in external world environment. Now that the pattern of Chinese modernization has been formed, this pattern will also dominate the future of the modernization in China. From outside, Chinese modernization is part of world modernization since modern times, and in the past few decades, Chinese modernization has been carried out in the state of globalization and opening-up, and it will continue to be carried out in the state of opening-up in future.

Therefore, on a global scale, countries have some common values or universal values for modernization, but modernization takes place in different countries under different civilizations, cultures, and national conditions, so there are also differences. This point is particularly manifested in the modernization of people. People have an abstract side, but they have a more concrete side, because all people are cultural people. No individual can choose the culture in which he or she was born. For this reason, human modernization and cultural modernization are inseparable, and the two can be said to be the same process, influencing each other. Because people are the root and core of modernization, the difference in the human coordinate leads to different people's cognition of material modernization. Furthermore, it is also because of the difference in the human coordinate that result in the difference in the institutional coordinate. If the institution is to regulate the relationship between material and people, then the institution must be suitable for people's needs for material and institution.

From this point of view, both convergence and divergence are part of modernization process. It is because all countries have a universal pursuit of the value of modernization that modernization has become converged in character. At the same time, all countries are pursuing their own modernization in line with their own civilization, culture and national conditions, and modernization has become a diverged nature. Convergence and divergence have constituted the modernization course of the world and also have constituted the course of Chinese modernization. This is true of fact and experience, and it is also true of people's understanding of modernization.

CHAPTER 3

Globalization and Modernization

In China, as the concept of modernization points to, Chinese modernization began in modern times. In other words, "modernization" is not only a historical concept, but more importantly, it implies different historical meanings. When concepts such as "slave society" and "feudal society" are mentioned, people tend to have a lifeless and spiritless image in their minds, while the concept of "modernization" gives people an image full of vitality, endless life, and constant change.

Empirical evidence also proves this point. There is not much consensus in the social sciences, but there is a consensus that "meaningful changes in human beings began in modern times". Historians have found that in fact, whether slave society or feudal society, they are not static, and they also have the power of change, otherwise it is difficult to explain the transformation of human society from one social form to another. As a matter of fact, many factors contributing to the occurrence of modernization have already arisen under the previous feudal society. But for all that, the changes that human beings have undergone before modernization cannot be compared in the same breath with the changes that human beings have undergone since modernization, which are two completely different changes. The economic statistics from the economist Angus Maddison show that the economy of thousands of years before modern times has

Z. Yongnian, *The Great Convergence VS. The Great Divergence*,
https://doi.org/10.1007/978-981-96-7846-4_3

almost been static, maintaining the edge of subsistence economy. Another economist, Angus Deaton, believes that:

> Many of the great episodes of human progress, including those that are usually described as being entirely good, have left behind them a legacy of inequality. The Industrial Revolution, beginning in Britain in the eighteenth and nineteenth centuries, initiated the economic growth that has been responsible for hundreds of millions of people escaping from material deprivation. The other side of the same Industrial Revolution is what historians call the "Great Divergence," when Britain, followed a little later by northwestern Europe and North America, pulled away from the rest of the world, creating the enormous gulf between the West and the rest that has not closed to this day. Today's global inequality was, to a large extent, created by the success of modern economic growth.
>
> We should not think that, prior to the Industrial Revolution, the rest of the world had always been backward and desperately poor. Decades before Columbus, China was advanced and rich enough to send a fleet of enormous ships under Admiral Zheng He—aircraft carriers relative to Columbus's rowboats—to explore the Indian Ocean. Three hundred years before even that, the city of Kaifeng was a smoke-filled metropolis of a million souls whose belching mills would not have been out of place in Lancashire eight hundred years later. Printers produced millions of books that were cheap enough to be read by people of even modest means. Yet those eras, in China and elsewhere, were not sustained, let alone taken as starting points for ever-increasing prosperity. In 1127, Kaifeng fell to an invasion of tribes from Manchuria who had been rashly employed to help it wage war; if you enlist dangerous allies, you had better make sure they are well paid. Economic growth in Asia kept starting and kept being choked off, by rapacious rulers, by wars, or by both. It is only in the last two hundred and fifty years that long-term and continuing economic growth in some parts of the world—but not in others—has led to persistent gaps between countries. Economic growth has been the engine of international income inequality.[1]

Although Deaton is talking about human inequality here, this passage points to several important aspects related to modernization and globalization. First, mankind's escaping from deprivation began with the Industrial Revolution. Previously, human beings had been living in a high

[1] Angus Deaton, *The Great Escape: Health, Wealth, and the Origins of Inequality* (Princeton and Oxford: Princeton University Press, 2013), pp. 4–5.

degree of deprivation of material life. Second, only the material changes after the beginning of the Industrial Revolution became universal, that is, the Industrial Revolution diffused and transmitted from Europe to the rest of the world. Although there were times of economic prosperity in some areas before the Industrial Revolution, this prosperity was not universal. It is because of the diffusibility and transmissibility of the Industrial Revolution that human society has experienced wave after wave of globalization since modern times. Third, the diffusion and transmission of the Industrial Revolution was not only uneven, but outside Europe and North America, its development was often interrupted. Fourth, the Industrial Revolution created wealth, but it also created inequality. Inequality existed not only within a country, but also between countries.

Although people still debate about why industrialization started in Europe and not in China or anywhere else in the world, there is no doubt that industrialization started in Europe. Industrialization first promoted the changes and development in Europe, and then soon diffused from Europe to every corner in the world. In this sense, industrialization and globalization meet each other in the same direction. In other words, it is industrialization that drives globalization.[2]

[2] It is necessary to explain the similarities and differences between the "Great Convergence" and the "Great Divergence" discussed here and those discussed in the field of economic history. There is a long history of what economic historians call the "Great Divergence", which studies why the Western world overcame its growth constraints to surpass Eastern countries such as China and India in the nineteenth century. In academia, scholars have put forward a variety of theories about the causes of the "Great Divergence", involving factors including geography, culture, institution, colonialism, aggression, resources, "historical accidents", and so on. Some scholars believe that the Great Divergence occurred during the Industrial Revolution in Britain in the eighteenth century, but others believe it can be traced back to earlier times, such as the period of the Renaissance and the Great Geographical Discovery in the rise of mercantilism and capitalism caused by the Commercial Revolution, or the period of Pre-Globalization and Scientific Revolution in the rise of European colonial empires, or the Age of Enlightenment. In a traditional view, there is a relatively consistent consensus that the Great Divergence should occur in 1750 before the Industrial Revolution, when European countries surpassed China, Japan, and the Middle East. However, the "revisionist" view of the California school, led by Professor Kenneth Pomeranz, argues that the Great Divergence should begin around 1800, after the Industrial Revolution. The gap caused by the Great Divergence peaked just before the First World War in the twentieth century, and remained there until the early 1970s. Over the next two decades, as most Third World countries had a significantly higher economic growth rate than that of the First World countries, the Great Divergence was also replaced by the Great Convergence in the late 1980s. Professor Kenneth Pomeranz's book *The Great Divergence: China, Europe, and the Making of the Modern World*

Globalization, driven by industrialization, is not comparable to any form of globalization in the past. Before modern industrialization, human society had already experienced different forms of globalization. During the Imperial age, some huge transcontinental empires, such as the Roman Empire and the Han Empire, also achieved some degree of globalization. What people call the Silk Road today is a symbol of globalization in the age of empires. Within the empire there are different local regimes, ethnic groups, races, tribes, etc., which are more inclusive than modern countries since modern times. Although modern countries are considered to be "modern", because they are based on sovereignty, modern countries have strong exclusiveness and their inclusiveness is far less than that of the empires before modern times. According to China's concept, the empire is "pluralistic and integrated". Not only is there frequent trade between different units within the empire, but trade between empires is

Economy is to answer the question: why was Western Europe the first region in the world to transform to a modern economic growth model, while China, once similar to it, has taken a completely different path after the eighteenth century? To answer this question, the first thing to clarify is the fact that how China and Western Europe exactly developed in modern times. What Kenneth Pomeranz presents in the first and second parts of this book is a picture that most scholars cannot believe: until 1750, East Asia and western Europe, or more specifically, Jiangnan, the most developed part of China, had a myriad of surprising resemblances with England, the most developed part of Western Europe—the two regions had very high similarities in terms of population, capital accumulation, technology, land, factor market and household decision-making, and so on. But when the perspective turns to the luxury consumption and capitalist system, Kenneth Pomeranz finds that there are indeed differences between the East and the West, but they are not enough to create an East–West divergence. In particular, from the degree of ecological constraints, the core regions of China (and Japan) and the core regions of western Europe are almost equally stressed. The third part of *The Great Divergence* explains the main factors of the divergence between China and the West. According to Kenneth Pomeranz, the divergence between Europe and the Old World in the nineteenth century was largely due to the advantageous geographical location of coal resource distribution and the discovery of the New World. Both of these made it irrelevant whether Europe used land intensively or not, and has contributed to the growth of its resource-intensive industries. The global situation has made the Americas the main source of primary products needed by Europe, greatly easing ecological constraints in Europe. This luck enabled Europe to switch to a resource-intensive and labor-saving path. At the same time, Asia has fallen into the dead end in development, moving further and further down the original labor-intensive and resource-saving path. What the present book wants to discuss is whether the "Great Convergence" achieved by China and the world under the condition of hyper-globalization, which begans in the 1980s, will cause the "Great Divergence" again because of today's anti-globalization. Therefore, if historians explain the past, then the intention of this book is to predict the future.

also common. The religious era in Europe is regarded as the Dark Ages by European scholars, but in fact the religious empire is also global. As a belief or thought, religion has no boundaries and exhibits an impetus for infinite expansion until it is blocked and stopped by another religion.

But why are neither empires nor religious empires endowed with modernity? This involves the second dimension of modernity we have discussed earlier, the human dimension. Indeed, from an empirical point of view, the concept of modernity is always associated with the concept of people. In the Western world, the concept of people originated in the European Renaissance. The long religious era before the Renaissance was called the Dark Middle Ages in Europe. God was regarded as the source of all things, everything served God and everything also depended on God. The Renaissance shifted the center of the secular world from "God" to "people", and people began to become the yardstick for measuring everything, even the only yardstick.

Thus, although the industrialization that began in Europe gave a great impetus to the process of modernization, the concept of modernity should be said to have begun in much earlier Renaissance era. At the same time, industrialization has prepared material conditions for the expansion of the concept of modernity. As mentioned earlier, the changes brought about by industrialization are objective phenomena, and the modernization driven by industrialization resulted in profound changes in all aspects of human society. It is because of these and other changes that various progressive ideas including freedom, independence, equality, and democracy have emerged one after another from the Renaissance to the Enlightenment in Europe. The systematic social science we see now is the product of intellectuals' observation and interpretation of these changes.

Material modernization has spread from Europe to all parts of the world not only because countries with material modernization are often relatively stronger countries, and they can defeat countries with no modernity or less modernity on the battlefield, but also because material modernization conforms to human nature. Material modernization has changed the conditions of "people". At the minimum, it has enabled human beings themselves to acquire modernity. For example, at the lowest level, they can stay away from hunger and fear. At the maximum, it endows human beings with the ability to exert their potential and achieve "well-rounded human development" (in Marx's words).

It is because the concept of modernity is always associated with people that modernization has promoted the changes in people and also contributed to the changes in institutions at the same time. It has been found that not only do different institutions lead to different material modernization, but even in the same case of material modernization, different institutions also lead to different "conditions" of people. In the intellectual history, the concern for institution has also been a unique knowledge phenomenon since modern times. The problem of development and inequality discussed by Deaton above is people's concern about the linkage between different institutions and inequality.

In the past few decades, it has been the mainstream of academic circles to discuss the changes in the material level and the human level from the institutional elements, which is manifested in new concepts such as institutional economics, institutional sociology, and institutional politics. In effect, the discussion of institution issues is not only a subject that cannot be ignored by scholars studying modernization today, but also an object that all political economists have been diligently studying since modern times. If the focus of the Renaissance in Europe is the change from "God" to "people", then the focus of the Enlightenment is the change from "people" to "institution". In the view of the Enlightenment advocates, people are the source of all things, but human behavior needs to be regulated by institutions, which can mold people into the ones needed by the society they yearn for.

Institutional exploration has been the subject of all political economists since modern times. Modern classical political scientists such as Adam Smith and David Ricardo have explored the problem of how a country pursues wealth and gets rich. Adam Smith wrote *An Inquiry into the Nature and Causes of The Wealth of Nations*, discovering the correlation between the market institutional arrangement by "an invisible hand" and wealth. David Ricardo advocated the division of labor and comparative advantage, and believed that wealth could be pursued through free trade. Most classical political scientists agree that private property rights and the protection of private property can achieve social enrichment. But at the other end of the spectrum, and also from modern times, at least since Rousseau, many thinkers in European society have argued that private property rights are the root of human injustice. Rousseau denounced the private property system. Marx revealed the operation of capital, mainly to explore the problem of social equity. Therefore, the West has two routes: One is to explore how to create wealth, represented by Adam Smith, and the other is to discuss how to realize social justice with Marx as the representative. After that, the world has developed two approaches to solve the problem. One approach is pure private ownership advocated by European scholars, or "private property is sacred and inviolable". Today, no matter whether it is neoliberalism or new institutionalism, Western economics and political economy all place special emphasis on private property rights and the protection of private property rights. However, the pure private property system is a hard route. As a matter of fact, from the stage of primitive capitalism described by Marx to the later stage of welfare capitalism, Europe experienced a long-term and even very violent socialist movement. Today, the welfare societies in the West are also in a difficult process of evolution. Such countries as Britain and the United States, which implement typical private property rights system, have not solved the problem of wealth and equity. People hate poverty and backwardness, as well as wealth but injustice.

The other approach is pure public ownership, that is, state ownership. The most typical is the Soviet Union's planned economic system. The public ownership system of the Soviet Union is the foundation of the Soviet national mobilization system, which has also made brilliant achievements in the early stage. The 1920s and 1930s saw a situation in Europe where everyone called himself a "socialist". The Soviet model did have a significant impact on the Europe and even the whole world. However, the Soviet model finally collapsed. So, it is a failure.

From these two processes, two experiences are relatively clear. First, neither pure private ownership nor pure public ownership succeeded. Second, private ownership was a little more successful than public ownership, because despite many problems in the West, private ownership survived, whereas pure public ownership in the Soviet Union did not. It should be pointed out, however, that this fact does not indicate in any sense that the public property system will inevitably die out, while the private property system will exist forever.

Today, both approaches gain survival and development in their own way. The typical private property system in the West (typical in Britain and the United States) is facing a profound crisis and is also changing. In fact, even in countries collectively referred to as capitalism, capitalism is no longer a singular concept, but has been divided into plural concepts, namely the so-called different "variants" of capitalism. There are the neoliberal economies typical of Britain and the Unites States, the "social market" capitalism of Germany, the high welfare capitalism of Northern Europe and strategic capitalism of Japan. Similarly, countries such as

China and Vietnam, once dominated by public ownership, have developed into veritable mix economies where public ownership and private ownership coexist. If we put aside ideological factors, it is not difficult for people to find the elements of integration in terms of the development of economic institutions.

No matter it is for European scholars or Chinese scholars, it is impossible to overestimate the profound impact of European and American modernization on China. The impact is manifested in the three aspects mentioned in this book, including material modernization, human modernization, and institutional modernization. The German philosopher Hegel was in the midst of drastic changes in modern Europe. Compared with the drastic changes in modern Europe, he even came to the conclusion that "China has no history". It is also obvious that "the unchanging history of China" mentioned by Hegel is also the reason why China's traditional countries have been repeatedly defeated by modern countries rising in the West since modern times. China was defeated by the Western "strong ships and strong artillery", but the technology possessed by the West is only one of its powerful elements, not the whole. Even the strength of the West is not also due to the wealth it owns. As Deaton pointed out, China's history was once prosperous and powerful, but it was not sustainable. The strength of a country does not lie in the momentary economic wealth it possesses, or even in its science and technology it possesses. While Western scholars are discussing development, progress, and strength, the elites from all walks of life in modern China are also striving to explore the century proposition of how to make China strong. Because China was defeated by the big guns of Western powers, the early Chinese elites saw first and foremost modernization as military modernization. This is nothing wrong with that, because imperialism prevailed in the world at that time, and the modernity of a country was often measured by whether it could defeat another country militarily. However, simple military modernization has not made China rich and strong. After being defeated by Japan, a former student, China's elites in various fields tried to modernize in different fields, putting forward national building goals such as "business war", "strengthening China through industry", and "strengthening China through education". Although all these attempts have limitations, they are of great significance to the times, and are the modernization for a weaker country to survive. Looking back today, how painful it was and how high the price was paid for this explorative process! But the final conclusion is correct, that is, the strength of a country is based on its "modernity" in all aspects, including military, science and technology, economy, culture, education, political system, and so on.

The period from the late Qing Dynasty to the May Fourth Movement can be said to be the stage of China's Enlightenment. This process produced progressive ideas (although most of them were imported from the West) and constantly gave birth to the organizations of modernity that pursued these ideas. The Communist Party of China (CPC) is not only a product of this process, but also has become the political party with its most modernity in this process, pursuing its own and the country's modernity in the most radical way. The process of pursuing modernity is undoubtedly also a political process. Whether it is the politics between the Qing government and the Government of the Republic of China, or the politics between Kuomingtang and the Communist Party, all revolve around what kind of modernization China wants to carry out and what kind of country China wants to build.

After establishing its political power, the Communist Party of China has led China through two waves of modernization, that is, the modernization in Mao Zedong era and the modernization started in Deng Xiaoping era. It should be emphasized that although the concept of "modernity" originated in the West, China's process of pursuing modernity or modernization is consistent with the international trend, and the difference is only the method. The goal is the same, but the methods used in different eras are different, which depends on the domestic and external conditions of the time. From this perspective, in the era of Mao Zedong, there was a "small divergence" between Chinese modernization and the Western world. In the early days of the founding of the People's Republic of China (PRC), China adopted a "one-sided" strategy toward the then-Soviet Union. This was inevitable at that time. As has been said before, there have been two paths to modernity since modern times: the Western path and the Soviet path. Now that the United States-led West has closed its doors to China, there is only one option left for China, and that is the Soviet model. After the deterioration of the relations with the Soviet Union, China embarked on a path of exploring independent modernization again, and had a "small divergence" not only with the Western world, but also with the Soviet Union. For a long time, China was isolated by both the socialist camp and the capitalist camp, and was in a state of being completely enclosed. It also shows that "weak countries have no diplomacy". This is true even for a country as large as China and its domestic affairs are deeply affected by its international environment. In view of this international environment, Mao Zedong defined the international situation at that time as "war and revolution". Although China's diplomacy was highly defensive, it was often "radical" in the eyes of the outside world. China was regarded as a country that "exported" the communist revolution. As a result, the relationship between China and some countries, especially neighboring countries, often fell into a vicious circle. China was not only in a state of tension with the Soviet Union at that time, but also was seen by Southeast Asian countries as a threat to them. This situation did not end until Nixon's visit to China and the normalization of Sino-US relationship.

But from the perspective of modernization, China embarked on a "small divergence", that is, it pursued the goals of the West and the Soviet Union in its own way. On the one hand, China competed with the Soviet Union in the communist camp at that time, and on the other hand, it also hoped to overtake Britain and the United States. The modernization of this period is mainly manifested as a "catch-up type", that is, how to catch up with the developed countries in the fastest way. "Catch-up" modernization often manifests itself as one-way modernization. In this era of "small divergence", China has proposed to achieve the "Four Modernizations", namely, the modernizations of industry, agriculture, national defense, and science and technology. Generally speaking, the "Four Modernizations" basically belong to the "material modernization" defined in this book. This is the first wave of modernization led by the Communist Party of China. Although there are many lessons to be summed up in this wave of modernization, if there is no modernization under this wave of "small divergence", it will be difficult for us to understand the second wave of modernization embodied as the "great convergence" in the era of reform and opening-up. The reason is very simple. China's independent political and economic system was established in the era of "small divergence". In particular, it should be emphasized that the independent political and economic system established in the era of "small divergence" has also provided institutional conditions for China to maintain its independence while realizing its development in the era of "great convergence". Today, when discussing the world significance of Chinese modernization, people emphasize that Chinese modernization has offered an "alternative modernization option" for those developing countries that want to both develop and maintain their independence. Empirically speaking, this is true. In the process of modernization, many countries have failed to deal with the relationship between integrating into the world for development and maintaining international independence: Either they have not been able to integrate into the world for development, or they have lost their independence in order to integrate with the world. The reason why China can achieve the two goals of development and independence at the same time has its historical roots. This is the meaning of the "small divergence" era.

CHAPTER 4

Great Convergence: Hyper-Globalization and Modernization

From the perspective of policy, what economists call hyper-globalization is the product of the policy combination of two types of sovereign countries with global influence. One is the reform and opening-up policy that China began to carry out under the leadership of Deng Xiaoping and the other is the neoliberal economic policy with the Thatcher Revolution in Britain and the Regan Revolution in the United States as its core.

China's reform and opening-up policy is a product of the environment. As mentioned in the previous chapter, after the founding of the People's Republic of China in 1949, the first wave of modernization in China took place under the environment of the "small divergence" between China and the world in Mao Zedong era. The "small divergence" is not a voluntary choice of China, but a result of the international environment. Although Chinese modernization in the isolated state has made great achievements, it has not led to the powerful country that people hoped for. The present situation of the country on the eve of reform and opening-up was later regarded by Deng Xiaoping as "poverty socialism". The goal of "catching up with Britain and the United States" in the Mao Zedong era has not only failed to realize, but also has led to a widening distance between China and Western countries. In other words, "catch-up" modernization has not achieved its goal. More importantly, China was lagging far behind its Asian neighbors. In 1949, Shanghai was also

Z. Yongnian, *The Great Convergence VS. The Great Divergence*,
https://doi.org/10.1007/978-981-96-7846-4_4

advanced compared with other Asian cities, including Tokyo and Hong Kong, but 30 years later, Shanghai, while still the most advanced city in mainland China, has fallen far behind Tokyo and Hong Kong. Indeed, during the 30 years that China was isolated, Japan has become the second largest economy in the world after the United States. After Japan, the "Four Asian Tigers" (South Korea, Singapore, Taiwan and Hong Kong) have achieved their economic take-off. Although these economies also belong to the Confucian cultural circle, they all have modernized. Why can these economies realize modernization?

In Deng Xiaoping's view, the original intention of socialism is to pursue the strength of the country and the prosperity of the people. Therefore, "poverty" should not be associated with "socialism", and the current situation of poverty socialism in China must be changed. To change this, isolation must be broken. Deng Xiaoping thus made a strategic judgment of "peace and development" on the world situation. Obviously, from an empirical point of view, this does not mean the international situation at that time has presented the condition of "peace and development". On the contrary, it has been still in the state of the Cold War between the United States and the Soviet Union, and the East and the West were divided. As far as China itself was concerned, it has just ended the "Cultural Revolution", a period known as "civil strife", and also has just ended its war of self-defense counterattack against Vietnam. The reason why Deng Xiaoping was able to make such a strategic judgment was mainly based on one "need", one "goal", and one "objective reality". One "need": China needs a peaceful international environment to pursue its internal development, and also needs such an environment to enable China to return to the international community; one "goal": Peace and development should be the international goal pursued not only by China, but also pursued by all the countries in the world; one "objective reality": In view of the Cold War situation between the United States and the Soviet Union, the United States objectively needs China's help to balance the Soviet Union. This objective fact also shows that the Western system dominated by the United States will be willing to accept China. All these factors prompted Deng Xiaoping's generation of Chinese leaders to define "peace and development" as the theme of the times, and under this theme, decide to implement the policy of reform and opening-up.

And what about the situation in the West? Why do Western countries, dominated by the United States, have motivation and willingness to accept China? Generally speaking, this is the product of the combination of two elements: capital and state, which are moving toward the same direction. As for the United States and other Western countries, the most important structural factor is the Cold War between the two camps of the United States and the Soviet Union, and the cooperation with China will constitute an effective balance to the Soviet Union and contain its expansion in Asia. From this perspective, China's war of self-defense counterattack against Vietnam was the action by China to check the power of the Soviet Union, because Vietnam was an ally of the Soviet Union in Asia at that time.

But it was the Thatcher Revolution and the Regan Revolution that really contributed to globalization and China's integration into the Western-dominated world economic system. These two revolutions, on both sides of the Atlantic, were not caused by international factors, but by domestic factors in Britain and the United States. During the whole Cold War, the Western economies with the United States as the main body have realized two levels of globalization: On the one hand, it was the globalization within the Western economies, and the economies between Western countries have formed a high degree of interdependence; on the other hand, the Western globalization has gradually extended into the sphere of non-Soviet influence, including Japan and the "Four Asian Tigers". However, this internal globalization in the West not only fails to meet the requirements of capital expansion, but also restricts the free expansion of capital. In the case of economic policy, the most effective constraint comes from Keynesianism.

Keynesianism began in the Great Depression of the 1930s in the West, and eventually evolved into an institutional arrangement called "embedded liberalism" by John Ruggie, a professor at the Kennedy School of Government of Harvard University, who once served as the assistant secretary-general of the United Nations. This institutional arrangement combines the four aspects of class compromise of democratic socialist model (welfare state system), the role of demand-side state intervention, financial supervision, and capital control as well as the free trade system into an organic whole, laying a solid foundation for the economic revival and sustained prosperity of Western countries after the war. Although the Cold War between the East and the West broke out after the second World War, this system was not completely connected with the reconstruction of post-war international security order. Its starting point was mainly to take care of the interests of the core members of the Western bloc and its peripheral members (mainly the non-Western allies of the United States), while the Soviet bloc at that time formed its own mutual economic assistance organization in socialist countries. Objectively speaking, this system led and created by the United States did play a dominant role in the world economic system and provided a favorable structural condition for the international peace after the war. Globalization within the West has taken place under this institutional arrangement.

The concept of "embedded liberalism" points to the key supporting design of the post-war liberal international order, which is through domestic economic and social institutional arrangement, to effectively control and harness the economic instability that Marx has long discovered that capitalism will inevitably bring, and to curb its destructive and predatory tendencies, so that the survival and development opportunities of most social groups can be reasonably guaranteed, so as to maintain social sustainable development. And this is to lay a solid foundation for the establishment of liberal international order in the United States after the war, that is, the domestic legitimacy foundation of the liberal international economic order.

After World War II, the reason why the system "embedded liberalism" was favored by the political elites in the Western developed countries has its special historical conditions. After Western countries experienced the painful lessons of the Great Depression in the 1930s, the classical liberal economics represented by Friedrich Hayek, was completely abandoned by the political elites in Western countries. Classical liberalism is convinced of the allocative efficiency of the free market, and firmly believes that the market can achieve the general equilibrium of automatic full employment. These core assumptions have been questioned. And Keynesian economics, which advocates that government actively uses fiscal policy and monetary policy to adjust the business cycle and selectively interferes with the price formation mechanism from the demand side, has stepped onto the historical stage and become the mainstream macroeconomic thought widely pursued by Western countries in the following half century. From 1932, when President Roosevelt came to power in the United States to implement the New Deal, the Swedish and German governments then adopted the policy suggestions of Keynes, and there was also a policy debate in Britain about how to effectively combat the Great Depression. In the practice of more and more Western countries,

Keynesian economics has exercised the control over the recurring problems of sharp business cyclical fluctuations and large-scale financial crisis to a considerable extent.[1] In this sense, Keynesian economics became the ideological basis for the "embedded liberalism" adopted by the post-war Western countries.

The political function of "embedded liberalism" is to maintain the compromise of class co-existence and co-prosperity reached by all social strata in Western society under the realization of various forms of democratic socialism, so as to prevent the rise of the radical left-wing political forces and effectively counter the spread of the Soviet model in the international community at that time. Under the system of "embedded liberalism", capitalists were forced to accept "regulated capitalism". Through such mechanisms as market supervision, anti-monopoly, labor legislation, financial nationalization, progressive taxation at a high level, and fiscal transfer payment, the state has curbed the destructive effect of capitalism on society and the predatory tendency toward vulnerable groups, corrected the bipolarization tendency of wealth and income that inevitably resulted from unequal exchange in the market between capital owners and laborers who sell their labor, and greatly weakened the most important structural power of capitalists, namely, the flow of capital, through strict capital regulation and financial repression. Under the condition that capital cannot move freely across borders to transfer the maximum profit returns, Western countries can maintain long-term balance and stability of power relations between classes.

More importantly, "embedded liberalism" provided a solid foundation of social support for the post-war US-led liberal international economic order. The state-led compensation and assistance mechanism enables those with potential interests damaged under the open economic system to get appropriate assistance and protection. Meanwhile, the popularization in education, job training, medical security, sound infrastructure, and public services has allowed more market participants to adapt to international market competition and explore new market opportunities. The "embedded liberalism" system is helpful for Western society to maintain the openness of the economic system and form a firm social consensus across classes, across regions, and beyond left–right political competition. And it is also conductive to the rapid reconstruction and revitalization

[1] For the spread of Keynesianism, see Peter A. Hall, ed., *The Political Power of Economic Ideas: Keynesianism across Nations* (Princeton: Princeton University Press, 1989).

of the Western economy as well as the establishment of an open trade system.

However, this system began to show its drawbacks in the 1970s, especially after the oil crisis, and it had no ability to solve the widespread problem of economic stagflation in the West. The shortcomings of this system are obvious, and two of them are fatal. First, in order to maintain the increasingly large welfare state system, the enterprises in Western countries are facing increasingly high tax rates. Even in a typical capitalist country with less welfare like the United States, there is also a "quasi-confiscation" tax rate. The high tax rate has seriously curbed the enthusiasm of enterprises (capital), and how to evade taxes has become the main consideration of capital. In other words, the efficiency and effectiveness of the tax system are increasingly becoming a problem.[2] Second, also in order to maintain the increasingly large welfare state system, the bureaucracies in Western countries are expanding and becoming increasingly bloated, inefficient, and ineffective.

Because Keynesianism advocates the state intervention, the criticism of this system also focuses on the state and the carrier of the state—the bureaucracy. In the 1970s and 1980s, there were numerous works criticizing the bureaucratic economic system in Western academic circles, which was a direct reflection of social sentiment of that era in academic circles. Thatcher did a good job of summing up what people thought of government and bureaucracy at that time. She defined government as "the cause of the problem" rather than "the solution to the problem". US president Ronald Reagan also took a similar view. The revolution initiated by Thatcher and Reagan was regarded as neoliberal economic revolution. In this revolution, Keynesian economics was replaced by neoliberal economics, government was replaced by market, and high taxes were replaced by low taxes. The key to implement neoliberal economic policy was privatization and financial liberalization, that is, loosening and even abandoning financial regulation. Under this condition, capital has gained unprecedented freedom. Capital and technology with capital have rapidly flowed from the West to all parts of the world, providing a huge impetus for globalization.

In a word, China's reform and opening-up and the neoliberal economic revolution in the West contributed to China's relatively smooth

[2] Emmanuel Saez and Gabriel Zucman. *The Triumph of Injustice: How the Rich Dodge Taxes and How to Make Them Pay*. New York: W. W. Norton & Company, 2019.

entry into the "liberal international order" dominated by the United States. That's the economic condition. As mentioned above, the United States needed China's cooperation to balance the Soviet Union at that time, which constituted the political condition for China to join this order.

Looking back, people can clearly see that China's entry into this system should be said to be relatively smooth compared with other countries because it has seized the great historical opportunity, though this does not mean that China did not encounter difficulties in this process. Although this Western-dominated system is open, that is to say, it can also accommodate other countries and regions, such as the above-mentioned Japan and the "Four Asian Tigers" economies in Asia, yet not all countries and regions can be absorbed. The will of the country that wants to enter this system and the consent of the existing members of this system are the two most basic conditions. In the case of both refusal, there is either isolation from each other or little contact. Even if one is willing and the other is unwilling, it is difficult to move toward integration. This kind of difficulty is particularly serious for a big country.

The Soviet Union and later Russia are typical examples. Although Russia's goal in modern times has been to catch up with the West, integrate into the West, and turn itself into a Western country, yet it has not succeeded to this day. The October Revolution in the Soviet Union, as Lenin put it, was a revolution that broke away from the "chain" of Western imperialism. After the revolution, the Soviet Union carried out modernization in its isolation from the West. In the early days, the Soviet Union also made great achievements. But two main reasons led to the ultimate failure. First, isolation. After decoupling from the Western chain, the Soviet Union has never been able to "hook up" with the West, so the Soviet-style development was in an isolated way, and there were no other markets for the Soviet Union except the bloc organized by the Soviet Union itself (namely the Warsaw Pact). At the same time, because of its isolation, the technological innovation of the Soviet Union's national system quickly lost its momentum. Technology can only advance in an open state, because only in an open state can competition be maintained. Without sufficient market, it was difficult for the economy of the Soviet bloc to achieve sustainable development. Second, highly centralized, centrally planned economy. As mentioned above, the Soviet Union was a typical public ownership model, with almost all the economic power centralized in the central bureaucracy, and local governments and enterprises had neither autonomy nor motivation for development. It can be said that the Soviet system and the Western system are two completely different systems, without any point of intersection. Even if both sides have the motivation to accept each other, there are no institutional conditions.

What about Russia after the collapse of the Soviet Union? From Mikhail Gorbachev, the last leader of the Soviet Union, to Boris Yeltsin, the first president of Russia, and then to Vladimir Putin, in his early days, they were all pro-Western, or at least tried to be. During the Yeltsin era and the early Putin years, Russia even contacted the United States (the West) to discuss whether Russia would join the NATO. But none of these discussions came to fruition. Apart from Russia's position, there is no incentive for the United States (the West) to accept Russia. In fact, the reason is very simple. The US-led NATO wants neither an external challenger nor an internal challenger. If Russia joins NATO, then it will become a major power second only to the United Sates, and it is possible to challenge the United States from within. On the outside, if Russia is strong enough, then it will challenge the United States from the outside. For the United States, the most rational choice is to weaken and contain Russia from the outside. This is also the core of American policy toward Russia for so many years. Obviously, this external environment of Russia profoundly restricts the direction and path of Russia's modernization.

In any case, China's ability to join or connect to the so-called "liberal international order" in the West is due to both China's own factors and those of the United States (the West). These two factors are indispensable. However, it should be emphasized that neither accession nor connection does mean the integration of China and the West. On the contrary, there has been a tension between China and the Western-dominated international order from the beginning. If this tension between the two cannot be seen, it will be difficult to understand today's situation.

This "liberal international order" dominated by the West is made up of three pillars.

The first pillar is to take economic interdependence as the economic foundation. As far as China and the world economy are concerned, the economic interdependence between the two is caused by globalization after the 1980s, and China is not only an active participant and promoter, but also a beneficiary of globalization. China's integration into the world economy has formed an interdependent relationship with the Western world. Interdependence does not mean that there are no contradictions among countries, but only means that the benefits of interdependence for the countries concerned are higher than the costs it entails. In view of this reality, all countries are willing to resolve their contradictions within the framework of interdependence. For example, in the past few decades, the World Trade Organization (WTO) has undergone several rounds of reforms. Although the reform process is not satisfactory, yet it at least shows that all countries hope that this organization will play a bigger and better role in advancing the globalization process.

The second pillar is the recognition of the international security system with the United Nations at its core. China has fully and actively participated in the management and construction of major international institutions. Within the United Nations, there are different forms of struggles among big countries and between big and small countries, and all countries have always had different voices on how to reform the United Nations system. But in any case, all countries agree with and have a consensus on the international security system with the United Nations at its core. At least all countries believe that the United Nations system plays an important role in maintaining world peace and stability. For example, for many years, among the five permanent members, only the United States often deviated from or even abandoned the United Nations system and engaged in unilateralism. Many other countries, even if they are not satisfied with the behavior of the United States, they have basically refrained from openly antagonizing the United States. If we borrow the concept of economist Albert Hirschman, although people have "voice" of dissatisfaction with the United Nations system, they do not choose "exit", but remain "loyalty", hoping the United Nations system can improve its own performance.[3] Under these circumstances, many countries still believe that the United Nations system plays a key role in maintaining international security. After all, the United Nations system is the only international system after the war.

The third pillar is the value identification of modernity. As mentioned above, modernity originated in the West and it comprises a whole set of progressive values, including humanity, science, rationality, fairness, justice, freedom, democracy, etc. As far as the West is concerned, this

[3] For Hirschman's concept, see Albert O. Hirschman, *Exit, Voice, and Loyalty: Responses to Decline in Firms, Organizations, and States* (Cambridge: Harvard University Press, 1970).

whole set of values has developed greatly from the Renaissance to the Enlightenment. It should be pointed out that these values are not unique to Western civilization, and also embodied in the major world civilizations to varying degrees. Humanity, secular rationality, fairness, and justice are also the core of Chinese civilization. Fairness and justice are almost the core values in all civilizations. Nevertheless, since modern times, modernity has spread from the West to the non-West. In this whole set of value systems, there are elements that promote material modernization, elements that promote institutional modernization and elements that promote human modernization. But in the real level, it is difficult to separate these elements. It is precisely for this reason that in many non-Western countries, people often equate modernization with "total and wholesale westernization", and think that only by fully borrowing or transplanting this set of value systems can the country achieve the modernization. In this process, non-Western countries have all obtained different modernization experiences, and Russia, Japan, Turkey, China, and other countries are all looking for a modernization model that works for them, or a model that obtains modernity. But this process is not easy. Japan acquires its modernity through the Westernization model, that is, Japan's so-called "breaking away from Asia and merging into Europe" model. Turkey also has similar experiences, while Russia acquires its modernity through the model of decoupling from the West. The Cold War between the United States and the Soviet Union caused the isolation of the world, and the world was divided into three parts: the Western group with the United States as the core; the Eastern group with the Soviet Union at its core and in between were the Third World countries, including India and later China.

What should be emphasized is that although the world is separated, all countries identify with modernity, and pursue and acquire modernity in their own ways. The attainment of modernity is not only the pursuit of people of all countries, but also the pursuit of governments of all countries. The reason is very simple. From the individual point of view, modernity means progress, and people all pursue a better life, so it is in line with the pursuit of dignity by human nature. From the national point of view, modernity means being strong, not being bullied by other countries in the international community, and is a symbol of national dignity. The unity at both individual and national levels makes the pursuit of modernity the theme of the world history since modern times. That is to say, all kinds of civilizations and all countries in the world agree with a whole set of concepts of modernity formed in the West from the Renaissance to the Age of Enlightenment, whether it is for the pursuit of individual dignity at the individual level or for the pursuit of collective dignity at the national level. The difference between the Western and non-Western worlds lies in two aspects. First, the pursuit of these values in different countries has different historical stages. Although modernity manifests itself as a whole set of values, yet these values cannot be realized at the same time. Even in the West, the realization of various values comes in stages, especially in the developing countries. Second, there are different ways to realize these values. All kinds of "isms" that have emerged since modern times such as liberalism, socialism, anarchism, nationalism, can all be understood as different approaches to the pursuit of modernity.

It should be emphasized that although modernity as a whole set of values was formed in the West from the Renaissance to the Age of Enlightenment, this in no way means that this whole set of values only belongs to the West. In fact, the Western history in that period presented the characteristics of openness and inclusiveness. Following the disintegration of the Roman Empire, the West fell into a religious era for several centuries, that is, the Western Middle Ages, or the "Dark Ages". In the Middle Ages, religion was the main body of Western society, and Western society could be called "religious society". Religion is also used to explain everything. The Renaissance was a transformation, because it shifted the focus of society from religion to humanity. Humanism was the core of the Renaissance movement. Humanism, science, and rationality constitute the axis of the Renaissance. In the Age of Enlightenment, people added new values on the basis of the values of humanism, science and rationality, including freedom, equality, fraternity, people's sovereignty(democracy), national sovereignty (national independence) and so on. It should be realized that in this process the West has absorbed and incorporated many values from other civilizations and cultures. To put it simply, the values integrated by the Renaissance and the West after that include three categories, namely, ancient Greek civilization, science in the Arab world, and the secular rationalism in the East.

Among them, China's contribution to Western civilization is enormous. Briefly speaking, it can be divided into three categories. The first category is technology, especially what is traditionally called "Three Great Inventions" or "Four Great Inventions". Francis Bacon, a modern British thinker, indicated in his *The New Organon*: "In fact these three things (printing, gunpowder and the nautical compass) have changed the face and condition of things all over the globe: the first in literature; the second in the art of war; the third in navigation; and innumerable changes have followed; so that no empire or sect or star seems to have exercised a greater power and influence on human affairs than those mechanical things". Karl Marx took up his argument and said: "Gunpowder, the compass, and the printing press were the three great inventions which ushered in bourgeois society. Gunpowder blew up the knightly class, the compass discovered the world market and founded the colonies, and the printing press was the instrument of Protestantism and the regeneration of science in general; the most powerful lever for creating the intellectual prerequisites". Friedrich Engels in his *The Peasant War in Germany* explicitly pointed out: "A succession of more or less important discoveries, the most prominent of which were the invention of gunpowder. As has now been shown beyond doubt, gunpowder came to the Arabs through India from China, and they brought it through Spain to Europe along with fire-arms".

Although Bacon and Marx did not attribute these three inventions to China, later historians all put them under the inventions of China. On the basis of Bacon, the British sinologist Walter Henry Medhurst emphasized: "Their (Chinese) inventive genius has been manifested in various particulars, and at early periods. Three most important discoveries (compass, printing and gunpowder), which have given an extraordinary impulse to the progress of civilization in Europe".[4] The sinologist Joseph Edkins was the first to add the papermaking to the above three great inventions. When comparing China and Japan, he pointed out: "But it should always be remembered that they(Japan) can boost of no remarkable inventions and discoveries, such as printing, papermaking, the properties of the loadstone, and the composition of gunpower".[5] The American scholar Thomas Francis Carter first clearly put forward the statement of "Four Great Invention" in the introduction of his book *The Invention of Printing in China and Its Spread Westward* published in 1925: "Four great inventions that spread through Europe at the beginning of the Renaissance had a large share in creating the modern world. ......In these

[4] W. H. Medhurst, *China, Its State and Prospects, with Especial Reference to the Spread of the Gospel* (London: John Snow, 1838), pp. 101–107.

[5] Joseph Edkins, *Religion in China* (London: K. Paul, 1884).

inventions and others as well, China claims to have had a conspicuous part".[6]

The second category is the institution type. Particular emphasis needs to be placed here on China's bureaucratic system or civil service system. China has formed a complete bureaucracy during Qin and Han Empires. It is in this sense that the famous political scientist Francis Fukuyama called China "the first modern state".[7] However, as "the first modern state", the influence of Chinese system on the West has always been underestimated. It was only in modern times that the West began to develop the similar bureaucratic system, and it was affected by the Chinese system. The first to discover and systematically apply the Chinese bureaucratic system was the British East India Company, and then this institution was imported into Europe and the United States again and absorbed into the European political system. The Chinese bureaucratic system stresses the values of hierarchy, rationality, centrality, meritocracy, openness, etc. The West later developed the democratic political system, but without this set of bureaucracy, it would have been almost impossible for a democratic system to operate normally. The effective operation of a democratic system depends on the distinction between "politics" and "administration", with political figures coming and going but bureaucrats (or civil servants) stable.[8]

The third category is the idea type. The influence of Chinese ideas upon the West is all-around. Here are a few examples. In the field of economy, the thought in the ancient Chinese classics *The Book of Changes* and the Taoist idea "Wu Wei" are regarded as the ideological core of the world's first political economy school, that is, the Physiocratic School in France. In Physiocracy, "Wu Wei" is expressed as "non-intervention" and "economic freedom". This thought also profoundly influenced Adam Smith's ideas on the market economy. In the field of education, the Chinese Confucian thought of "education for all without discrimination" has become the ideological root of mass education gradually formed

[6] Thomas Francis Carter, *The Invention of Printing in China and Its Spread Westward* (New York: Columbia University Press, 1925).

[7] Francis Fukuyama, *The Origins of Political Order: From Prehuman Times to the French Revolution* (New York: Farrar, Straus and Giroux, 2011).

[8] For the discussion of the influence of the Chinese bureaucratic system with meritocracy as its core upon the West, see Zheng Yongnian, *Civilization and The Chinese Body Politic* (New York and London: Routledge, 2023).

in Western modern times. Although the economic foundation of mass education is industrialization since modern times, China's "education for all without discrimination" is its ideological basis. Mass education also has a profound impact on Western democracy, because the quality of democracy depends on the people's educational levels. If the people cannot think rationally, then democracy will be inferior. In the social field, the classical Chinese concept of "Great Harmony Society" has a high degree of consistence with the concept of socialism that began to take shape in Europe since the early modern period. Just because of this, after modern socialist thought was introduced into China from Europe, Chinese intellectuals accepted it without any difficulty.

What should be pointed out is that there are many ideas that have not been realized in China due to material and institutional constraints, and because industrialization and modernization started in the West, Western countries have the material conditions to realize these ideas before China. Mass education, based on the concept of "Education for All Without Discrimination", is a typical example. On the other hand, it is also because the West is subject to many institutional constraints, some ideas advocated by the West have not been realized in the West, but they have been realized in China because China has the institutional conditions that the West does not have. The idea of socialism is a typical example. The West, especially the contemporary United States and Britain where neoliberalism prevails, is too dominated by capital, and the components of socialism is few and far between. Although China's level of economic development is not as high as that of Britain and the United States, yet China has the institutional conditions and achieved basic social equity. In the more than 40 years after the reform and opening-up, the fact that China has helped nearly 800 million people get rid of absolute poverty is a typical case.

Because the Industrial Revolution and Scientific and Technological Revolution in modern times transmitted and diffused from the West to non-Western countries, the people in non-Western countries thought that the concept of modernity belonged to the West, and Western countries also deliberately forgot their own historical experience of "learning from non-Western countries". This has created a situation like this: On the one hand, the West strives to push toward non-Western countries the values of modernity it identifies with and the institutional arrangement that the West believes can realize these values. On the other hand, some non-Western countries believe that these values belong purely to the West and strive to resist these values. But this is not in line with the actual situation. As mentioned above, these values stem from multiple civilizations and cultures, and it's just that the West has integrated them all into one system. Even those countries that strive to shape non-Western value system, still contain Western values in their systems. The reason is that the so-called Western value system itself contains non-Western values.

In any case, only after the beginning of globalization in the 1980s did all kinds of "isms" in pursuit of modernity obtain a rare historical opportunity and tend to "converge". After the disintegration of the Soviet Union-Eastern European bloc in the early 1990s, globalization extended to all the corners of the world at an unprecedented pace, and was regarded as hyper-globalization, with the rapid flow of production factors such as capital, technology, and talents across the globe. These are, to a large extent, only globalization at the material level and have once occurred in history, but the scale and extent are different. However, for the West, these material levels of globalization will inevitably lead to the changes on institutional and human levels. Globalization is seen as a process of economic and technological diffusion, involving the growing trade, investment, and the spread of technology between countries. These technologies make many things—such as knowledge and information in Wikipedia—at your fingertips. Therefore, globalization is also a process related to the political, social, and moral changes.

The perception in the West is manifested as: the Cold War is over and the world seems to have come together. The Cold War contest between communism and capitalism finally ends with the victory of capitalism. All countries have become more interdependent economically. The Internet is ready to facilitate global exchanges. Democracy has been expanded, and the world seems to have a high degree of consensus on a set of Western universal values—freedom, equality, individual dignity, pluralism, human rights.

In the 1990s, British sociologist Anthony Giddens argued that globalization has changed our current state of life and become a part of our current life. It involves the intensification of global social relations. Globalization is about the integration of worldviews, products, ideas, and cultures. The international society has been replaced by the global society.[9]

[9] Anthony Giddens, *The Third Way: The Renewal of Social Democracy* (Cambridge: Polity Press, 1998).

Actually, after the disintegration of the Soviet Union, the West presented a generally optimistic atmosphere, believing that the Western liberal democracy is the best institutional system in human history, and it is also the last kind of institutional system. This optimistic atmosphere is directly reflected in Fukuyama's argument of "end of history".[10] Without this optimistic atmosphere, Fukuyama's books would probably be hard to sell so well. Anyway, although this optimism was not without its doubters, there was no other system in the world that could compete with the Western liberal democratic system at that time. That is to say, in the eyes of the West, liberal democracy has been accepted by the whole world as the mainstream ideology of the world, and it is a political modernity that must be pursued necessarily and inevitably by all countries.

This perception is highly consistent with the Western modernization theory. People think that as all countries integrate into globalization, they will become more like "us" in the West, namely the countries that have modernized.[11] The West has full confidence in the Western system, thinking that non-Western countries all over the world will admire the success of the Western democratic countries and try to follow suit, and believing that as all countries modernize, they will become more inclined to bourgeoisie, consumerism, peace—just like the West. Along with the modernization of society, the people in non-Western countries will become more secular, just like the people in Europe and the United States. Their driving force is much more from the desire to make money than to conquer others. They are more inclined to settle in the suburbs than to pursue fanatical ideology or have that kind of desire for prestige and conquest that has caused human beings to undergo hundreds of years of wars.

This general optimism in the West has also influenced the Western perception of Chinese modernization to a large extent. Although China is a socialist country with its own unique historical experience, development model, political system and civilization paradigm, and it has not and cannot become a Western-style country, yet for a very long time, the West has held an illusion about China, firmly believing that China's reform and opening-up will one day promote the evolution of China into another

[10] Francis Fukuyama, *The End of History and the Last Man* (New York: Free Press, 1992).

[11] James M. Fallows, *More Like Us: Making America Great Again* (New York: Houghton Mifflin Harcourt, 1989).

Western-style country. Since the reform and opening-up, the successive leaders of China have stressed time and again that it is impossible for China's system to evolve into a political system similar to the West, and they have been reforming at the policy level. On the one hand, they oppose China's system sliding into the Western style, and on the other hand, they actively build a political system that conforms to Chinese civilization, culture, and national conditions. However, political figures in the West believe that these efforts by Chinese leaders will eventually prove to be in vain, because liberal democracy is a universal system that human beings should accept and there is no force that can stop liberal democracy from happening. This is the general attitude of the West to accept China. It should also be pointed out that the discourse change among China's domestic intellectuals is also an external source of this Western optimism. At that time, many intellectuals in China also held the similar view, believing that globalization driven by the reform and opening-up would not only contribute to material progress, but also promote China's institutional and human modernization, and ultimately achieve the world commonwealth.

There are two more factors that have also greatly reduced the political pressure from the West upon China. First, for a long time, though Chinese leaders have opposed the evolution of China's political system into a Western style, yet under the principle of "seeking common ground while shelving the differences", China has also actively engaged in dialogue with the West and sought political peaceful coexistence. This attitude of China is actually a direct reflection of Chinese civilization. As one secular civilization, Chinese civilization is characterized with inclusiveness and openness, and has never refused to deal with any civilization. Although Chinese civilization will not and has not evolved into another civilization, its inclusiveness and openness allow Chinese civilization to absorb the elements from other civilizations to the maximum extent, and transform them into part of Chinese civilization. Second, after the disintegration of the Soviet Union, Western democracy gained enough room for expansion. For many years, the Soviet Union and Eastern European countries have become the focus of concern for Western countries. This has also objectively eased the pressure on China in terms of political democratization.

CHAPTER 5

Chinese Modernization Under Great Convergence

The "convergence" of globalization and modernization has brought unprecedented momentum for change to China. From the perspective of globalization, at least the changes in the following major aspects are the direct products of the "Great Convergence" of globalization and modernization:

1. **Outward-looking or Export-oriented economy**

In this respect, the development trajectory of China, Japan, and the "Four Asian Tigers" economies is similar, that is, by connecting with the Western-dominated economic system, an outward-looking or export-oriented economy has been formed. Today people talk about "external cycle" or "international circulation", but in fact the cities in the coastal areas including the Yangtze River Delta and the Pearl River Delta have grown up under the international circulation from the very beginning, that is, they have grown up under the open conditions. Starting from the 1980s, China's foreign trade enterprises, especially processing trade enterprises have adhered to the development strategy of "two ends outside, big import and big export", and embarked on the track of development by taking Original Equipment Manufacturer (OEM) for the foreign brands as the main way. They import raw materials from abroad and then sell

Z. Yongnian, *The Great Convergence VS. The Great Divergence*, https://doi.org/10.1007/978-981-96-7846-4_5

their products abroad after processing them at home, thus placing the "two ends" of the production process in the international market. In 2013, China has become the world's largest trading country in goods and this development model of "big import and big export" contributed significantly. In fact, because of globalization, the cities in China have occupied a very favorable position in the international division of labor system. In the Pearl River Delta region, for example, today, Guangzhou's status as an international business and trade center city has been strengthened, Shenzhen has sprung up from a small fishing village to a first-tier city in China and has become a city of scientific and technological innovation or the "Silicon Valley" of China, and Dongguan and Foshan are manufacturing cities. These are all related to the international division of labor arising from globalization. The rise of the urban belts in the Yangtze River Delta and other regions also took place under the same background.

If China does not join the world economy, it is hard to imagine the high-speed urbanization since the reform and opening-up. Urbanization does not simply build tall buildings, but requires economic activities. The outward-looking economic activities are a main driving force behind the high-speed urbanization of China.

2. Technological progress

Since the reform and opening-up, China has become the largest application market of technology in Western countries, especially the United States. Since the Trump administration, the United States has been accusing China of "stealing" American technology, which is of course slandering and demonizing China. If it is "stealing", the United States also "stole" the technology of other countries at the beginning of its development. Worldwide, Britain was the first country to realize its industrialization, and then industrialization diffused to other countries. This diffusion process is the process of technology diffusion. In Europe, compared with Britain, Germany, France, and Italy are post-developing countries. These countries all learn from Britain, and in this process, the government plays an important role. The United States also learned from Britain and other European countries in the early stages of its industrialization. The government not only helped enterprises "steal" European technology, but also practiced mercantilism to protect national industry. Only after the national industry grows up will the opening-up policy be implemented. And furthermore, it must be pointed out that the diffusion of technology from the United States and other Western countries to China, is mutually beneficial for both sides. China's application of American technology has effectively assisted the domestic technological upgrading in the United States. American enterprises export a lot of technology with low added value to China, while making a lot of money from China, which is very conductive to the domestic technological upgrading in the United States. It is a simple fact that the United States has never exported the real high technology to China. What should be stressed more is that the United States and other Western countries have transferred some manufacturing industries to China, and for many years, China has paid a huge price for environmental protection.

For China, we should realize that since the reform and opening-up, China indeed has made technological progress from the process of Western technological diffusion. What needs to be emphasized is that up to now, China has been still mainly the application market of Western technology, and the original technology for Chinese enterprises themselves has been still very insufficient. The Pearl River Delta region has become a symbol of "made in China", but we must have a correct understanding of "made in China". Before the 1980s, when people said "made in Germany", "made in the United States", or "made in Japan", these countries mostly produced the whole products, because globalization at that time was limited globalization, restricted to traditional investment and trade. But the globalization after the 1980s was completely different. The neoliberal policy that began with the Regan Revolution in the United States and the Thatcher Revolution in Britain, led to what people would call hyper-globalization later. Under the hyper-globalization, capital, technology and talents have gained a great deal of freedom and can flow around the world, which greatly promoted the international division of labor, and thus the industrial chain and supply chain systems have also emerged on a global and regional scale. In this context, the connotation of "made in China" has undergone great changes. "Manufacturing" is no longer creation or production in the original sense. More scientifically speaking, it is "China assembly". Many parts of a product are produced in other countries, especially in other Asian countries, then transported to China, assembled in China and then exported to all countries in the world. Today, people use concepts such as "created in China" or "intelligent manufacturing in China", which actually refers to "manufacturing" before the 1980s, that is, the transformation from the application of technology to the creation of original technology.

3. **Release of demographic dividend**

Economists have been emphasizing the importance of the demographic dividend on economic development, which is not wrong. However, the release of the demographic dividend requires conditions. Since modern times, the most important condition has been economic development driven by industrialization. Empirically, there is a demographic dividend in many countries, but only after industrialization takes off can the demographic dividend be fully released. China's demographic dividend did not come into being after the reform and opening-up. As a matter of fact, before the reform and opening-up, China had a demographic dividend. At that time, it was considered that the population was too large, and the economic development could not keep up with the demands of population, which also became the basis for the implementation of the family planning policy in the 1980s. China's demographic dividend has been released because of globalization. As far as the Pearl River Delta region is concerned, industrialization in the context of globalization has empowered the Pearl River Delta region, which has attracted a large number of "immigrants" from all parts of China, namely the migrant-worker "immigrants". For many years after China's accession to the World Trade Organization, the Pearl River Delta region has become the manufacturing hub of China, absorbing about 30 million migrant workers every year. Shenzhen has developed from a small town in the early 1980s to a metropolis with a population of 20 million today, which can be said to be the product of "immigration". The United States says that China has "stolen" American jobs, but it is actually the direct product of the globalization of capital. Indeed, after the 1980s, the technological development in the United States did not bring jobs to the United States, because American technology was exported to many developing countries including China, which brought employment to these countries. In a sense, migrant workers in the Pearl River Delta region are actually the "working class of the United States".

4. **Rise of private enterprise clusters**

The present mixed economic system in China has evolved from the planned economic system before the reform and opening-up, and it was the development of private economy that contributed to the formation of mixed economic system. Since the reform and opening-up, there are three main sources for the growth of private enterprises in China.

The first source is that the fields outside state-owned enterprises (SOEs), mostly developed from the early self-employed (or *getihu*). The private enterprises that grew up in the 1980s were all self-employed at that time. Although township and village enterprises (TVEs) in China belong to collective-owned ones in terms of ownership, yet they are also part, or even the main part of the self-employed group. Most of these township and village enterprises have evolved into private enterprises through restructuring in the later days.

The second source is privatization. Privatization in the mid-1990s has transformed many state-owned enterprises to private enterprises. At that time, the reform policy of state-owned enterprises called "grasping the large, letting go the small" (or *zhuada, fangxiao*) was carried out. The reason is that many state-owned enterprises at the time had low efficiency in productivity and could not effectively push forward the country's economic development. Instead, privatization of a large number of small and medium-sized state-owned enterprises became an effective measure of "reducing their burdens" for governments at all levels, that it, "letting go the small". At the same time, governments at all levels began to restructure major state-owned enterprises into large-scale enterprise groups (or *qiye jituan*), that is, "grasping the large". Until today, whether it is a state-owned enterprise or a private enterprise, its basic pattern has been formed under the policy of "grasping the large, letting go the small".

The third source is foreign capital. After foreign capital entering China, it is mainly distributed in the fields of manufacturing and high technology. Briefly speaking, the application of Western technology in China is realized through foreign capital. Owing to the constraints of the system, foreign capital does not cooperate too much with state-owned enterprises after entering China, and mostly with private enterprises. From an empirical point of view, private enterprises that grow up through foreign capital have strong vitality, because these enterprises are often technology-oriented and connect with the international market. Certainly, many private enterprises have separated from foreign capital, and become completely local enterprises. As far as the relationship with the West is concerned, China's state-owned enterprises have never been systematically integrated with the international economic system, which is not only due to the system, but also because the West has ideological and political bias against China's state-owned enterprises. And this part of private enterprises that grew up through foreign capital has been related to the world economy from the very beginning, or they are originally part of the world economy.

In other words, private enterprises have always been the main part and grasper for China to integrate with the world economy. This point has been seen very clearly since the Trump administration launched the trade war against China. From Trump to Biden, the US government has been doing everything possible to decouple from China's economy and trade, but it has not succeeded. Empirically, China's state-owned enterprises have no real connection with the Western economy, and they are either forced to decouple or take the initiative to decouple. The failure of decoupling between China and the United States is mainly the result of private enterprises in China. In the international economy, China's private enterprises have shown a very strong resilience in the international industrial chain and supply chain systems.

These economic changes directly caused by globalization have also contributed to institutional changes or modernization in all aspects of China. As we can see today, although China's transformation has not led to Westernization at the institutional and human levels, yet as far as China's own history is concerned, globalization-driven modernization is undoubtedly in all directions. We can at least discuss it from the following levels:

1. **Modernization of ideology**

During the period from the May Fourth Movement to the reform and opening-up, China transformed into a highly ideological society due to the revolution-style and "continuing revolution-style" mobilization for a long time. Ideology guides everything and measures everything. Here it refers to the ideology of political mobilization type that adapts to the planned economic system. The reform and opening-up made China accept the market once again. Before this, the market was regarded as only the product of capitalism, and China's socialist system could not allow the market to exist. But Deng Xiaoping's generation of Chinese leaders solved the problem. In Deng Xiaoping's opinion, the market itself has no ideological component, and it is just a tool for human beings to create wealth. Therefore, capitalism can make use of the market, and socialism can also make use of the market. This de-ideological market consciousness undoubtedly accords with the historical and realistic situation. Historically, over China's thousands of years of history, for most of the period, China's market existed and was quite developed. Only in several short periods did the government adopt the policy of economic statism hostile to the market.[1] In reality, apart from the Soviet Union and some countries in Eastern Europe, market also exists under different political and economic systems. In 1992, the 14th CPC National Congress, after Deng Xiaoping's South Tour Speeches, formally put forward the concept of socialist market economy and wrote it into the Constitution, thus the governing party completed its ideological transformation. From the perspective of globalization, this transformation is not only a product of globalization, but also a prerequisite for China to integrate into the world. It is hard to imagine that how China can achieve its connection with the rest of the world and go outside under the ideology of planned economy. Until today, there are still a few economies that reject the market economy and remain outside the world economic system.

It should be emphasized that the ideological transformation mentioned here refers to the ideology at the official level. At the level of social ideology, Chinese society is more and more characterized by diversity, and its views and attitudes toward the market also vary widely. There are those who believe in the market economy, and those who do not believe in the market economy; there are those who benefit from the market economy and those who suffer from it; there are those who advocate the complete marketization and those who advocate the elimination of the market economy. The ideological forces at the social level manifest themselves in different ways from time to time, and try to influence the government's decision-making. Although the governing party and its government will inevitably be affected by social ideological forces, and their internal views on the market are not always be consistent, the market has gained ideological and legal legitimacy.

[1] See Zheng Yongnian and Huang Yanjie's book *Market in State: The Political Economy of Domination in China*, which has been translated into Chinese by Qiu Daolong (Hangzhou: Zhejiang People's Publishing House, 2021).

Whether it is the diversified market ideology at the social level, or different views on marketization within the government, differentiation itself is an important symbol for modernization. Regardless of the West and the East, the main feature of traditional society is "consistency", while the main feature of modern society is "pluralism". It is more appropriate to use the concept of "pluralism and integration" to describe the ideological status quo of Chinese society.

2. Modernization of the governing party

In China, the Communist Party of China is the main political force, so Chinese modernization in all aspects depends first and foremost on the modernization of the governing party itself. In other words, the governing party leads the modernization of the country and society with its own modernization. As mentioned above, under the globalization, China has developed a variety of economic elements, that is, today's "fixed economy". This objective situation requires the governing party to transform. Just as Marx revealed, economy is the foundation and politics is the superstructure. When the economic foundation has changed, the superstructure should also change with it. In other words, economy is modernized, the superstructure should also be modernized with it. Like the Communist Party in other parts of the world, the traditional purpose of the Communist Party of China is also to abolish private ownership and eliminate the bourgeoisie. This was also done before the reform and opening-up. After the reform and opening-up, the governing party kept pace with the times and overcame ideological resistance. First, it amended the Constitution to give legal legitimacy to all kinds of legal property (including private property), and then formulated the *Property Law of the People's Republic of China* and the *Civil Code of the People's Republic of China*, to provide legal protection for all kinds of legal property. In the meantime, the governing party has also gradually opened up its political process, allowing and encouraging private entrepreneurs to join the Communist Party. In this way, the governing party has been transformed, at least in theory, from a closed party representing a specific class to an open party that can represent the social interests of the majority. During the revolutionary period, the Communist Party without doubt should rely on the specific social strata with revolutionary nature, but after becoming the governing party, it needed to transform, and became the leader for all social strata. This transformation of the governing party is a milestone of China's politics, and it is also the most significant change in the field of China's politics. Western academics and policy research circles often fail to see this and view China's reform model as one that is "only economic reform without political reform". This is also an important reason why the West still has the difficulty understanding China so far. In fact, the Communist Party in the Soviet Union and Eastern European countries were eliminated by history because they could not keep up with the times, while the Communist Party of China has not only realized its own transformation and development, but also effectively led the country's modernization. Although Western society perceives the Communist Party of China as conservative because it has not evolved into a Western-style political party, yet from an empirical perspective, the Communist Party of China can be said to be the most modern political party in the world. Once the Communist Party of China views a system or phenomenon as modernity, it will pursue it and achieve it without hesitation. It is very simple because only by doing so can the Communist Party of China keep pace with the times and lead the times. From the perspective of consolidating and strengthening the leadership of the Party, the West regards the Communist Party of China as "conservative", but from the perspective of changing self and self-revolution, the modernity of the Communist Party of China is self-evident.

3. Modernization of the bureaucracy

Although China was the first country to establish the bureaucratic system in the world, yet this set of bureaucratic system established in 1949 when the People's Republic of China was founded, entirely served for the planned economy at that time, and administered various economic and social activities. This set of bureaucratic system was incompatible with the market economy, so the reform of bureaucratic system has always been the focus of reform. From the 1980s to the late 1990s, through many bureaucratic reforms (or institutional reforms), China has established a set of bureaucratic system that basically adapted to the market economy. The most extensive reform took place during the time when Zhu Rongji was the prime minister in the 1990s. At that time, in order to join the World Trade Organization and connect with the world, China has carried out a comprehensive reform of its own legal, regulatory and policy systems, which has provided huge impetus for institutional reforms.[2] After entering the twenty-first century, the focus of the reform of the bureaucratic system has shifted to the reform of "super-ministry system". This was also the need to continue to integrate with the world. Under the "super-ministry system", the functions of the government should be transformed from directly engaging in and intervening in economic activities to regulating economic activities and providing services for enterprises. Today, this task is far from complete, but the direction is clear.

4. Modernization of the economic system

In the times of planned economy, the "trinity" of government, society and enterprise constituted a strict management and control system. One enterprise is also a social and political body. In the case of absence of separation of organizational functions, China has no basic construction of state system. After the market economy began, the "trinity" system soon failed to meet the needs of the times. By far, although the state-owned enterprises and government have not been separated, Chinese society has basically achieved functional separation, that is, the enterprises and their social functions have been separated, and government functions and economic functions have been separated. This requires the construction of an economic system compatible with the market economy. Great progress has been made in this respect. China has set up the basic state system to support the market economy, including the tax-sharing system, the central bank system and the financial system. At the same time, under the mixed economic system, China has also basically achieved the basic balance between state-owned sectors and non-state-owned sectors, large state-owned enterprises and small and medium-sized private enterprises, thus achieving the basic balance between the government and the market.

5. Modernization of society

[2] For a discussion of the impact of globalization on China's institutional transformation, see Zheng Yongnian's book *Globalization and State Transformation in China*, which has been translated into Chinese by Yu Jianxing and He Ziying (Hangzhou: Zhejiang People's Publishing House, 2009).

As mentioned earlier, before the reform and opening-up, China organized the society by its ideology. Obviously, the different groups in society are divided by political ideology, and also are managed and controlled by it. This reached its peak during the "Cultural Revolution". The so-called "land, rich, counter, bad, right" ("*Five Black Categories*": landlords, rich peasants, counterrevolutionaries, bad elements, and rightists) and so on are all highly politicized labels and hats. After de-ideologization, Chinese society returned to nature and transformed into a class and interest-oriented society. Although the class and interest-oriented society will also have many problems, mainly manifested in multi-level differentiation, such as income differences, class differences, and related cognitive differences and belief differences, yet compared with the ideology-oriented society that requires consistency, the society with pluralistic interests and consciousness is much more in line with human nature, and therefore it has much more modernity.

In other words, in the past few decades, Chinese modernization in all aspects has been realized in the state of globalization. Globalization has provided the most direct dynamic mechanism for Chinese modernization. So, the question now is, how will anti-globalization affect Chinese modernization? Will anti-globalization slow down or even interrupt Chinese modernization? Under the condition of anti-globalization, how will China continue to promote its modernization? Beginning from the next chapter, we will discuss these issues.

CHAPTER 6

From Hyper-Globalization to "World Chaos"

Why is the world undergoing a transition from hyper-globalization to anti-globalization?

As the ancient Chinese saying "thirty years to the east of the river, thirty years to the west of the river" reveals, today not only is hyper-globalization no longer, but the world has entered the era of "troubled times". Although globalization will continue at the level of goods trade and capital flow, and the diffusion of technology will not cease, yet globalization as the driving logic of world affairs has ended. Economic competition has converged with geopolitics, political system, ideology, morality, and other competitions to become a competition for global dominance. As the interconnected points among countries promoted by hyper-globalization in the past are decoupled one by one, more and more people are worried that the world is splitting into one Western region centered on the United States and one region centered on China. If this trend cannot be reversed, the cold war in the style of the United States and the Soviet Union will become inevitable. Some people even worry that China and the United States have already entered the state of the cold war. Now what needs to be worried is whether there will be a hot war between the two countries. Between 1875 and 1914, the world also experienced a similar wave of "hyper-globalization". By the beginning of the twentieth century, Norman Angell wrote a book *The Great Illusion*,

Z. Yongnian, *The Great Convergence VS. The Great Divergence*, https://doi.org/10.1007/978-981-96-7846-4_6

arguing that the globalized nations in that era would not break out of war because of their excessive inter-dependence in economy.[1] Nowadays, people regard it as a negative textbook, and believe it is only an illusion to facilitate human events and unite all nations together with material forces, such as economy and technology. The decades of "hyper-globalization" before 1914 eventually led to the world war, and it was not one war, but two wars. Today, people have no reason not to worry that history will repeat itself, or repeat itself in another way.

The dramatic changes in today's international environment are indeed a bit surprising. But from the perspective of big history, such changes are also normal. Just as globalization does not unfold linearly, modernization also does not unfold linearly, and globalization and modernization even do not always converge. Whether it is globalization or modernization, each progress is promoted by different factors and has different influences on all countries. Similarly, the reasons for each regression are also different, and their influences on all countries are more different. All countries need to seek and analyze the reasons for progress or regression, because progress is what people want and regression is what people do not want.

Although modernization began in the West, and then diffused to other countries around the world, yet non-Western countries are definitely not only a passive role, but also not simply respond to the modernization that extended from the West. Even if it is a response, different responses have different endings. Since modern times, the different modernization models of non-Western countries such as Japan, Russia, Turkey and China have illustrated this point. It should be noted that even in the West, modernization varies from country to country. The Industrial Revolution started in Britain, and when it extended to France, Germany, Italy, and other countries, modernization took different models.

The same is also true of globalization. Empirically, in the past wave of globalization, those countries that refused to join or refused to be involved in the wave of globalization did not change much, but for those countries that chose to join or were passively involved in the wave of globalization, the outcomes are also not the same. Whether it is the process of modernization or the wave of globalization, once involved, it will produce

[1] Norman Angell, *The Great Illusion: A Study of the Relation of Military Power in Nations to their Economic and Social Advantage, 3 ed.* (New York and London: G. P. Putnam's & Sons, 1911).

winners and losers. But who is the winner and who is the loser does not necessarily depend on who is the initiator or who is the follower. Modernization started in Western Europe, but Western European countries are not always winners. The late-comers including Japan and the "Four Asian Tigers" economies in Asia, not only caught up with the western Europe, but even surpassed it. Globalization is the same. As mentioned above, the United States and Britain are the initiators and promoters of this wave of globalization, and China and India are the followers, but as the initiators, the United States and Britain now call themselves the "victims" of globalization, while China and India are viewed as the winners. Indeed, just as the development of China and India over the past few decades has been inseparable from globalization, the populism prevailing in Britain and the United States today is also the product of globalization.

From this point of view, it is of great significance, especially for China, to find and analyze the reasons of today's international disorder. As a major country, China has been a participant of globalization over the past decades and also benefited a lot from globalization. As discussed above, Chinese modernization has made great progress in the process of globalization. How to effectively deal with the chaos of today's international order and then achieve sustainable modernization requires us to make an objective and rational analysis of the situation. Because China is an internal part of this process, there is no reason to attribute the causes of "regression" and "chaos" solely into "external factors". Only by assuming its share of responsibilities that should be borne, can China make sense of its roles in the future.

The chaotic situation in today's world is caused by a variety of intricate factors, but four of them are the most important: the COVID-19 pandemic, the conflict between Russia and Ukraine, the "re-feudalization" of the international order, and the decoupling between China and the United States.

1. The COVID-19 pandemic

If we understand history, it is not difficult to find that there have been many times in history when wars and conflicts walked hand in hand with the pandemic. Unfortunately, this time the COVID-19 pandemic once again walked together with war and conflict. This time, the COVID-19 pandemic came first, and the conflicts followed later. In the past few years, the COVID-19 has had great impact on various countries, and from the occurrence to the circulation, various countries have been deeply affected and tired of coping with it. However, with the weakening of the virulence of the novel coronavirus variant strain, human beings are returning to normal life. Still, no one can claim that the COVID-19 pandemic has completely disappeared, and many societies have not recovered from the negative impact caused by the COVID-19 on the supply chains and the industrial chains.

On the whole, European and American countries have basically been unsuccessful in fighting the pandemic. In the past, it was very difficult for us to understand this failure in Europe and the United States, because established capitalist countries like the United States and Britain owned developed medical systems and huge resources that the developed economies can mobilize, and they should do better than China. On the other hand, China, in some respects, is still an undeveloped country compared with developed countries like Britain and the United States. China's per capita GDP will only reach $12,000 by 2021, while the per capita GDP of these developed economies in Europe and the United States all exceeds $50,000, which is much more developed than ours. However, China's prevention and control of the COVID-19 pandemic has been very successful this time compared with other countries. What is the reason for this?

The COVID-19 pandemic has exposed the weakness of various state systems. China owes its success to what we call the capabilities of institutional mobilization. In contrast, in the West, although the state resources are very strong, many contradictions arise between the state and society and between the government and the people when it comes to governing the crisis. These also have something to do with the differences between the individualism-centered culture in the West and the collectivism-centered culture in Asia. Because not only China, but other Asian countries and regions have been generally much more successful than the West, in responding to the COVID-19 pandemic. Even those societies such as Japan and South Korea, which are heavily influenced by Western culture, have been much more effective than Western countries in prevention and treatment of the COVID-19 pandemic. This time the COVID-19 pandemic has tested the system of every country.

The COVID-19 pandemic not only divided the country, but also divided the society. When human beings face the crisis, all kinds of weaknesses will be revealed, not only in the question of whether people and novel coronavirus can coexist, but also in the question of whether people can coexist with each other. The COVID-19 crisis has greatly divided American society. China, to some extent, also has the similar problems, but the difference only lies in its controllable or uncontrollable—we are controllable, but many Western countries are out of control. Naturally, the society is divided not only because of the impact of the COVID-19 pandemic, but also because of the impact on the society of the huge economic rescue plans launched by various countries and governments during the COVID-19 pandemic. In essence, the huge financial and fiscal plans of various countries are mainly used to rescue social crisis, but the economic resources allocated by the state instead aggravated social injustice. This is very obvious in American society.

The ongoing fermentation of the COVID-19 crisis has also affected the relationship between countries. There are few exchanges between countries, and the aviation industry all over the world has suffered a disastrous impact. The decrease in state-to-state interaction naturally leads to the decrease in people-to-people interaction. In other words, the so-called decoupling occurs not only between countries, but also between people. In terms of Sino-US relationship, since the outbreak of the COVID-19 crisis, China and the United States not only has decoupled from each other in economy and trade, but also generated serious opposition in ideology, governance philosophy, values and other aspects. The people of the two countries have quarreled with each other on social media.

If people pay attention to social media, they will find the COVID-19 crisis has led to the rise of populism in various countries. If it manifests itself in populism at home, it manifests itself in nationalism on the international political stage. In the United States, this populism is also manifested in disputes between various races. Since the COVID-19 crisis, the living environment of Asian Americans and other ethnic groups has become bad, while the nationalist sentiment has profoundly been influencing the US foreign policy toward other countries.

2. The conflict between Russia and Ukraine

The Russia-Ukraine conflict is expected. Although it was initiated by Russia, the root of the conflict lies in the US-led NATO. NATO is a product of the Cold War, and its enemy at that time was the Warsaw

Pact, that is, the Soviet Union—Eastern European bloc. After the disintegration of the Soviet Union—Eastern European bloc, the Warsaw Pact also disappeared, but NATO not only did not dissolve, but began to its expansion one round after another. NATO expanded eastward five times in a row until Ukraine also wanted to join NATO, pushing Russia to its doorstep and posing a threat to Russia's national security.

Some people think this conflict was caused by the personal character of Russian President Putin. This is the rhetoric that Western media and Western political figures push the main responsibility to Putin alone. It is not scientific to exaggerate Putin's personal role, and the root cause of the conflict does not lie in Putin. Gorbachev, the former leader of the Soviet Union, was very pro-Western. After the disintegration of the Soviet Union, Yeltsin, the first president of Russia, was also pro-Western, and even Putin himself was also pro-Western in his early days. They all wanted to join the Western camp and even NATO, but the West refused Russia's request.

It is also a fact that Putin does not like the West. Then people will have to ask, why did Putin, who was very pro-Western in his early days, later become an anti-Western figure? Quite naturally, this is the result of the long-term interaction between the West and Russia. The eastward expansion of NATO has made Russia feel unsafe as a country. Even if there is no Putin, as long as the NATO's eastward expansion threatens Russia's security, there will also be another Putin.

So, what will the future hold for the Russia-Ukraine conflict?

The first possibility is that Russia will fail completely, and even some people say that it will cause a second disintegration of Russia. In various ways, the West sanctioned Russia with the unprecedented tools. The Russia-Ukraine conflict is not only the conflict between Russia and Ukraine, but soon becomes a conflict between Russia and Ukraine as an agent of the West after the conflict begins. The NATO countries led by the United States are not directly involved in the conflict, but they pay, contribute, and supply weapons. Ukraine is actually an agent in disguise. However, historically, the big countries are hard to be defeated. The Russian nation is full of disasters. After the October Revolution in 1917, the whole West has also tried to contain the communist revolution of the Soviet Union. For half a century after 1945, the West has all been fighting against the Soviet Union. Despite the disintegration of the Soviet Union, Russia was still a big country after that. There is no possibility that Russia will completely fail.

The second possibility is that Russia will win completely. That is to say, Russia has achieved its goals, such as Ukraine not joining NATO, the demilitarization of Ukraine, Ukraine not allowing foreign countries to set up military bases, recognizing the independence of Crimea. This possibility is also very small. Ukraine is larger than Germany, and it is difficult for Russia to annex the whole of Ukraine. On social media, many people are discussing what Putin is going to do, but most of them are the speculations of Western media and Western political figures, because people have no idea what Putin really wants. The final result could be a partial failure and a partial success for Russia.

The Russia-Ukraine conflict indicates the disintegration of the international system with the United Nations as its center established since World War II. When the United Nations cannot impose its checks and balances in any effective ways to make its member countries to comply with the rules, it shows that the United Nations system has failed. The United Nations is not a country, but a system composed of one set of rules. When its rules are useless and non-binding on its member countries, this system composed of rules is basically in the state of disintegration.

"There is no winner in the war". But in the short term, the United States is the winner. The United States has achieved what President Biden called two "unity". The first is the unity among European countries, because the Russia-Ukraine conflict has given European countries another common enemy. The second is the unity between the United States and Europe. The United States in Trump's time has "withdrawn treaties and organizations" everywhere, and has not attached importance to the relationship between the United States and its European allies. After Biden came to power, the first priority was to restore the relations with its European allies on the international level, and the Russia-Ukraine conflict undoubtedly helped the United States realize the unity. In addition, there is also another unity, that is, the United States has realized the "unity" between China and Russia. However, it is obvious that this unity is "being united", which is the result of Western political figures and media tying China and Russia together, and the Western ongoing efforts to shape the concept of "China-Russia axis" in the narrative of international discourse.

In the long run, though, the United States is both a winner and a loser. Why do we say that?

First, on the surface, it seems that the United States and Europe are united, but in fact they are not. The first thing, Europe is experiencing a very serious energy crisis. Overall, European countries rely on Russia for about 40% of their energy, while Germany relies on Russia for more than 50% of its energy. For a long run, they can propose de-Russification, but it will undoubtedly be a disaster for Europe to let European countries cut off their relations with Russia in a short period of time when there is a high degree of dependence. No government can afford it and no enterprise can afford it. The next, Europe is also experiencing a food crisis. Ukraine and Russia can be said to be the breadbasket of Europe, especially Ukraine. Then there is the supply chain crisis. In the short term, although the Russia-Ukraine conflict has little impact on the United States, European countries will have to bear the crisis brought about by the conflict. Although the United States (the West) sanctions Russia, this decoupling and de-Russification can be described as "hurting enemy by one thousand, losing eight hundred by themselves". Russia is a "fighting nation", the tolerance of its people is very high, but countries like France, Germany, and Britain are used to being rich and their people's tolerance is very low.

Second, there is an issue of remilitarization of Germany. What impact will Germany's remilitarization impose on Europe? This is much easier to understand from the perspective of our neighbor Japan. How many years has Japan been trying to amend its pacifist constitution and militarize it again? However, this is not only difficult to reach a consensus in Japan, but also will lead to a strong backlash from Asian countries. The remilitarization of Japan will have a very profound impact on the whole geopolitics of East Asia.

Germany is taking advantage of the Ukrainian crisis to remilitarize this time. Everyone is very supportive, at least no country explicitly opposes it, and the United States is also pushing toward. The military budget of Germany suddenly rose to 2%. What does the remilitarization of Germany mean for Europe? What impact will it have on France? What impact will it have on the national relations between Britain, France and Germany? Professor Huntington of Harvard University in the United States has written a book entitled *The Clash of Civilizations and the Remaking of World Order*, arguing that after the end of the Cold War, different wars will happen between different civilizations, while there will be no more wars between European countries.[2] However, Huntington's judgment

[2] See Samuel Huntington's book *The Clash of Civilizations and the Remaking of World Order*, which has been translated into Chinese by Zhou Qi, Liu Fei, Zhang Liping and Wang Yuan (Beijing: Xinhua Publishing House, 2010).

may be wrong. We should know that World War I and World War II took place between European countries, between countries within the same civilization, the same culture, and even between countries with similar political systems and economic development levels. The remilitarization of Germany will impose a very significant influence on the geopolitics of Europe in the long run.

Third, the problem of nuclear proliferation will be more severe. Because of the conflict between Russia and Ukraine, some countries like Belarus have amended their constitutions to allow countries to have nuclear weapons. Some countries have also put forward the concept of "nuclear sharing", including Japan and South Korea in Asia, who want to share nuclear weapons with the United States on the grounds of North Korea. And countries such as Poland have decided to allow the United States to deploy nuclear weapons in Poland. The nuclear proliferation caused by the Russia-Ukraine conflict will become a new wave of threats, which will undoubtedly bring a greater insecurity to the world, including the United States itself. Although some scholars in the area of international relations also argue that if every country possessed nuclear weapons, would the world become more peaceful? Although people can have different assumptions, yet one factor is enough to make people draw a pessimistic conclusion—this world not only will not become peaceful, but will also be more dangerous. This factor is that people can never guarantee that no leader will "go crazy", and use nuclear weapons at will, leading to nuclear proliferation and nuclear war.

In addition, the Russia-Ukraine conflict also shows the failure of American diplomatic capabilities in disguise. Not only has China and Russia been tied together by the United States, but the United States itself has also kidnapped Europe. The United States has its own unique geopolitical advantage, surrounded by only two countries—Canada in the north and Mexico in the south. Now some people think that if the United States supports Ukraine, will it turn "Ukraine battlefield" into another Afghanistan battlefield? Afghanistan is in the Middle East, far from the United States and far from Europe. But now this "battlefield" is in Ukraine, in the very core of Europe. If Ukraine becomes another Afghanistan, the whole of Europe will suffer. Therefore, the United States has in fact kidnapped European countries. In dealing with the Russian issue and the European issue, the United States still proceeds from its own interests, not from the interests of European countries. Although Biden claims that the United States and Europe have realized unity because of the Russia-Ukraine conflict, yet this unity may be very fragile, which has been increasingly confirmed by the recent developments.

Even more important is the impact of this conflict on globalization. This influence is both profound and all-round. People can at least discuss this from the following aspects:

In the first place, this conflict has led to people's reconsideration of globalization on the ideological level. The Russia-Ukraine conflict has ended the myth that globalization brought world peace. In this respect, Larry Fink, Chairman and CEO of BlackRock in the United States has a typical thinking. After this conflict began, Fink warned in a chairman's letter to the group's shareholders on March 24, 2022 that Russia's "invasion" of Ukraine would reshape the world economy and "put an end to the globalization we have experienced over the last three decades". Fink wrote in this open letter, "Russia's brutal attack on Ukraine has upended the world order that had been in place since the end of the Cold War, more than 30 years ago. The attack on a sovereign nation is something we have not seen in Europe in nearly 80 years—and most of us never imagined that in our lifetimes we would see a war like this waged by a nuclear superpower".

Fink argues, "The ramifications of this war are not limited to Eastern Europe. They are layered on top of a pandemic that has already had profound effects on political, economic, and social trends. The impact will reverberate for decades to come in ways we can't yet predict". He pointed out, "In the early 1990s, as the world emerged from the Cold War, Russia was welcomed into the global financial system and given access to global capital markets. In time, Russia became interconnected with the world and deeply linked to Western Europe. The world benefited from a global peace dividend and the expansion of globalization. These were powerful trends that accelerated international trade, expanded global capital markets, increased economic growth, and helped to dramatically reduce poverty in nations around the world".

However, "The Russian invasion of Ukraine has put an end to the globalization we have experienced over the last three decades. We had already seen connectivity between nations, companies, and even people strained by two years of the pandemic. It has left many communities and people feeling isolated and looking inward. I believe this has exacerbated the polarization and extremist behavior we are seeing across society today. The invasion has catalyzed nations and governments to come together to sever financial and business ties with Russia. United in their steadfast commitment to support the Ukrainian people, they launched an "economic war" against Russia. Governments across the world almost unanimously imposed sanctions, including taking the unprecedented step of barring the Russian central bank from deploying its hard currency reserves".

In the next place, this conflict immediately led to a rapid and comprehensive decoupling of Russia from Western economies. As it is well known to all, after this conflict began, Western governments dominated the comprehensive decoupling of the Western economy from the Russian economy. But these efforts to decouple from Russia not only occurred at the level of Western governments, but also went deeper into the level of enterprises and companies. We continue to quote Fink's point of view. Fink noted, "Capital markets, financial institutions and companies have gone even further beyond government-imposed sanctions.......access to capital markets is a privilege, not a right. And following Russia's invasion, we saw how the private sector quickly terminated longstanding business and investment relationships".

Fink said, "The speed and magnitude of company actions to amplify sanctions has been incredible. Iconic American consumer brands have suspended their operations of non-essential products. And financial services companies have taken similar steps to further isolate the Russian economy from the global financial system. These actions taken by the private sector demonstrate the power of the capital markets: how the markets can provide capital to those who constructively work within the system and how quickly they can deny it to those who operate outside of it. Russia has been essentially cut off from global capital markets, demonstrating the commitment of major companies to operate consistent with core values. This 'economic war' shows what we can achieve when companies, supported by their stakeholders, come together in the face of violence and aggression".

With regard to the impact of the Russia-Ukraine conflict on Western countries, enterprises, and customers, Fink argues, "And while dependence on Russian energy is in the spotlight, companies and governments will also be looking more broadly at their dependencies on other nations. This may lead companies to onshore or nearshore more of their operations, resulting in a faster pull back from some countries. Others—like Mexico, Brazil, the United States, or manufacturing hubs in Southeast

Asia—could stand to benefit. This decoupling will inevitably create challenges for companies, including higher costs and margin pressures. While companies' and consumers' balance sheets are strong today, giving them more of a cushion to weather these difficulties, a large-scale reorientation of supply chains will inherently be inflationary".

Howard Marks, co-founder of US Oaktree Capital Management, L.P. also expressed similar views in a letter to investors. He highlighted Europe's dependence on Russian energy and the security risks of outsourcing computer chip manufacturing in the United States. In a memorandum to the clients published on March 23, 2022, Marks proposed, "The invasion of Ukraine has shown that Europe's importation of oil and gas from Russia has left it vulnerable to a hostile, unprincipled nation (worse in this case—to such an individual) at the same time that winding down nuclear power generation has increased the region's need for imported oil and gas. The practice of offshore procurement similarly makes countries and companies dependent on their positive relations with foreign nations and the efficacy of our transportation system".

Marks continued, "The recognition of these negative aspects of globalization has now caused the pendulum to swing back toward local sourcing. Rather than the cheapest, easiest and greenest sources, there'll probably be more of a premium put on the safest and surest. For example, both US and non-US companies have announced that they intend to build new foundries to produce semiconductors in the US. And I imagine many US importers of materials, components and finished goods are looking for sources closer to home. Similarly, it's now less likely that Germany will follow through on its plan to turn off its three remaining nuclear reactors on December 31 and more likely that it will reactivate the three it retired at the end of 2021 (and perhaps, with the rest of Europe, recalibrate the balance between energy imports and domestic energy production)".

Marks added, "If the pendulum continues to move for a while in the direction I foresee, there will be ramifications for investors. Globalization has been a boon for worldwide GDP, the nations whose economies it has lifted, and the companies that reduced costs by buying abroad. The swing away will be less favorable in those regards, but it may (a) improve importers' security, (b) increase the competitiveness of onshore producers and the number of domestic manufacturing jobs, and (c) create investment opportunities in the transition. For how long will the pendulum swing away from globalization and toward onshoring? The answer depends in part on how the current situations are resolved and in part on which force wins: the need for dependability and security or the desire for cheap sourcing".

Marks finally said in his memo, "If you substitute the words 'off-shoring' and 'domestic sourcing' for 'free markets' and 'regulation,' then this passage just as accurately describes the choice between the cheapest sourcing and the most secure sourcing. This absence of perfect, permanent solutions is characteristic of pendulums—it's why they swing. And after many decades of globalization and cost minimization, I think we're about to find investment opportunities in the swing toward reliable supply".

Once more, this conflict accelerated the process that the West, led by the United States, creates world bipolarization by shaping the narrative of "China-Russia axis". After the outbreak of this conflict, China not only expressed its regret over the conflict, but also believed that the expansion of NATO is the main cause that led to the conflict. As a matter of fact, most non-Western countries hold this view. However, the United States once again adopted the policy of "Either you are with us, or you are with the enemy" toward China after the "September 11 Attacks", cooperated with some Western countries, and took this conflict as an opportunity to shape the diplomatic narrative of "China-Russia axis", which accelerated its process of creating world bipolarization. To a large extent, as far as globalization is concerned, the negative impact brought by this diplomatic narrative is much more profound than the COVID-19 pandemic and the decoupling efforts led by the US government, and it is much more toxic to China's international business environment.

Edward Alden, a senior fellow at the US Council on Foreign Relations (CFR) who studies US economic competitiveness and trade policy, said in an interview with US media that the bigger concern for China is that the risk assessment around China has changed due to the close relationship between China and Russia, and China's refusal to condemn Russia's aggression. Alden said, "I think a lot of Western companies are rethinking their business in China. They have seen the results of Russia's invasion of Ukraine. Their economic interests in Russia have disappeared overnight, and this operation cost tens of millions of dollars to the Western companies. Now there are many Western companies with deep investments in China saying, what will happen if China does this to Taiwan? What will happen to our value of investment in China? Will it disappear overnight? Therefore, I think you are going to see a massive withdrawal of Western capital from China, which would be much bigger than the consequences of a trade war or a pandemic that we're seeing". Alden said, "For me, this is much more direct harm than Western sanctions". Indeed, since the outbreak of the Russia-Ukraine conflict, the United States and Europe have been creating ideas such as "China is unreliable" and "doing business with China is toxic".

The conflict between Russia and Ukraine and the narrative of "China-Russia axis" by the United States and European countries have not only worsened the Sino-US relationship, but also worsened the Sino-European relationship. These factors have not only made European countries withdrawal their capital from Russia, but also triggered European governments and private organizations to re-evaluate China in depth. The Russia-Ukraine conflict has disturbed the already fragile trade supply chain between China and Europe, while exacerbating the soaring costs of energy and raw materials. The geopolitical factors are also affecting the companies operating in China. According to Bloomberg, in late March 2022, before Shanghai was "locked down", a survey of 391 members of European Union Chamber of Commerce in China found that most German companies said that the crisis caused by the Russia-Ukraine conflict was impacting their China strategy. One-third of respondents said that they expected to put on hold the planned business or investment, while 46% saw a decrease in the attractiveness of Chinese markets. Some 10% said that the existing business was likely to move out of China, and 27% said that they expected Asia to accelerate its diversification.

Joerg Wuttke, president of the European Union Chamber of Commerce in China, pointed out that China's attitude toward Ukraine has had a big impact on its public image. Coupled with China's dynamic zero-COVID policy and related business disruptions, now the really dangerous idea of "China becoming unreliable" has been deeply rooted in people's heart.

In fact, the relationship between European Union and China has quickly deteriorated in recent years, mainly because the European Union has imposed sanctions on China for the so-called "human rights issues in Xinjiang". China has also fought back against the members of European parliament, resulting in the deadlock of EU-China Comprehensive Agreement on Investment (CAI).

3. The "re-feudalization" of the international order

Before the emergence of the modern international system in which sovereign states were supreme, the world has presented a feudal pattern in which multiple empires coexisted with obvious hierarchies and separation from each other. Because the modern international system is built on the sovereign states constructed since modern times, by borrowing the concept of "feudalism" before the rise of modern sovereign states, we can say that the current international situation has also produced new "feudal" characteristics. Following the decline of the United States as "one hegemonic superpower", other major powers in the world began to "compete on the Central plains"—all wanted to establish the spheres of influence, regional and even international order centered on themselves, which we call the "re-feudalization" of the international order.

In history, there have once been several eras when empires coexisted, such as the Roman Empire, the Qin and Han Empires in China. Although there were also population movement and trade within these empires, and there were also some trade exchanges between these empires, yet the scale was very limited. For example, China's Silk Road, Tea Horse Road and other trade routes were extremely limited in scale compared with the total amount of the intra-imperial trade at that time. In general, the coexistence of empires is mainly manifested as mutual isolation, and wars often occur due to the expansion of empires and the contradictions between different religions, races, and nationalities.

With the rise of modern sovereign states in the West, international relations have evolved into what scholars in the area of international relations call the international society, and every country is a member of the international society. If the members of a society are individuals, then the members of the international society are sovereign states, and in principle sovereign states are equal with each other. International relations based on "equal" sovereign states are not the same as feudal societies defined by Marxism. The former manifests itself as equality, at least in theory, while the latter manifests itself as hierarchy. For example, China's tributary system is hierarchical, and other countries also accept this hierarchy. As a matter of fact, the tributary system was not only manifested in China before 1840, but also existed within various empires around the world. The Indian Empire and the Roman Empire were all hierarchical without exception. It is only because China entered the form of modern sovereign states later than the West that China's tributary system was so prominent, but the tributary system is not the invention of China.

After entering the modern times, wars often occurred under the international system with sovereign states as the main members, the most typical ones were World War I and World War II, and the main battlefield took place between European sovereign states. However, the bipolarized international order during the period of the Cold War between the United States and the Soviet Union cannot be called "feudalism". The term "bipolarity" refers to the two large blocs, the United States and the Soviet Union, with the larger US-led Western markets on the one hand, and the smaller Soviet markets on the other hand. At the same time, few of the vast Third World countries could avoid these two big markets. They either had more relations with the West, or had more relations with the Soviet Union. The Cold War between the United States and the Soviet Union was the international system divided by ideological camps.

The "re-feudalization" of the contemporary international order refers, first and foremost, to the collapse of the US-led world integration promoted after the end of the Cold War. The first manifestation of integration is that the bipolarization during the period of the Cold War has never existed again, and the United States has become the sole hegemony. Second, it refers to the reconstruction of the world order by the United States after it has become "one hegemonic superpower", which includes both the reconstruction in military security and the reconstruction in economic globalization. However, as already discussed earlier, there are several basic conditions for the emergence of integration: The first condition is that globalization is dominated by the United States, and most countries, including China, have also accepted the world economic system dominated by the United States; the second condition is that the collective security provided by the United Nations at the international level, can coordinate the actions of countries, and the United Nations has a certain degree of binding force on major countries; the third condition is that it has formed the common values that are comparatively recognized around the world, highlighting the modernity of the international system. This further demonstrates that globalization is not only about the globalization of currency, goods and trade, but also with the disintegration of the Soviet Union, the values of democracy and freedom advocated by the West have become a dominant ideology on a global level. At least that is what the West thinks.

However, the existence of the integration of world order was short-lived. It is because many countries, including China, have not, and will not, become a system like that in the West. Before that, there had been a naive fantasy in the West: Even if China's political system is based on its civilization, China's reform and opening-up will eventually facilitate the transformation of China into a Western-style system. But, in fact, China actively conducts multi-dimensional dialogues with the West in order to seek common ground while shelving differences, and try to find common interests.

Nowadays, the United States is just like the king of Zhou during the Eastern Zhou Dynasty in China, it is no longer "one hegemonic superpower", its role as the world police has become unworthy of its name, and it is very difficult for the United States to maintain the world system headed by itself with its own strength. This is mainly manifested in the following aspects: One is that the excessive expansion of the American empire has brought out the problem of excessive costs. The United States is too selfish. Under the circumstances of "one hegemonic superpower", the United States has been pretending to serve the public for its private gains, wantonly expanding its territory, and becoming a new empire. However, due to the excessive expansion of the empire, the United States is unable to support this system. This is the direct reason why the United States has withdrawn from various international organizations, withdrawn from international affairs, and reduced its commitments to its allies in Trump's time. Biden changed this practice after he took office, but the problem raised by Trump still exists—the United States wants to maintain its hegemony in the international system, but its national power is difficult to maintain; the second is that there has been a strong backlash from other countries. Because the excessive expansion by the American empire, especially the eastward expansion of NATO led by the United States five times in a row, has caused a backlash from Russia. And the conflict between Russia and Ukraine is a manifestation of this backlash; the third is that emerging major countries such as China, India, Turkey, and Indonesia, have risen to share the world power with the United States.

When it comes to major-country competition, everyone thinks of the competition between China and the United States, just like the competition between the United States and the Soviet Union during the Cold War. What we cannot ignore, however, is that today's major-country competition is not just the one between China and the United States. During the period of Mao Zedong, we called the superpower the First World, besides which there were the Second World and the Third World. Now we still consider ourselves the largest Third World country, and we also represent the interests of the Third World countries, but from the perspective of other countries, China and the United States are now two superpowers. Just as the United States and the Soviet Union could not determine the whole world during the Cold War, China and the United States cannot determine the affairs of the whole world today. In fact, other big countries are playing increasingly significant role in today's international affairs.

Today, a remarkable phenomenon in international relations is that although Sino-US relationship is indeed important, yet major-country relations are not just Sino-US relationship. Many countries do not necessarily have to choose sides between China and the United States, the two major countries. Contemporary situations are very different from the situation during the Cold War when the United States and the Soviet Union were competing for hegemony. More countries are no longer simply "choosing one from the two" and each country is ensuring its national security in its own way. Simply put, the structure of international relations is moving toward "feudalization".

The most obvious one of these is Russia. As mentioned before, NATO as a bloc, if there are no restrictions from external forces, will never stop its expansion, and Russia has always felt insecure because of this. Therefore, it is understandable that Russia wants to counter NATO by establishing a bloc similar to "Mini Soviet Union", because only in this way can the expansion of NATO be stopped and Russia's basic national security be guaranteed.

India is also becoming a major country that has made a difference on the international political stage. India's attitude toward the Russia-Ukraine conflict is similar to that of China, and it even brazenly buys Russian energy for profits from it. In recent years, the United States has implemented the Indo-Pacific strategy to counterbalance China, and some people think that India will stand on the side of the United States to condemn Russia, but India has not done this. Why is that? Traditionally speaking, India has had a good relationship with the Soviet Union, and its military and equipment systems are also basically from the Soviet Union and Russia. Furthermore, India is also a country with its civilization, such a big country will not entirely lean against the United States, and the United States also has not enough abilities to "incorporate" the whole of India. Despite the similar positions between India and China, India has not been under great international pressure.

Turkey has played an important role in the Russia-Ukraine conflict this time, which is impressive. To some extent, Turkey has so far been the only winner in the development of this event. Turkey not only condemned the actions by Russia, but also condemned NATO's failure to properly deal with the relations with Russia. In the meantime, Turkey also displayed its superb diplomatic prowess by bringing Russia and Ukraine together and holding several rounds of negotiations in Istanbul, the capital. During the conflict between Russia and Ukraine, Turkey also took advantage of the favorable international environment to cross the border to attack the armed forces of the Kurdistan Workers' Party (PKK) in northern Iraq. Turkey was once a Muslim empire, and since modern times, it has changed from a former Muslim religious country to a secular country. However, the current President Erdogan has been promoting "re-religionization" and "de-secularization" after he came to power, to build a Turkish alliance and empire with ambitions. If he succeeds, with the impact of Turkey on the "Xinjiang Separation" forces all along, it will have a big influence on the situation in the northwest frontier in China.

Indonesia in Southeast Asia is also a major country with a population of several hundred million. If the role of Indonesia in the Association of Southeast Asian Nations (ASEAN) can be restored to what it was under Suharto before 1970, its primacy position in Southeast Asia cannot be ignored. Indonesia has also been pursuing a major-country status in the region, and has its own independent policy toward the United States and China. For China's Belt and Road Initiative (BRI or B&R), especially the "Maritime Silk Road", Indonesia is a top priority. The rise of Indonesia has undoubtedly had a big impact on the relationship between China and Southeast Asia.

Japan to the east of China is also another major country. Although China's economic aggregate has greatly surpassed Japan's since its rise, Japan, after all, was once the second largest economy in the world and it is now the third largest economy in the world. Up to now, Japan is still a big country with great capabilities in terms of technology, economy, and other aspects. With its technological and economic abilities, and the help of the United States, Japan has been pursuing its own bloc. Japan is now the main economy in the Comprehensive and Progressive Agreement for Trans-Pacific Partnership (CPTPP), and its economic power is the strongest in CPTPP. China formally applied to join the CPTPP in 2021, and it is regarded as China's "second accession to the WTO", but whether it can be realized will largely depend on Japan's attitudes toward China's entry into the CPTTP. Japan is more the main obstacle for China to resolve the Taiwan question.

4. The decoupling between China and the United States

The Sino-US relationship is not one pair of simple bilateral relationship. The two countries, China and the United States, are more like the two pillars of today's world order, and neither of them can fall down. Our country has always stressed that if China and the United States cooperate, anything can be done. If China and the United States do not cooperate, nothing can be done. It is a pity that the grand strategy of the United States now is to deal with China.

During the Cold War, the so-called great triangle between China, the United States, and the Soviet Union has been formed. President Nixon facilitated the establishment of Sino-US diplomatic relations, and China and the United States basically stood together. Although it was not a formal alliance, it was in fact a quasi-alliance that worked together to deal with the expansion of the Soviet Union. After the disintegration of the Soviet Union, the United States began to lay its emphasis on China. The United States has long made its judgment that it will be difficult for Russia to rise again after the collapse of the Soviet Union. Russia, for the United States, can only act as a "troublemaker", and it will not impose a fatal impact on the global interests of the United States. This fatal impact can only come from China.

During George Walker Bush administration, the rise of new conservatism in the United States was directed against China, with an aim to establish an Asian "Mini NATO". But then, because the "September 11 Attacks" happened, and the focus of the United States temporarily shifted to counter-terrorism. Also because of counter-terrorism, China and the United States have found some common interests.

Is the US counter-terrorism a success or a failure? In fact, the United States has not succeeded in its counter-terrorism, but the United States has just changed its mentality, believing that terrorism is a norm and everyone may have to face the threat of terrorism constantly. The United States has come to think that the real threat to the United States is China. In so doing, Obama has put forward a new concept, namely "pivot to Asia". Trump formally proposed the concept of "Indo-Pacific Strategy". At the early stage, the "Indo-Pacific Strategy" was only some informal communications. During the Trump administration, the Quadrilateral Security Dialogue (QUAD) between the United States, Japan, Australia, and India was a ministerial-level dialogue, and during the Biden administration, it has been elevated to the level of heads of state, and turned into a summit meeting.

Why did the United States end the war in Afghanistan from the Middle East? Why did the United States break away from Europe before the conflict between Russia and Ukraine? It is quite simply that the big goal of the United States is to shift its strategic focus to the Indo-Pacific region. Today, the United States has formed a series of alliances that can be called "two, three, four, five and six plus". The "two" refers to the bilateral allies of the United States in the Asia-Pacific region, such as the United States and Japan, the United States and South Korea, and the United States and Australia. The "three" is AUKUS, that is, the alliance of the United States, Britain and Australia. The "four" refers to the QUAD that have mentioned above. The "five" is the "Five Eyes Alliance". The "six" means adding Singapore, Vietnam, and other countries on the basis of the four Indo-Pacific countries. Naturally, the United States can expand indefinitely its alliances, and become "six plus".

The main purpose of the United States is still to form an Asian version of NATO against China. The United States has been reconstructing different types of alliances. For example, it hopes to integrate the bilateral alliance between the United States and Japan, and between the United States and South Korea into a trilateral alliance between the United States, Japan, and South Korea. It is only because there have been historical scars between Japan and South Korea that the trilateral alliance has not been able to form. The expansion of NATO has caused the conflict between Russia and Ukraine in Europe, while the United States has been trying to form a "Mini-NATO" in Asia. If the United States succeeds in its integration, it will have a dramatic impact on the geopolitics in Asia. This will not only stop China from realizing its national reunification, but will also pose a huge threat to China's national security.

There are also many means for the United States against China. The first means of the United States is bipolarization, that is, the establishment of one pole centered on the United States and one pole centered on China. This action has long started. In the field of ideology, after US president Biden came to power, he simply defined Sino-US relationship as a confrontation between the so-called "American democracy" and "Chinese autocracy", which is a struggle for systems. As discussed earlier, after the Russia-Ukraine conflict, the United States tied Russia and China together, which further pushed bipolarization a step forward. The United States describes itself as "democracy" and "civilization", while it describes China and Russia as "autocracy" and "barbarism". This is typical of ideological struggle.

The second means of the United States is decoupling. First of all, there is the decoupling of high technology. The United States has put a stranglehold around China's neck. For example, in the area of high technology such as chips, it is very obvious. Then there is decoupling in the aspects of economy, trade, investment, and finance. What is more serious is the decoupling of talents. The United States has now restricted Chinese students from studying abroad. It is becoming more and more difficult for Chinese students who have graduated from polytechnic to study in the United States because the so-called safety review (actually political review) is getting stricter and stricter.

After the conflict between Russia and Ukraine, some people are asking whether the United States is placing its emphasis on Europe again and is not going to shift back to the Asia-Pacific region. That is less likely. The Russia-Ukraine conflict only delayed and consumed some of the energy of the United States, while the grand strategy of the United States will not change, and it will still be placed in the Indo-Pacific region, with China as its target. Although the United States took advantage of various means to impose sanctions on Russia after the outbreak of the Russia-Ukraine conflict, yet the United States has never forgotten Taiwan, nor has it forgotten the South China Sea. In response to the conflict between Russia and Ukraine, the basic judgment of the United States is that Russia is only a "troublemaker", and their real main competitor and main enemy is China. The grand strategy of the United States will not change.

Under the influence of these four factors, the three pillars of the world order discussed earlier—economic interdependence, recognition of the international security system with the United Nations as its core, and recognition of the values of modernity—are being shaken at an accelerating pace. To a large extent, it can be said that the international system with the United Nations as its core since World War II has tended to collapse, and the world is heading for chaos. The chaos of the world is manifested in the following aspects:

1. **The dramatic deterioration of global economic and trade arrangements**

Economic interdependence is an important economic pillar of the world order, but what challenges economic interdependence is precisely the advocator of the liberal international order—the United States. Part of the reason for this situation can be contributed to the contradiction between economic and political logic of globalization itself. In developed countries, the main dividends of globalization have eventually flown to capital providers and high-skilled workers, which aggravates economic inequality between ordinary workers, white-collar workers, and capital owners. Some economists argue that this does not affect the necessity of globalization, because "the overall welfare of a society will increase". But it has been proved that the political consequences caused by gaps in income cannot be ignored. The wave of anti-globalization has begun to emerge. The anti-globalization sentiments bred by the sense of injustice have led to Brexit in Britain and the rise of populist political leaders such as Trump, the reversal of the economic policy for opening up to the outside world, and the collapse of capital in a highly politicized and toxic international environment. The Laissez Faire capitalist ideal of "capital can always benefit from globalization" has eventually come to a direct conflict with the secular politics under the system of "one person, one vote".

A report from *The Economist* in Britain said that between 2008 and 2019, the world trade has fallen by about five percentage points relative to global GDP. A series of new tariffs and other trade barriers are piling up. The flows of immigration are lower, too. Between 2016 and 2019, the global flows of long-term investment have fallen by half.

The stability of the international trade organization has also been challenged, and this challenge has still come from the United States. Since the Trump administration in the United States has adhered to the foreign policy of "America First", and launched a unilateral trade war against its trading partners including China, the recognition of the World Trade Organization has continuously been weakened. In the meantime, the trend of grouping in trade and investment is strengthening, and countries have begun to launch a new trade framework with themselves as the center, showing a tendency of "feudalization". The United States is leading the establishment of a so-called "value-based blocs" or investment framework. The European Union is strengthening the tendency of political and moral values of its trade policy. Japan is dominating the CPTPP. Turkey is constructing an economic bloc with Turkish as its core. All the other major countries such as India and Indonesia are also framing their trade and economic blocs with themselves as the core. During this process, "de-Sinicization" and "de-Russification" have become a core of the policy narrative of the United States and Western countries, and have become the leverage for the West to divide the world. If this trend has continued, the trading system based on the World Trade Organization will eventually be replaced by regional and grouping trade arrangements one by one. This has undoubtedly facilitated the disintegration of the economic foundation of the established world order, that is, the interdependence of the global economy.

2. **The rapid deterioration of global collective security organizations**

First of all, the proliferation of nuclear weapons is increasingly difficult to be effectively curbed. Nuclear proliferation is an old problem, and it is only a matter of time before Iran and North Korea acquire nuclear weapons. As discussed earlier, the Russia-Ukraine conflict has caused more and more medium-sized countries, and even small countries to attempt to get nuclear weapons to safeguard national security. Belarus has already amended its constitution to provide a legal foundation for the possession of nuclear weapons. Japan and South Korea, which have long pursued anti-nuclear policies, also made a big shift and proposed to "share nuclear weapons" with the United States. Secondly, the United Nations has gradually lost its ability to restrain the behaviors of major countries, and appeared increasingly irrelevant. After the "September 11 Attacks", the US war on terrorism has bypassed the United Nations, and unilaterally waged a war against Iraqi, which has seriously violated the legitimacy of the United Nations as a collective security organization. The Russia-Ukraine conflict, which has not yet ended so far, once again proved that how limited the ability of the United Nations to restrain the behaviors of major countries is. Under such circumstances, military powers will be inclined to establish "law enforcement agencies" centered on themselves to maintain regional security, or in other words, regional security organizations centered on regional powers will become more and more common. Russia has built Collective Security Treaty Organization (CSTO) as early as 2002. The United States, on the one hand, strengthens the cohesion of NATO by attacking Russia. On the other hand, it establishes a new military alliance around China in the Indo-Pacific region, that is, the Asian version of NATO.

3. The crisis of shared values

Today, despite the active efforts of promotion from the West, democracy and freedom have no longer become universal values that can be accepted by people for the simple reason that this institutional arrangement is difficult to respond to all kinds of challenges human beings are facing. Human civilization has entered the process of comprehensive modernization at the beginning of the twentieth century. However, while modernization has brought material prosperity to human beings, it has also planted the seeds of crisis, including food crises, energy crisis, public health crisis, social crisis, environmental crisis, and demographic crisis. In poor countries, food crisis has risen and fallen one after another, not because of natural disasters, but because these countries have been deprived of the basic ability to produce and distribute food under unfair international institutional arrangements. Those countries that have made achievements in modernization have also been facing crisis in the same way. For example, in the United States, social crisis is quite severe. The huge gap in wealth has led to the reduction of the middle class and the prevalence of racism and populism. In East Asian and European countries, societies have fallen into the demographic crisis of zero population growth and negative population growth. Although this wave of COVID-19 pandemic crisis that lasted for several years has passed, yet it does not mean that global public health crisis has also gone away with it. As a matter of fact, different types of global public health crisis have emerged over and over again. The development of modernization needs to be based on social organism, but the current modernization, to a great extent, is destroying rather than nourishing social organism. The dividends brought by modernization are increasingly difficult to compensate for the losses brought by it. In the past, many crises have been covered up by economic development. However, with the decline in the growth rate of world development, people have increasingly begun to reflect on the drawbacks of modernity. Modernization has begun to enter the period of bottleneck.

The crisis of modernity is the crisis of values for human civilizations. Modernization is the product of the European Enlightenment. Under the influence of the Enlightenment, human beings began to realize that reason could bring happiness, freedom, and order to human beings. Though this kind of thought has the dark side of colonialism and racism, its spread in Asia, Africa, and other regions has objectively brought ideological progress and economic development for the people in these regions. As mentioned earlier, after the twentieth century, many kinds of ideologies have emerged in human beings. Despite the great differences in their contents, they all recognize the pursuit of modernity in fact. Liberalism, socialism, and communism are, in the final analysis, the manifestations of the pursuit of modernity by all civilizations and countries in different approaches. Pursuing modernity has been almost the value orientation of all countries since modern times.

However, nowadays, the drawbacks and crisis of modernity are becoming more and more apparent. One myth has been pervading in human society: Is modernity still a value that is worth pursuing? Although the vast majority of countries take the pursuit of modernity as the key strategy for their national development, yet through the phenomena such as populism in the United States, the rise of Islamic religious radicalism and the economic status quo in Russia, we can still see that a new feudalism based on modern industry, and science and technology is rising. Whether it is at the individual level or at the group level, people have begun to call the value of modernity into question, but for the present there has not been any other kind of values that can take place of modernity. There has been a tendency for the backward traditional elements to recover in an all-round way, and ignorance, barbarism, cults, and violence are prevailing, which has been affecting not only ordinary people, but also political figures. Since human society entered modernization, the vacuum of values has been emerging for the first time.

All these above phenomena are not only different manifestations of the disorder of the international order, but also mean the end of the old international order. People could argue that the chaos of the world is because major countries have lost their abilities to provide international public goods. An effective international governance requires each major country to provide sufficient public goods. In the past, whether it is for globalization or for international security, its essence is public goods. Therefore, when each major country does things in its own way, and is unable to provide adequate international public goods, the world will fall back into the state of separation. In this aspect, the United States is particularly typical, not to mention that it has had no ability to provide international public goods. During the Trump period, the United States has shown that it has no willingness to support its allies, or even "withdraw from the group".

What's worse, on the global scale, various countries are producing more international public bads, mainly displayed in the respect of environment and security crises. These pressing crises also include public health crisis, energy shortage, food crisis, and nuclear proliferation. If there are no good international public goods provided by major countries, these crises will more and more exacerbated. Naturally, when the crisis comes, small countries will bear the brunt of this crisis. For example, in this conflict between Russia and Ukraine, Russia, a big country, has a large territory after all, and despite the war, it remained its resilience, while Ukraine, a small country, can only rely on the support from Western countries. Small countries are very vulnerable in the face of crisis. The purpose of the United States to provide economic and military assistance is to let Ukraine take the place of the West to confront Russia. Although the United States and Russia have not yet engaged in the direct military conflict with each other, this process of "proxy war" is also manifested as the confrontation between major countries. Not only are there no good international public goods to talk about, but also more and more international public bads have been produced at present.

CHAPTER 7

Globalization and the Crisis of Human Society

In July 2022, the resignation of British Prime Minister Boris Johnson and the attack on former Japanese Prime Minister Shinzo Abe happened almost at the same time, then came the bankruptcy of the Sri Lankan government, while more economies have been on the blink of bankruptcy. A lot of people have been shocked that these things are happening. As a matter of fact, although these things occurred accidently, historically speaking, once human beings enter the era of chaos, whatever happens is possible. Since the US Trump administration launched the Sino-US trade war, the world has tended to throw into the chaos.

People do not need to trace back to the long history. Since modern times, whenever the world entered the chaos, whether it is all kinds of violence at the domestic level, or the conflicts and wars at the international level, all kinds of phenomena will happen. It is often the case that people have not yet reacted to one phenomenon, while another phenomenon has followed.

People who have been concerned with the current world chaos often tend to ignore the influence of domestic politics by countries on international politics. The Prussian military theorist Carl von Clausewitz has said two things: The first thing is that "diplomacy is an extension of internal affairs" and the second thing is that "war is the continuation of politics with other means". The former Speaker of the US House of

Z. Yongnian, *The Great Convergence VS. The Great Divergence*,
https://doi.org/10.1007/978-981-96-7846-4_7

Representative, Tip O'Neill, has also said that "all politics is local". If these three sentences are put together, people can detect the relationship among internal affairs, diplomacy, and war. To put it simply, international conflict is the result of the changes in internal affairs. Therefore, to answer the question "for the current world chaos, where is the chaos", people must begin by studying internal affairs of various countries.

In recent years, some hot spots of public opinion within the United States have provided us with a good entry point. In 2022, the Supreme Court of the United States made four important decisions, which not only have caused a sensation in American society, but also have stirred up world public opinion. The first is to allow more people to legally bear firearms in public. The second is to eliminate constitutional protection of women's right to abortion. The third is to allow public funds to subsidize religious institutions, including church schools. The fourth is to limit the power of the federal government to reduce greenhouse gas emissions from power plants. Various public opinions from the perspective of human progress made the criticism that this is the degradation of society. In response to the elimination of constitutional protection of women's right to abortion, the US president Biden made a remark, "the Court literally taking America back 150 years".

As a matter of fact, these changes are difficult to be described only by using concepts such as "regression" and "degradation", and they are also difficult to be judged by the existing standards for ideology and morality. These changes indicate a more profound transformation, and whether people like them or not, these changes will be real.

From Brexit, the Sino-US trade war, and then to the Ukraine crisis, where is the root cause for the world chaos in recent years? On the surface, it is chaotic in the internal affairs, but in fact it is chaotic in the people's hearts. The chaos of the people's hearts is the deepest chaos.

Within the context of the West, the means to control chaos is the rule of law, and the rule of law is the proudest achievement for the Western world since modern times. But if individuals, groups, and organizations do not obey the laws, even the governments do not also obey the rules, and political figures often take the lead in disobeying the laws, then the rule of law will be of no help, and it will be a common phenomenon that the laws cannot be held accountable to the public. This situation further extends to the international society. As discussed in the previous chapter, our international system is similar to anarchy. The United Nations is not a sovereign state, but a system composed of a set of rules. If member countries all deviate from the rules of the United Nations, then the United Nations is in name only. If everyone does not obey the rules, this set of rules are equivalent to ineffectiveness. Although the United Nations system still exists, yet more and more countries do not take it seriously, which indicates that the United Nations is becoming less and less relevant to real-world affairs.

We further question closely, what are the reasons why people do not follow the rules and disobey the laws? Quite simply, this is because the society has lost its moral foundation. Society is a community, and it can be as small as a small family, a village, and as large as a country, an international society. The operation of this community needs a certain moral basis. The formation of laws is based on morality. If people think that the laws are not in line with people's moral standards, they will not abide by the laws, and even they will rebel against the laws. The closest thing related to morality is people, so we need to explore why people have lost faith in the moral foundation of the society.

What is the foundation of morality? This foundation is basic social equity. When society loses its basic fairness, the moral foundation will be shaken, thus disintegrating the social community. In the theory of *Guanzi*, a book about Chinese classical economics, there is a saying that "those who have a fixed property for their livelihood will have a stable heart", that is to say, the middle class is an important social foundation to maintain social stability. This can be used to explain the instability in European and American societies. The effect of economic globalization has caused the wealth imbalance of the middle society in Europe and the United States. After the middle class has shrunk dramatically, it is no longer the main body of society. The original olive-shaped society has gradually presented bipolarization. As a result, the rich are getting richer and richer, and the poor are getting poorer and poorer. The dumbbell-shaped society is characterized by great wealth and great poverty. When a large amount of wealth in society is concentrated in the hands of a very small number of people, and the poor cannot get class jump through fair channels, it is easy to generate the emotions of polarization. When all these social problems accumulate to a certain extent, they will erupt, which can cause social unrest at the mildest, and also can cause disintegration of the existing order at the worst.

The crisis within the United States is extraordinarily profound. On the surface, it is a crisis of governance, but in fact it is a crisis of morality.

The United States has now evolved into a typical plutocratic society. On the surface, it advocates democracy, freedom and the rule of law, but in fact it practices fist politics and power politics. For example, everyone knows the harm guns will do to the society, but bloody incidents such as school shootings have constantly come to the stages, while mandatory gun control has not been enforced. There have always been vested interests that have legalized gun ownership, and now it has even gone from bad to worse, allowing citizens to legally carry guns in public from the level of the Supreme Court. More than that, the loss of constitutional protection of women's right to abortion and racial discrimination have still been tearing American society apart step by step.

In a word, the super-globalization in the past several decades, while creating a huge amount of wealth for the United States, has led to a high degree of social differentiation, thus leading to the disintegration of human community. It has been manifested at the domestic level as the disintegration of society, and at the international level as the disintegration of the international community.

The difference between human beings and the animal world lies in that human beings possess values, while animals do not. Human behaviors are often driven by forces that run deeper than their own economic and political interests. At least since the Western Enlightenment, more and more people have thought this way. This perception is not difficult to understand.

To start with, human beings identify with politics or have sense of community. Human beings are political animals by nature. Human beings are group animals, but they belong to different groups, and the identities from different groups are contradictory to each other. Human beings are strongly driven by the desire to be recognized, which is a desire that needs to be seen, to be respected, and to be appreciated. If people are made not to feel noticed, respected, and appreciated, they will become angry, resentful, and vindictive. They will think that this kind of belittling is unfair, and will respond to this with aggressive indignation.

But globalization has undermined, if not still make it disappear entirely, the sense of community in human beings. Over the past few decades, global politics has been a machine that has been producing enormous social injustice. In one country after another, groups of urban elites with higher education have risen, controlling media, university, and culture, and usually having political power. There are many people who have felt that they have been looked down upon or ignored. In one country after another, populist leaders who took advantage of these discontents have begun to get the upper hand, Trump in the United States, Modi in India, and Le Pen in France.

Next, the majority of people have a strong loyalty to the class and country to which they belong. But in the past several decades, many people have felt that their positions have been left behind and that their national honor has been threatened. In the heyday of globalization, multilateral organizations and transnational corporations seemed to drown out the voices of nation states. But today, in order to uphold national sovereignty and restore national pride, highly nationalistic movements led by political strongmen have sprung up in one country after another. India is led by Modi, Turkey is led by Erdogan, the United States is led by Trump, and Britain is led by Johnson. These political strongmen have sent a message to the world: There is no cosmopolitanism and global convergence in the world; we will in our own way make our country great again.

In addition, human beings are driven by moral longings—namely their attachment to their own cultural values, and their desire to defend their own values when they seem to be attacked. In the past several decades, globalization seemed to be this kind of attack to many people.

After the Cold War, Western values have dominated the world through movies, music, political dialogue, and social media. Thus, one theory of Western globalization is that world cultures will in the main achieve convergence surrounding these liberal values. But the problem lies in the fact that this is not the case. The values of the West are not the values of the world, and the values which are considered as universal by the West are actually not universal. Even in the West, there are also more and more people who have realized that Western values are special cases, not universal ones. Joseph Henrich has written a book *The WEIRDest People in the World*. In this book, through hundreds of pages of data, he has presented that how rare it is exactly for these people who have Western, Educated, Industrialized, Rich, and Democratic (WEIRD) values. He even wrote, "We WEIRD people are highly individualistic, self-obsessed, control-oriented, nonconformist, and analytical. We focus on ourselves—our attributes, accomplishments, and aspirations—over our relationships and social roles".[1]

For a very long time, Western countries, especially the United States, seem to tend to transform all phenomena into "rights". In China, people call these people who hold this tendency "white left" (*baizuo*). The problem is that what is regarded as a right by the "white left" in the West may not necessarily be understood and accepted by those people from other civilizations and cultural backgrounds. In non-Western countries, people feel strange or even unacceptable to Western concepts of gender roles. When they saw the fanatical defense of the right of sexual minority (LGBTQ) in the West, they felt that they could not understand it. The idea that everyone has the right to choose their own identity and values may be purely Western, and it may be a pure fallacy to many non-Western people. In the West, the purpose of education is to instill critical thinking skills and to liberate students from the perceptions of their parents and the social communities they belong to. This view is considered absurd to many people in non-Western countries.

As a matter of fact, even in the West, the views of "white left" are not accepted by all the people, or even by most people. For example, 44% of US high school students said in the report that they always have feelings of sadness and hopelessness.

Although the United States and the West have strongly promoted globalization in the past several decades, and Western culture has also globalized with it. However, this by no means indicates that the cultures of the world have converged. The actual situation is just the opposite. If a person is local, then he or she cannot be global; but if a person is global, then he or she must be local. Super-globalization has not only failed to make world cultures converge, but it has intensified the differentiation of cultures of various countries, and thus local cultures have gained a rise. Economists Femando Ferreira and Joel Waldfogel have studied the pop music charts from 22 countries between 1960 and 2007. This research found that people preferred music from their own countries, and that this preference has increased since the late 1990s. People don't want to

[1] Joseph Henrich, *The WEIRDest People in the World: How the West Became Psychologically Peculiar and Particularly Prosperous* (New York: Farrar, Straus and Giroux, 2020).

integrate into a homogenous global culture, and they want to keep their own culture.

Every few years, the World Values Survey (WVS) research project will ask people all over the world about their moral and cultural beliefs. Every few years, a part of these survey findings will be synthesized into a map showing the relationships between different cultural zones. In 1996, the Protestant cultural zone and English-speaking zone in Europe have formed into a large cluster with other global zones. Western values are different from those in Latin American zone and Confucian zone, but they have been interlinked. But the cultural map in 2020 looks different. The Protestant cultural zone and English-speaking zone in Europe have been far away from other cultures of the world, and they are now as abrupt as a cultural peninsular outside of the world.

The World Values Survey Association in its summary of survey findings and various viewpoints pointed out, concerning issues such as marriage, family, gender, and sexual orientation, "There has been a growing divergence between the prevailing values in low-income countries and high-income countries". The West has long been in disengagement. Nowadays, the distance between the West and the rest of the world is getting bigger and bigger.

Finally, the desire for order drives people strongly. For the majority of population, there is no worse than chaos and anarchy. Cultural changes in Western style, and the paralysis of effective governance, which often appear at the same time, make people feel like social chaos, like anarchy, which leads people to seek order at all costs. However, in more and more places of the world, people cannot have access to this order.

There are all the signs that indicate that under hyper-globalization, the liberal democracy of which the West has been proud is also declining. A US Non-Governmental Organization (NGO) in the *Freedom in the World in 2022* pointed out, "The world has experienced a democratic decline for 16 consecutive years". The *Freedom in the World in 2021* of this NGO said, "The countries experiencing deterioration outnumbered those with improvements by the largest margin recorded since the negative trend began in 2006. The long democratic recession is deepening".

Western countries had originally expected that globalization would make the world become more "similar to the West", and that more countries would accept Western-style democracy. In the heyday of hyper-globalization, democratic regimes were widely regarded as stable and authoritarian regimes were widely seen as "turning into the ashes of history" sooner or later. But today, more and more Western democratic countries or Western-style democratic politics have become less stable than what they once were. As a matter of fact, some countries with democratic regimes, including the United States, are even experiencing profound governance crises, while many countries that are perceived by the West as authoritarian regimes have become more stable. The United States, for example, has been regarded as a model and beacon of democracy since its founding, but now it has slipped into bipolarization and is not functioning well.

There is an inherent tradition for the United States that its internal affairs outweigh diplomacy, and its internal crises have shown a new type of imperialism externally, which has been specifically manifested in shirking its responsibilities to the outside world. Today, the United States has almost described all internal democratic crises as threats from Russia and China, and has attributed the democratic crises in the United States to threats from "autocratic" China. This logic is absurd in itself. Internal affairs are threatened from the outside world, which is a typical political discourse for developing countries in the past, and it also reflects the fact that the United States and the West have interfered with politics of developing countries. But this set of political discourse has now become the main measures to shirk the responsibilities to the outside world for the United States which has now been the largest democratic country and has long been regarded as a "beacon of democracy". This fact itself is a huge political tragedy for the United States. At present, for the US Congress members, most have become anti-China pioneers, and shifted responsibilities to China on various China-related issues. Whether it is COVID-19, 5G communications or carbon emissions, they all regarded China as the biggest threat, and even if the United States wants to launch a war, the root cause will be attributed to other countries. This kind of initiative, of having no internal reflection and shirking all the responsibilities to external forces, is the practice of poor and weak countries in the past, but now is being imitated by the United States. This is a phenomenon that needs a deep thinking with depth.

The United States once supported and led the construction of the international system and promoted global free trade, while now the United States opposes the order it has established and dominated, and engages into group gangs. When the most powerful member state in the United Nations does not abide by the rules, then this set of system of rules will be equivalent to disintegration, and thus there are "feudalization" and "gangsterdom" appearing in the international order.

The so-called "value-based blocs" that are packaged with morality by the United States are fragile. As discussed in the previous chapter, if today's United States is compared to the king of Zhou during the Eastern Zhou dynasty in China, the king of Zhou cannot hold on and then feudalization and competing for hegemony among princes can be understandable, but now the United States itself has also become a member striving for hegemony, which shows how far it has fallen.

The decline of global hegemony for the United States, in the final analysis, is the trend toward mediocrity for the Western world in every aspect.

In the first place, it is reflected in the trend toward mediocrity for political figures. "The Best and the Brightest" of the bygone days in the United States have all gone forever. Political figures such as Nixon, Kissinger who can take the interests of the whole into account and put ideological disputes aside, have disappeared. Instead, they have been replaced by the intense debate between two elderly Americans, and some of Trump's supporters have not so far recognized the results of the election, and even caused the "Capitol Hill chaos" at the instigation of Trump.

In the next place, economic elites are extremely self-interested. Economic elites and magnates have held their wealth tightly, and companies like the Ford factory have been increasingly rare. In those days, the Ford factory have transformed the American working class into the middle class, and made great contributions to American society. If we look at the giants such as Apple, Amazon, and Facebook now, they have had no time to care about American life.

More important is the depravity in intellectual circles. Intellectuals in the traditional sense have collectively lost their voices, while a large number of intellectuals have followed politicians to scold China. Ideological intolerance, mutual cursing, and demonization have become the main stream. Since the 1960s, despite the constant crises in the United States and the West, yet there has been no decent thinker in the Western world.

Indeed, the Western world we see today is the product of the Renaissance, the Reformation and the Enlightenment that the West has experienced in modern times. Religious freedom, scientific rationality, and progressive concepts such as freedom, democracy, human rights have all developed in the process of modernization. The various phenomena of re-religionization, anti-secularization, and anti-globalization that we are witnessing today, actually announce the end of this process that once brought progress to human beings.

Moral crisis has become the deepest crisis in human society today. The crisis has given rise to revolution, war and religious interference and involvement in politics. This has become a world phenomenon. For example, the corresponding trends of re-religionization, de-secularization and militarization in Turkey, Afghanistan, and Myanmar are becoming more and more obvious. Many countries are performing a tense confrontation between religion and secularism, and the struggle between the two is equally fierce within the United States. The centrists in the United States are becoming less and less. And the left and the right are polarized and opposed: The "White-Left" extremely proposed to "abolish history", while the conservative right forces are also strong, winning one after another on the issues such as guns, abortion rights, and religions.

This phenomenon was immediately reflected on the ballot papers. As a matter of fact, in a normal election event, the voter turnout of about 30% is sufficient, and there is no need to vote in a society where people trust each other. In the past, there were many centrists in the United States, but now the centrists are getting smaller and smaller, and people support either the Republican Party or the Democratic Party. Everyone only has to believe in themselves, and only has to believe that one vote in their hands can change reality. However, the result is just the opposite. Democracy has evolved into populism, putting the greatest achievement of the Enlightenment project into a profound crisis. The more divided the political map in the United States is, the more obvious the partisanship is, and the more extreme political figures and policies will emerge one after another.

These sharp internal conflicts have been spread and expanded through social media as an emotional amplifier, making mob politics more and more profound. The phenomenon of political polarization is typical of the United States. Embodied in the whole Western world, and reflected in the international order is that "the world is in chaos".

But the chaos itself also contains solutions. For example, revolution, war, religion, and so on will come one after another in the chaos. Most of them have become the factors which aggravate the chaos, but some of them have also become the origin of good governance and progress. For example, in history, the Glorious Revolution in Britain, the Civil War in the United States, and the revolutions in China since modern times, were all the motives before the dawn of new human society.

The chaotic world is like the up-and-down stock market, with troughs, peaks, and rebounds. After World War II, we once thought the world has been climbing up to the peak of great harmony of human beings, but now we are on the pathway to moral decline. People cannot see clearly when there is a low point and when it will rebound.

To put it simply, diplomacy is the continuation of internal affairs and war is the extension of politics by another form. The disintegration of the international order in this round cannot ignore the externalized impact of internal political crises in the United States and other Western powers. The reason why the world is chaotic lies in the chaos in people's heart and in the collapse of moral foundation. The international order and human society are also facing and will face much more baptism in different forms such as revolution, war, and religion. The moral concepts such as democracy, freedom, and human rights and their meanings once put forward by Western countries led by the United States will also be reconstructed. The international order is in a broken but unestablished chaos, and human beings are faced with a big moral test.

As discussed earlier, the shared belief in the progressive values established from the Renaissance to the Age of Enlightenment has constituted the driving forces behind the pursuit of modernity by the vast majority of countries in the world since modern times. What is different is only the different stages (emphasizing different values in stages) countries have been in and different approaches (manifested as "isms") they have adopted, in the process of pursuing these values. However, whether it is in the East or in the West, the course of pursuing modernity is not linear. There are times of progress, there are times of regression, there are times of optimism and there are times of pessimism. If the great convergence between globalization and modernization over the past 40 years has led to optimism, then the great divergence between the two is now leading to pessimism.

Bret Stephens, an opinion columnist for *The New York Times*, published an article titled "Can We Still Be Optimistic About America?", on 10 May 2022. This article is a direct reflection of this kind of sentiments.[2] Here we might as well quote at length:

[2] Bret L. Stephens, "Can We Still Be Optimistic About America?". *New York Times*, May 10, 2022.

This is a season—an age, really—of American pessimism.
The pessimism comes in many flavors. There is progressive pessimism: The country is tilting toward MAGA-hatted fascism or a new version of "The Handmaid's Tale." There is conservative pessimism: The institutions, from primary schools to the Pentagon, are all being captured by wokeness. There is Afropessimism: Black people have always been excluded by systemic, ineradicable racism. There is the pessimism of the white middle and working classes: The country and the values they've known for generations are being hijacked by smug, self-dealing elites who view them with contempt. There is also the pessimism of the middle: We are losing the institutional capacity, cultural norms and moral courage needed to strike pragmatic compromises at almost every level of society. Zero-sum is now our default setting.
These various kinds of pessimism may reach contradictory conclusions, but they are based on undeniable realities. In 2012, there were roughly 41,000 overdose deaths in the United States. Last year, the number topped 100,000. In 2012, there were 4.7 murders for every 100,000 people. Last year, the rate hit an estimated 6.9, a 47 percent increase. A decade ago, you rarely heard of carjackings. Now, they are through the roof. Shoplifting? Ditto. The nation's mental health was in steep decline before the pandemic, with a 60 percent increase of major depressive episodes among adolescents between 2007 and 2019. Everything we know about the effects of lockdowns and school closures suggests it's gotten much worse.
Economics tells a similar story. "Twenty-first-century America has somehow managed to produce markedly more wealth for its wealthholders even as it provided markedly less work for its workers," observed Nicholas Eberstadt of the American Enterprise Institute in a landmark 2017 Commentary essay. It's in part from the loss of meaningful work—and the consequent evaporation of pride, purpose and dignity in labor—that we get the startling increase in death rates among white middle-aged Americans, often to suicide or substance abuse.
The list goes on, but you get the point. Even without the daily reminders of Carter-era inflation, this feels like another era of Carter-style malaise, complete with an unpopular president who tends to inspire more sympathy than he does confidence.
So why am I still an optimist when it comes to America? Because while we are bent, our adversaries are brittle. As we find ways to bend, they can only remain static or shatter.
This week brought two powerful reminders of the point. In Moscow, Vladimir Putin gave his customary May 9 Victory Day speech, in which he enlisted nostalgia for a partly mythical past to promote lies about a wholly

mythical present, all for the sake of a war that is going badly for him. Putin is belatedly discovering that the powers to humiliate, subvert and destroy are weaker forces than the powers to attract, inspire and build—powers free nations possess almost as a birthright. The Kremlin might yet be able to bludgeon its way to something it can call victory. But its reward will mainly be the very rubble it has created. The rest of Ukraine will find ways to flourish, ideally as a member of NATO and the European Union.

Meanwhile, in Shanghai, more than 25 million people remain under strict lockdown, a real-world dystopia in which hovering drones warn residents through loudspeakers to "control your soul's desire for freedom." Does anyone still think that China's handling of the pandemic—its deceits, its mediocre vaccines, a zero-Covid policy that manifestly failed and now this cruel lockdown that has brought hunger and medicine shortages to its richest city—is a model to the rest of the world?

For all its undeniable progress over 45 years, China remains a Potemkin regime obsessed with fostering aggrandizing illusions: about domestic harmony (aided by a vast system of surveillance and prison camps); about technological innovation (aided by unprecedented theft of intellectual property); about unstoppable economic growth (aided by manufactured statistics). The illusions may win status for Beijing. But they come with a heavy price: the systematic denial of truth, even to the regime itself.

Rulers who come to believe their own propaganda will inevitably miscalculate, often catastrophically. Look again at Putin, who really believed he had a competent military.

Which brings me back to the United States. Just as dictatorships advertise their strengths but hide their weaknesses—both to others and to themselves—democracies do the opposite: We obsess over our weaknesses even as we forget our formidable strengths. It is the source of our pessimism. But it is also, paradoxically, our deepest strength: In refusing to look away from our flaws, we not only acknowledge them but also begin fixing them. We rethink. We adapt. In bending, we find new ways to grow. We have a demonstrated record of defanging right-wing demagogues, debunking left-wing ideologues, promoting racial justice, reversing crime waves, revitalizing the political center and reinvigorating the American ideal. Our problems may be hard, but they are neither insoluble nor new.

Those without our freedoms will not be so fortunate.

The author here not only criticizes the United States, but also tries to demonize Russia and China. The way the author narrates itself is also the important reason why people feel so pessimistic about the world today. The traditional international order is facing a complete disintegration, and the international politics is being reshuffled, presenting a trend of competing with each other. The struggle in international politics is not only between the two major countries, China and the United States, but also between other major countries. The major countries seek to establish on the ruins of the old order a new international order or regional order which can contribute to the maximization of their own national interests. The conflict between Russia and Ukraine is only the beginning of this struggle. Major countries such as Turkey, India, Japan, and Indonesia are all preparing to make their moves, actively carrying out various major-country diplomacy and striving to play an important role in the process of constructing a new international order. By its very nature, the world has presented a "neo-feudal" situation, and will inevitably be manifested to a large extent in doing things by each one in its own way before the new order is established.

Though the world is facing the situation of doing things by each one in its own way, yet if countries have a shared understanding of modernity, then they can also coordinate their actions and jointly meet the challenges they are facing, because it is clear that the feudalization of the international order is not in line with the interests of any country. The tragedy is that people have no consensus on modernity, or have no shared values. Bret Stephens's narrative is a typical example of Western scholars and policy research circles. They fail to reflect on themselves, not only demonize others and shift responsibility to the outside world, but also condemn other countries from the perspective of a hypocritical morality. We should be aware that this is the general mood in Western intellectual circles. The Western world has completely lost the openness and inclusiveness they prevailed from the Renaissance to the Age of the Enlightenment. Now, the "West" itself has become an ideology. Viewing anything that is non-Western needs to obey this ideology. It can be said, to a large extent, that liberal democracy is like the Medieval God. That is to say, when the knowledge system in the intellectual class also presents feudalization, the feudalized state order has also its legitimacy.

CHAPTER 8

Great Divergence and Its Consequences

As mentioned earlier, people can draw a conclusion, that is, since the early 1980s, the combination of various international and domestic factors has given China the greatest opportunity for once, namely the "convergence" of globalization and modernization. In other words, globalization has provided an open and favorable environment for China's internal modernization, which has effectively contributed to the modernization of China in all aspects. What impact, then, will the dramatic changes in the international environment today have on the world modernization? Here, we are mainly concerned about the issues in the two broad aspects. First, the divergence of globalization and modernization. Over the past few decades, globalization and modernization have converged, promoting and strengthening each other. So, is today's international situation leading to the divergence of globalization and modernization? And how will this divergence affect Chinese modernization or globalization? Second, the divergence between China and the West. As mentioned above, in the past few decades, at the empirical level, the "convergence" between China and the West has been mainly manifested in the aspect of material modernization, while the institutional and human modernization levels have not really converged, and China has also opposed and prevented the convergence with the West at the levels of institutions and people. However, in the ideas of many people, whether they are Westerners or some social

Z. Yongnian, *The Great Convergence VS. The Great Divergence*, https://doi.org/10.1007/978-981-96-7846-4_8

groups in China, globalization and modernization will eventually lead to the transformation of China's institutions and even people into the Western-style. Then, when the West and China have lost this illusion, what kind of divergence will China and the West have at the institutional and human levels? And how will this divergence affect Chinese modernization or globalization?

To begin with, it should be emphasized once more that in the era of globalization, the globalization of a country affects the internal modernization process of a country. A brief comparison of the rise of Shenzhen with the decline of the "Rust Belt" in the United States can make this point clear. Shenzhen has developed from a small fishing village (town) in the early 1980s into its current super first-tier city. The population of Shenzhen has exceeded 20 million, and is still growing. The population development is due to the industry in Shenzhen, and with the industry, there will be employment in society and tax revenue for the government. And all these constitute the modernization of Shenzhen. The "Rust Belt" in the United States was very glorious until the 1980s. This region has risen due to the automobile industry, but because in the industrial changes caused by globalization the cities have not been transformed in time and become the "Rust Belt", which has led to the decay of cities and the serious crises the urban governance is facing. For many years, the social level in these cities has been so rampant with violence that the governance of the government has no longer been effective. That is to say, in Shenzhen, globalization and modernization are "converging", and moving toward the same direction, while in American "Rust Belt", globalization and modernization are "diverging", and running in opposition to each other.

Just as the Great Convergence, whether the convergence of globalization and modernization, or the convergence between China and the West, has produced great changes in China; and the Great Divergence, whether it is the divergence of globalization and modernization or the divergence between China and the West, will also have huge impact on China. The Great Divergence has just begun now, and the effects of all sides will unfold one by one. The Great Convergence has been driven primarily by the global flows of capital and technology, and the impact of the Great Divergence has also begun with the anti-globalization of capital and technology. Here are at least a few aspects in which the anti-globalization of capital and technology has been rapidly manifesting itself with worldwide consequences. Although the focus here is on the impact of the

Great Divergence on China, other economies face the similar impacts to a greater or lesser degree.

1. China facing the risk of decoupling from the Western world

The preceding chapter has discussed the manifestations and root causes of the chaos in the international order, while the international chaos has more influences on China's internal modernization environment. Among them, the most serious is that China faces the risk of decoupling from the world. There are several factors that put China at risk of decoupling from the Western world, including the US strategy of decoupling from China, the Russia-Ukraine conflict, the changes in the business environment during the COVID-19 pandemic, and the competition from Southeast Asian countries such as Vietnam. The impact of these factors on the international order has been discussed, and their impact on China will be discussed here.

The first is the US decoupling strategy. As discussed earlier, whether it is in the East or in the West, the internal modernization of a country is basically a change in all aspects trigged by economic and technological changes. Economy and technology are more effective leverage in promoting globalization. Globalization in the past several decades began with the movement of capital around the world, which promoted the movement of technology, talents, and labor around the world. The United States began to engage in a trade conflict with China from the Trump administration. Trump has engaged in the trade conflict mainly in order to realize his so-called trade balance issue, and the subjective intention is not for the decoupling between China and the United States. However, some of the conflict measures he has taken, such as the blockade of China in the field of high science and technology, have actually started the process of decoupling. Since Biden took office, the United States has taken a further step in decoupling, and has systematically decoupled from China in various aspects such as economy, trade, and technology. The systematic decoupling is much more toxic than the stranglehold on high science and technology that began from Trump. The stranglehold on high science and technology is mainly aimed at China's technological progress, that is, not allowing China to realize its technological upgrading. However, the systematic decoupling means removing the ladder of Chinese industry. Without doubt, since modern times, the entire industrial base is on the basis of Western science and technology, and also it was first developed and established by the West. Although China's development has its autonomy, yet the industrial base is still inseparable from the Western system. Once the systematic decoupling between China and the West is realized, then the foundations of many industrial sectors in China will be affected in a very negative way.

Up to now, China and the United States have not decoupled from each other, and this is mainly due to two factors. On the one hand, the United States itself has been weak in pandemic prevention, and it is difficult to realize the so-called "re-industrialization" that has begun since Trump, that is, the return of industrial and supply chains to the United States. This means that the United States and other Western countries still need China's industrial and supply chains, and naturally they cannot decouple from China. On the other hand, China has controlled the spread of the COVID-19 pandemic in the early stage of its outbreak, and resumed work and production at the fastest speed, which has basically ensured the security of the international supply and industrial chains. At the same time, private enterprises in China have grown up in the state of openness, and they are part of international economies, showcasing strong resilience in the face of the pressure of decoupling from the United States and other Western countries.

The efforts by some Western countries, mainly the United States, to decouple from China are still going on. Although this decoupling will not succeed, yet the decoupling action by the United States has had a negative impact on private enterprises in China. For example, the decoupling of science and technology, has already had a great impact. Shenzhen is a city where high-tech enterprises are very concentrated, but its GDP growth rate has slowed down since the trade conflict between China and the United States. Because Huawei has made a great contribution to Shenzhen's economy, the crackdown on Huawei by the United States has not only deeply affected Huawei itself, but also directly affected the overall GDP growth in Shenzhen. What is deeply affected is not only economic growth, but also employment and taxation associated with it.

The second is the impacts of the conflict between Russia and Ukraine. The United States has desperately exploited the Russia-Ukraine conflict to worsen the business environment in China from two aspects. For the first thing, the United States has been trying to tie China and Russia together and shape a diplomatic discourse of "China-Russia axis", which has put tremendous pressure on Western capital in China and also forced them to move away from China. For the second thing, in such an environment, the international business environment for Chinese enterprises has also been deteriorating at an accelerated pace. Western politicians and media have demonized Chinese enterprises and prevented Chinese enterprises and Chinese products from "going global". Although people do not want the economy and politics to be so closely linked, yet politics has become the most important part of the business environment. This is a fact that we have to accept.

The third is the changes in the business environment that have occurred during the COVID-19 pandemic. The negative impacts of the pandemic that has lasted for couple of years on China's economy, are ever more not allowed to ignore. The persistent pandemic has hindered development of many small and medium-sized enterprises in China, and constantly small and medium-sized enterprises, especially micro enterprises, have been closed down. Small and medium-sized enterprises are big employers in China, and their difficulties often bring enormous pressure to employment. In 2022, the pandemic caused by the Omicron variant strain of the COVID-19 broke out continuously in Shanghai, Shenzhen, Guangzhou, and other big cities, and similarly large private enterprises have been heavily affected. For example, the suspension of work and production in Shanghai has still more led to the disruption of product supply chains in many fields. The automobile chip manufacturer, On Semiconductor (Onsemi), has announced during the pandemic in Shanghai that due to the impact from the global pandemic, especially the pandemic in Asia-Pacific region, and the prevention and control management in Shanghai, Onsemi has decided to shut down its Global Distribution Center in China and transfer its industrial capacity overseas.

Internal difficulties have also been prompting some major external risks to accelerate fermentation. Some politicians in the United States and Europe want to decouple from China in terms of industrial chains and finance, but this has been difficult to realize in the past few years. One is that in previous years the pandemic in the West went out of control which made it impossible for its enterprises to resume work and production, while China's scientific pandemic prevention has ensured the resumption of work and production of its enterprises. The resilience of a large number of private enterprises in China has ultimately contributed to a strong rise in foreign trade, and China's linkage with the world trade has been much closer. Another is that the Sino-US interest rate spread and China's financial opening-up have attracted a large amount of Western capital to continue to flow into China, and the financial ties between China and the West have also been strengthened. However, since 2022, the resumption of production in the West, the risk of the suspension of production that faced private enterprises in some parts of China, and the reversal of long-term interest rate spread between China and the United States, have made the situation more and more unfavorable to China. The outflows of industry and capital have begun to accelerate, with some part returning to the West, and some part flowing into countries such as India and Vietnam. The Indo-Pacific Economic Framework (IPEF) that is being accelerated by the United States and led by it has also been intensifying and consolidating these trends. Although it is normal that some capital outflows to Southeast Asia have been caused by the rising costs of land and labor in China, yet some capital outflows have been affected by strict pandemic control measures, such as the decisions by some foreign-funded companies in Shanghai to move their headquarters to Singapore.

The fourth is the competitions from Southeast Asian and South Asian countries. In particular, it should be emphasized that some countries in Southeast Asia and South Asia, including Vietnam, Malaysia, and India, are rising rapidly and their business environment is improving rapidly. Countries such as India, Vietnam, and Malaysia have followed China's export-processing development model used in the 1980s and implemented more open and favorable investment policies by providing cheaper production factors such as land and labor, thus enhancing their attraction to foreign investment. Some countries in Southeast Asia have gradually opened their controls, even though the COVID-19 pandemic has not ended, thus increasing their attraction to foreign investment. For example, Vietnam saw an 88.3% year-on-year growth in Foreign Direct Investment (FDI) inflows in the first four months of 2022. One more obvious trend is that these economies are actively and diligently integrating with the West, reforming their internal economic structures and striving to meet the "values" demanded by the West. Vietnam is now a member of the CPTPP, and its reforms in the areas of state-owned enterprises, labor-capital relationships, the rule of law, and policy transparency have been particularly remarkable. As a result, they not only attract capital from all over the world, but also attract part of capital from China.

The manufacturing relocation , capital outflows , and immigration waves will increase the risks of China's decoupling from the world economy, undermine external confidence in China's future economic development, and lead to a vicious circle. In the long run that will affect the sustainable development, and even security of China's economy. As mentioned above, it is difficult for the unilateral policy of the United States to decouple the economy of China from that of the West, because Western enterprises in China have to take into account Chinese market factors. However, since 2022, affected by the COVID-19 pandemic, some Western enterprises have moved out of China. Once these enterprises leave China, it will be difficult to return to China again. It should be noted that in the world industrial chains and supply chains, China has been still at the middle and low end, and can be replaced. In the past, although the costs of labor and land have been rising, factors such as China's complete supply chains, industrial chains and market size have been still attractive to Western capital and enterprises. However, these enterprises could not absorb the immediate impact of the factors by the pandemic, so some enterprises began to move away from China. Today, economies such as Vietnam and India have posed strong competition with China in the middle and low end of industrial and supply chains. Once China's industrial and supply chains are transferred to these more competitive countries, it will be difficult to attract them back.

2. **Influencing the process of urbanization**

As mentioned before, the rapid urbanization along the coastal areas in China is related to the international division of labor resulting from globalization, that is to say, the development of manufacturing industry has been the biggest driving force of urbanization for a long period of time. Once the manufacturing industry declines, urbanization will be problematic. In particular, the division of labor between cities in the manufacturing sector has led to the homogenization of industries in some cities. The single industry means the risks of sustainable development of cities. The "Rust Belt" in the United States is a case in point, because its main industry is the automobile industry, as soon as the automobile industry declines, the whole city begins to decline. The development of many cities in China also illustrates this point. For example, in the era of planned economy, many energy-type cities were once glorious, but since the reform and opening-up, because they have not carried out industrial transformation in a timely manner, they began to decline. For many years, there has been a concern about whether the old industrial base in northeast China will become China's "Rust Belt". This concern is not unfounded. The strategy of "Revitalizing the Northeast" has been proposed for many years, but the situation has not improved. Today's Northeast is not only experiencing a shortage of talents, but also experiencing a shortage of population. Due to the shrinking of economic activities, there is a large outflow of population every year. The governments at all levels attach great importance to this, and have tried every possible means to revitalize the Northeast. However, in the absence of grassroots and market dynamics, the actions by governments have not changed the difficult situation. Today, for various reasons, especially the Sino-US trade war, whether it is in the Yangtze River Delta, the Pearl River Delta or other regions, this situation has also appeared in some cities. If a city is too dependent on several industries or several large companies, once these industries and large companies have problems, then the city will possibly have big problems. As discussed earlier, Shenzhen's relationship with Huawei is typical. Over the years, Huawei has made great contributions to the economic development and growth of Shenzhen, and Shenzhen is also highly dependent on Huawei. For these years, the US sanctions on Huawei has had a profound impact on Huawei, and this impact also directly affect Shenzhen's economy.

3. **The rise of online populist and nationalist sentiments**

Modernity also manifests itself as the changing mentality of the people. When globalization and modernization "converge", people tend to have a worldview, viewing problems from the international perspective; people also tend to be more secular in their outlook, looking at the relationships between people, groups, and countries from the rational perspective, and finding rational solutions when problems arise in these relationships. However, in the case of anti-globalization, internal development is held back, and then many problems come up to the surface. At the time of development, all these problems are shown as the problems in development and can be solved in the process of development. But once development is blocked, these problems become the real problems, and for the lack of effective solutions, they profoundly affect people's interests. In this way, people tend to be introverted, or by using a popular term today, tend to be "involuted". This situation has appeared among some social groups in China, which is manifested as populist sentiments internally and as nationalist sentiments externally. Nationalist sentiment is displayed as anti-West and xenophobe, while populist sentiment is displayed as hatred of the rich and anti-elites. Whether it is for nationalist sentiment or for populist sentiment, they are not a set of comprehensive and self-consistent political theory, such as Marxism, liberalism, conservatism, etc., but a collection of emotions. Under this sentiment, netizens' reactions to specific issues can quickly ferment into online public opinion or even online mobilization until the entire cyberspace is swallowed up by irrational voices. Where online populism sweeps through, it is full of language violences, personal attacks, and inciting words. Moreover, because there are still many irregularities in the process of exercising public power, online populism often takes advantage of this imperfection to enter reality from the network through malicious reporting and other means, which has a great impact on society and actually hurts personal rights of specific citizens. Therefore, this phenomenon deserves attention and response.

In summary, the modernization in the previous 40 years or so is the product of globalization, so once anti-globalization becomes the mainstream, modernization will inevitably be affected. It is self-evident that economic slowdown or economic shrinkage will have an impact on a country, and all aspects such as GDP growth, employment, taxation and people's livelihood will be negatively affected. Both foreign countries and China itself have a lot of experiences in this regard. Today, local finance has become a big problem in some cities in China because of economic shrinkage. The governments in a small number of cities have begun to pose an arbitrary charge on private enterprises and society because of financial difficulties, leading to tensions between the government and society. There is reason to worry that with the deterioration of the international environment, especially the intensification of the US-led decoupling movement, the economy in more places will shrink to varying degrees. As far as urbanization is concerned, people do not want to the American "Rust Belt" to happen in China. If it happens, it will be not only an economic, social, and political issue, but also a question that the process of modernization is affected as a result. Therefore, people must think about how to deal with the impact of the changes in the international environment on modernization.

CHAPTER 9

Evaluation of Great Divergence

The "Great Divergence" takes place at both subjective and objective levels.

The first is the subjective level. It refers to the strategic intention of the US hardliners on China, that is, to delay, curb, and contain China's sustainable economic development through decoupling from China, and even ultimately to terminate China's modernization process. In recent years, Chinese and foreign academic and policy circles have been discussing the two traps facing China, namely the "Middle Income Trap" and the "Thucydides Trap". The first trap points to whether China can achieve sustainable development or sustainable modernization internally, and upgrade itself to the status of an advanced economy. The second trap points to the Sino-US relationship, that is, whether a rising China is bound to challenge, and even eventually replace US hegemony. On this issue, Appendix 1 of this book has a special discussion. Although the Chinese side has been emphasizing peaceful rise and does not believe that "a strong country must be hegemonic", yet the United States is convinced of this. The "Thucydides Trap" theory or the view that "there must be a war between China and the United States" has been popular in US academic and policy research circles. From the Trump administration to the Biden administration, more and more people in US political, academic, and policy research circles have believed that China has a

Z. Yongnian, *The Great Convergence VS. The Great Divergence*,
https://doi.org/10.1007/978-981-96-7846-4_9

"hundred-year plan", that is, China's replacement of US hegemony has become China's most long-term strategic goal in modern times. Despite the strong conspiratorial overtones for these theories, such a perception has already had a direct impact on China Policy by the United States. As noted earlier, the Biden administration has clearly defined China as the only country that has ability and will to challenge the United States. By far, the US strategy has been crystal clear, that is, to avoid the "Thucydides Trap" by pushing China into the "Middle Income Trap". The logic here is clear. Once China falls into the "Middle Income Trap", then China will no longer be able to challenge the United States, thus avoiding the "Thucydides Trap". The United States has made it clear that it has abandoned the attempts to change China, and now is turning to tying China down by shaping its external environment. And decoupling is the main economic grip that binds China.

The second is the objective level, that is, the decoupling that is actually taking place. The reason for decoupling is from both the trade war launched by the US government and the economic factors themselves. The trade war has the most direct impact on decoupling, while the COVID-19 pandemic has also had some impact on the transfer of industrial and supply chains for some period of time. However, not all decoupling behaviors have been caused by the trade war and the COVID-19 pandemic. People do not need to look at this issue in an overly nationalistic or populist way. As mentioned earlier, capital and technology are inherently mobile. Along with the economic development of China, the domestic labors and land cost are also rising rapidly, and the requirements by the Chinese government for environmental protection are also being enhanced, all of which are increasing the operating costs of enterprises. As a result, it is a normal economic phenomenon for some foreign enterprises to leave China and move to other countries. This phenomenon has been happening long before the Sino-US trade war began.

Globalization affects the modernization process within countries, so for China, it is necessary to answer the question whether globalization will be interrupted. If it will not be interrupted, then, while the interdependence of economy and trade between China and the West will decrease, the two will not completely decouple from each other, and the modernization process can be sustained even if it is affected in some way. More importantly, as the author has repeatedly stressed, the globalization process is shaped by both subjective and objective factors, that is, the flow of factors such as capital, technology, and talents at the objective level, and the policies implemented by the governments of various countries regarding the flow of factors at the subjective level. In other words, even in the face of the policy of decoupling from China by some Western countries such as the United States, China can also respond to the US decoupling policy through subjective efforts at the policy level, alleviate the impacts and shocks posed by the US decoupling policy toward China, and even invalidate it. As far as China is concerned, another factor can be added, that is, China can take the initiative to promote globalization.

Whether these subjective and objective factors can play a role depends on what role rationality can play in our decision-making, while what role rationality can play also depends on whether we can make a new, correct, and precise judgment on the international situation. Whether it is over-optimism or over-pessimism, it will affect our rational play. Among them, the following judgments are extremely critical.

1. **Hyper-globalization is no longer there, but globalization will not end completely**

Historically speaking, capital and technology are the biggest driving forces for globalization. Given that the Fourth Industrial Revolution is in full swing on a global scale, it is difficult for people to imagine that globalization will disappear. It is more likely that, as has happened again and again through history, globalization has encountered political and social resistances and its speed slowed down. Political and social resistances can slow down the speed of globalization, but it is difficult to stop it. One side is politics and society, and the other side is capital and technology. The two sides are currently in the process of contest and each side will be constrained by the other side. Capital and technology cannot flow freely without constraints as before, similarly, politics and society do not have a full control over the flow of capital and technology.

We might as well imagine what the future world order bred by the Fourth Industrial Revolution will be like and how it will differ from today's world order. Information technology, biotechnology, new material technology, energy technology, and space technology will promote human progress in future, and this trend has already become more and more clear in the past 20 years. In these highly technologically advanced future worlds, the composition of power has changed dramatically. Countries with advanced technology and human capital will have more powers to shape the world order. In this world, the level of information technology and the scale of industry will determine countries' economic strength, biotechnology and information technology will redraw the boundary of human and intellectual resources, the discovery of new materials and new-type manufacturing methods will reshape the order of the global industrial chains, the progress of new materials and new energy will change the geopolitics of resources, and the world economic and political geography will be rewritten. With the rise of information technology and space military technology, the traditional military superiority on land, sea, and air will be further weakened and the foundation of global military hegemony will also be recast as a result. It is obvious that this "technological hegemony era" order, dominated by technology and human capital, is quite different from our existing international order, which was laid out by the outcomes of wars in the twentieth century. In today's world, most of human production still comes from manufacturing, human capital is limited by aging, materials are constrained by scarce natural resources and traditional industrial technology, energy is highly dependent on high-carbon fossil fuels, global security is built on the balance of nuclear weapons, and the world ecology is on the verge of limit. Undoubtedly, these restrictions have shaped the modern order, and they also have become the target that emerging technologies are determined to break through. The existing order will eventually be unable to imprison the emerging forces that master new technologies, and this is the fundamental reason why the modern world is difficult to sustainably stabilize.

From the perspective of technology-led changes in the international order, the United States is both the biggest defender and the biggest challenger to the international order, because of its international leadership position and well-developed emerging technology industry. In the former role, China is a competitor to the United States; in the latter role, China is the biggest potential partner to the United States. This is an important reason why its China Policy is entangled in "confrontation" and "cooperation". China's technological and economic potential, and its need for international security, also mean that China must manage the complex issue of Sino-US relationship. On key issues such as nuclear proliferation and carbon emissions, the cooperation between China and the United States is important for both sides. Just like the nuclear issue, the non-cooperation between China and the United States on environmental issues will push both sides to "ecological mutually assured destruction". Although the United States defines Sino-US relationship on the basis of ideology, yet ideology has become irrelevant and very harmful when it comes to issues such as environmental protection. China and the United States are both in the same boat, and neither can escape in the face of climate disaster.

In fact, as has been said before, the root cause of the crises of the international order lies in the fact that the world is increasingly producing international public bads, while the supply of good international public goods is insufficient. Without the cooperation between China and the United States, the world will not have enough capacity to provide good international public goods, or reduce international public bads. The United States can engage in world bipolarization to contain China and push China to fall into the "Thucydides Trap". However, given that China and the United States share the same earth, the actions by the United States seriously damage the interests of the United States itself while harming the interests of China. There is no doubt that international public bads are not only limited to climate changes, but also include public health crises like COVID-19, marine ecological crises, nuclear proliferation crises, etc. Once disaster strikes, no country can stay out of it.

Therefore, on the positive side, no force can stop the spread of capital and technology on a global scale. Political and social forces can impede and slow down the diffusion of capital and technology, but they do not have the capacity to terminate the diffusion. As far as China is concerned, as long as the United States and other Western countries are still capitalist societies, as long as we ourselves are open, then any ideological or other political factors can empower the United States to achieve the goal of world bipolarization. Even if it is achieved for a while, it will only be temporary. On the negative side, we are all in an interconnected global village, and no country can escape the impact of international public bads produced at the other end of this global village on itself.

China's sustainable modernization needs a stable world order, and this needs to be achieved through cooperation with the United States. Although the current world order is not the product of China's dominance, yet China can be said to be the biggest beneficiary of this order. The rapid development of China since its reform and opening-up for more than 40 years is the result of China's integration into the existing world order. Furthermore, China is dissatisfied with US hegemony in world affairs and US hegemony in its China policy. China has been calling for multi-polarization of the world order, that is, an international order with a more decentralized power. However, we also need to realize that although we have called for multi-polarization of the world order, yet from the current point of view, the world multi-polarization will not bring huge benefits to China. China is a country with a very strong economic externalities, which is completely different from the Soviet Union during the Cold War. Multi-polarization is conductive to those closed countries to resist external influences, but this is not the case for China. Not all multi-polarization is beneficial to non-hegemonic countries. Other country groups under multi-polarization will not choose China. For China, this means a more isolated geo-economic environment and a more fragile national economy. As a matter of fact, the carriers of contemporary multi-polarization are traditional major countries such as Russia and Japan, and emerging major countries such as India, Turkey, and Indonesia. All these carriers of powers are around China and their Asianization means that China will face a greater geopolitical challenge. It is natural that the existence and rise for these major countries not only share the international power of the United States, but also share the international power of China. In this regard, China and the United States can find a great room for cooperation. The "re-feudalization" of the international order indicates that it is difficult to have a high probability of success for the efforts by the United States to bipolarize the world order, and it is difficult for these carriers of powers to stand on the side of the United States against China. Meanwhile, this "re-feudalization" also means alliances among major countries, including China and the United States.

2. The United States does not represent the whole world

From the Trump administration until now, the tensions between China and the United States have quickly extended from trade conflicts to almost all aspects. Owing to economic interdependence, the decoupling between China and the United States takes time and costs very high. At the same time, the United States also lacks effective measures to counterbalance China. Therefore, the United States began to carry out value diplomacy around the binary opposition of "democracy-autocracy", demonized China's political system and demanded that all countries in the world follow the United States in counterbalancing and encircling "authoritarian" China on the grounds of ideological differences. China has also been defined as a "revisionist state" that seeks to subvert the Western liberal international order. After the outbreak of the Russia-Ukraine conflict, the United States and the West have been creating the concept of a "Russia-China axis", binding China and Russia together, and defining the conflict as a "world war" between "democracy" and "autocracy", and between "civilization" and "barbarism".

The US strategy of world bipolarization has indeed posed a severe challenge to China. However, we need to realize that the United States is not the whole world. China has already been the world's second largest economy, and has established economic and trade relations with various countries in symbiosis and common prosperity. The relationship between the United States and other countries to a large extent depends on how open the US economy is. Although the United States is still the largest market in the world, yet it has not been the market that could absorb almost all of the surplus products in the world after World War II, and its attractiveness has not been what it used to be. The rise of economic nationalism and trade protectionism in the United States is not without good reasons. As previously discussed, though globalization in the past several decades has created a huge amount of wealth for the United States, yet the American middle-class has been a victim. Trump therefore wants to promote "American greatness again" through trade protectionism. Although the Biden administration has returned to multilateralism on world affairs, yet on the aspect of trade it has still pursued the policies by the Trump administration, and there is no substantial difference between the "foreign policy for the middle class" by the Biden administration and Trump's "Make America great again". The Trump administration has withdrawn from the Trans-Pacific Partnership (TPP) in order to protect the America market. Although the Biden administration has returned to many of the international institutions from which the Trump administration has withdrawn, yet it has not returned to the TPP on trade issues. In order to deal with China, the Biden administration has shifted to construct the so-called "Indo-Pacific Economic Framework". However, for Asian countries, especially for ASEAN countries, whether the "Indo-Pacific Economic Framework" is attractive depends on the openness of the American market. If this framework means that ASEAN countries must "choose sides", that is, stand with the United States, then this framework cannot avoid the fate of ineffectiveness. Since China's reform and opening-up, almost all ASEAN countries have developed profound economic and trade relations with China. For them, the best situation is to maintain peace between China and the United States, because in this case, they can develop relations with both China and the United States at the same time. In the event of an open conflict between China and the United States, they will have to "choose sides", thus minimizing their national interests, especially for those countries which have a security relationship with the United States. For these countries, because their security system has been integrated into the American system, they do not have a lot room to say "no" to the United States. In other words, they have no choice in face of the United States. Meanwhile, they can have a choice when facing China. However, whether there is no choice or there is a choice, they all have to bear huge costs. And this is also the reason why in recent years, as the United States has shifted its strategy into the Indo-Pacific region, these countries have been more and more concerned about the conflict between China and the United States. Whether it is for Asian countries or for countries in other regions, there is no reason for those that have developed profound economic and trade relations with China, to give up the Chinese markets.

Moreover, even at the ideological level, the ideology of freedom and democracy advocated by the United States has raised doubts in Western society itself, and it has gradually lost its appeal in the non-Western world. The military behaviors by the United States in Iraq, Afghanistan, Libya and other regions have made the international community severely question American-style democracy. The wave of refugees caused by the US military movements in the Middle East and other places has led to severe social crises in Europe all the more. As discussed earlier, since the outbreak of the Russia-Ukraine conflict, the United States has been trying to isolate China by binding China and Russia together through the narrative of "China-Russia axis", but the actual results have not been as envisioned by the United States. The US-led NATO not only has constituted the root cause of the Russia-Ukraine conflict, but also has kidnapped European countries. Although European countries stand morally and ideologically with the United States, yet the United States does not bear the huge losses that the war has inflicted on European countries. The same is true of many other countries. Although these countries also condemn Russia for provoking the conflict, yet it does not indicate that they stand together with the United States against Russia. The irresponsible behaviors by the

United States toward the world have eventually caused an ideological vacuum for the world order.

Even for the United States, it is not composed of a single interest group and different interest groups have different attitudes and policy preferences toward China. Some interest groups have gained tremendous benefits from economic and trade relations between China and the United States. The Cold War faction and the hardliners on China in the United States do want to decouple from China, but Wall Street does not want to give up the Chinese market. Wall Street has also put pressure on China from time to time, but its main purpose is to get China to open up more so that they can be more profitable in the Chinese market.

3. **The parallel globalization of China and the United States will "converge" indirectly in third parties**

Anti-globalization started from the trade conflict between China and the United States, and the United States launched the Sino-US trade conflict in an attempt to gain advantages from Sino-US competition through non-economic measures such as politics and administration. Naturally, as the two largest economies in the world, the trade conflict between them immediately had a huge impact on the whole world. Over these years, in this discussion about what impact of major-country competition between China and the United States will have on globalization, the focus of people's attention has fallen on the speculation about where the future trends for globalization will go. As previously discussed, since the end of the Cold War, political, business, and opinion leaders in Western industrial countries all have tended to believe and accept the conception that expanding the cross-border flows of goods, capital, information, ideas, and people is inevitable and irreversible, and for the most part this is a positive development. In the words of Thomas L. Friedman, the columnist for *The New York Times*, "the world is flat". At that time, it was widely believed that globalization, namely the ever-closer integration of world economies and societies, will result in the increase in efficiency, the improvement in the levels of income and welfare in all countries, and the reduction in the gaps in the living standards between countries. Meanwhile, these tendencies will promote cross-cultural understanding, encourage the spread of Western liberal democratic norms and institutions, and enhance the prospects for international cooperation and peace.

But now there are not many people who hold such a universal belief any more. However, from another point of view, it is precisely because the goal of the Sino-US trade war launched by the United States is to target China that what the United States has done is not completely to cancel globalization, but to change the way that globalization is made, so that the balance of globalization is tilted in favor of the United States. Even Aaron Friedberg, a professor of politics and international affairs at Princeton University, who has been advocating that the United States should hold a hardline policy toward China for these years, also believes that the process of globalization will continue under the impetus of technology.

Friedberg has published one research in the winter issue of 2021–2022 in *Texas National Security Review*. In this study, Friedberg explored the possible impact of the intensifying rivalry between the United States and China on the evolving structure of the international economy, and anticipated five possible paths for economic globalization to continue to evolve. (1) Deglobalization, (2) reglobalization, (3) hegemony with Chinese characteristics, (4) regional blocs, and (5) value-based blocs.

The so-called "deglobalization" is not difficult to understand, that is, the disappearance of globalization. But as Friedberg himself said, globalization cannot disappear as long as there is a technological impetus.

The deglobalization we are facing today is the result of the decline of US hegemony. The hegemonic stability theory is the product of the United States, while European countries emphasize the balance of power. The theory of hegemonic stability assumes that a single preponderant power is needed to build an open international trading system. It is acknowledged that since World War II, especially since the 1980s, the United States has indeed played a key role in promoting globalization and maintaining the openness of the world economy. This is the international public goods that the United States has provided for the international community, but the United States also has gained tremendous benefits in doing so. Today, because the United States is no longer able to sustain an open world economic system, the international free trade system is on the verge of collapse and has begun to fragment into a series of countries, each pursuing its self-sufficiency or narrow national self-reliance. This phenomenon is also what we call "re-feudalization".

Reglobalization means that if the major members of the globalization system work together and, in particular, if they are able to make use of multilateral institutions to enhance communication and promote cooperation, it may be possible to preserve an open global economic order. For example, Friedberg suggests that if the United States renounces unilateralism, China commits to follow the path of liberalization, and all parties agree to strengthen existing dispute-resolution mechanisms and abide by their rulings, perhaps the current World Trade Organization-centered system can be saved.

The so-called "hegemony with Chinese characteristics" should be a path that is unlikely to be followed in the foreseeable future. Friedberg argues that through history, the decline of one hegemony has been followed eventually by the rise of a new one, most often in the aftermath of a system-shattering war.

The fourth path, regional blocs, refers to the fact that the global economy is not entirely fragmented into a collection of autarkic states, but could become divided into increasingly separate and distinct blocs. This is one scenario that theorists once anticipated in the 1970s.

The valued-based bloc is the fifth path proposed by Friedberg. He said, "it is a world in which the advanced industrial democracies of Europe, Asia, and the Western Hemisphere band together to form a free trade area and perhaps a full economic bloc". As the label suggests, such a grouping would resemble the partial Western system built by the United States during the Cold War.

Friedberg believes that a new trading bloc organized along this line will have a number of economic and strategic benefits for the United States and its partners. Creating a mega free trade agreement made up primarily of advanced industrial democratic countries, will likely increase the economic growth rates of all of its members, while diverting some trade that might otherwise have gone to China. The members of a "democratic trading bloc" can work together to force the Chinese government to modify its trade and industrial policies, otherwise they will deny or restrict China's access to their common market.

Here Friedberg is not so much looking to the future as analyzing the actual behavior of the United States. Anti-globalization is a reality. The regional blocs and the value-based blocs mentioned here are what the United States and some countries are practicing today. Within the tide of globalization in the past, regionalization and globalization moved toward the same direction, or the goal of regionalization is to promote regional integration into the tide of globalization. However, today, regionalization is showing a trend that we call "feudalization". The value-based blocs vigorously pushed by the United States are trying to split the world on a global scale. Friedberg made it very clear that the United States was doing this in order to divide the world into two, thus leading to the model of world order during the Cold War between the United States and the Soviet Union, and its purpose was to contain China.

As far as his mode of thinking is concerned, it is not difficult to understand Friedberg's definition of the globalization promoted by China as "hegemony with Chinese characteristics", because it is a typical practice of imposing the logic of Western behavior on other countries. The process by which Western scholars understand China often becomes a process of "self-externalization". Since modern times, Western countries have interpreted China's traditional tributary system as "Chinese-style hegemony" or "Chinese-style imperialism". Although China's tributary system is manifested as hierarchy or "hegemony", yet it does not have such character as Western hegemony or imperialism. In modern times, European countries have established the principle of sovereign states and used this principle to deal with relations between countries, or international relations. Although the principle of sovereign states emphasizes equality between countries, yet this equality is only formal, because in fact countries are not equal among themselves. The actual relations between European countries are also unequal, and hierarchical, except that no country is so overly powerful to make this country become a hegemony. European countries have therefore developed the principle of "balance of power" to handle relations between them. After World War II, when the United States became the core of Western countries, the situation has changed dramatically. From any point of view, the United States is the hegemony within Western countries, and the United States has undoubtedly developed the theory of "hegemonic stability" to demonstrate the importance of hegemony to the stability of the international order. In practice, the United States often transforms its own will into the will of the international community and imposes it on other countries, and even directly imposes its own will on other countries. On some occasions, the United States even has used international laws which it cannot accept to restrain and intervene in other countries. The United Nations Convention on the Law of the Sea (UNCLOS) is a typical example. The United States has not accepted it to date, but it has been using it to bind other countries.

China's diplomatic behavior is different from that of Western Europe and from that of the United States. From any point of view, traditional China has been the largest country in East Asia, the actual hegemony. Therefore, China has embraced a realistic attitude and does not think that countries are completely equal. But on the other hand, China also seeks to manage the relationship between big and smaller countries in the international relations that are actually unequal. As a result, China has developed the concepts of "the way of sage-king" (*wangdao*) and "the way of hegemony" (*badao*), believing that big countries should exercise the "kingly way" rather than the "hegemonic way" over smaller countries, and believing that if a big country exercises the "hegemonic way", it will eventually loose trust among smaller countries and lead to failure. The tributary system is the product of this thinking. In modern terms, people can understand the tributary system as a "unilateral policy of opening up" between the Chinese dynasty and smaller countries. There is no need to deny the hierarchical nature of the tributary system, that is, smaller countries need to recognize the Chinese dynasty and "kowtow" to the Chinese emperor by offering gifts to the Chinese court. However, it is unfair to judge the hierarchical nature of "kowtow" in modern concepts. At that time, there were various forms of hierarchical international relations among all East Asian countries. For example, the smaller Vietnam "kowtowed" to the big country China, but the smaller countries around Vietnam "kowtowed" to Vietnam as well. It is more important to emphasize that the contribution between China and smaller countries is asymmetrical. The actual situation is often that if a smaller country contributes $5 to the Chinese emperor, the Chinese emperor needs to give back $10 to this smaller country. In essence, the tributary system was a trading arrangement in which China opened up its trade to smaller countries after these countries had gained the recognition from the Chinese court, even though the Chinese court itself was not interested in trading with the smaller countries. Just because of this, the tributary system became unsustainable.

There is another conceptual reason why the West defines the tributary system of China as hegemony or imperialism. Before modern times in the West, similar situation existed, but after the formation of modern sovereign states, they began to emphasize equality between countries, at least equality in form. At this time, China has not accepted the Western concept of formal equality. This is a kind of difference in concept, and this difference is also the main reason why Chinese academic circles themselves have criticized the tributary system since modern times, arguing that the concept of tributary has not made China establish the concept of international relations, and the practice of international relations in the modern sense earlier. As discussed here, there is not much truth to this criticism. Since modern times, China's traditional countries have been weak and powerless in the face of modern Western countries. Both intellectual elites and political elites think that China needs to be built into a country like the West, and this understanding is also reflected on their understanding of China's traditional countries' diplomacy.

Since modern times, the Chinese people have not only accepted the concept of national equality, but also made great efforts to pursue equality, not only in form, but also in substance. This has enabled the traditional Chinese spirit of "kingly way" to still exist, and be expressed through modern forms. Up to now, China has reached free trade agreements with many countries and groups of countries (such as ASEAN), and in many respects China has a spirit of unilateral opening-up. Many international economic practices of multilateralism being practiced by China, including Asian Infrastructure Investment Bank (AIIB), The Belt and Road Initiative and the "BRICKS", all present two distinctive characteristics: First, they are inclusiveness, openness, and equality; second, they do not aim at any third country, but at issues of concern by all member states. To a large extent, the globalization that China is striving for is in fact similar to what Friedberg called "reglobalization" which is a regional multilateralism moving toward the same direction with globalization. This has formed a remarkable contrast with the exclusive trading blocs against third countries that the United States is practicing.

As a result, the United States and China are practicing their own models of globalization. In the short term, these two models are likely to show the parallel development trend, that is, they do not intersect with each other. In the West people have also realized that this value-based blocs by the United States may possibly lead to the formation of a vast economic bloc organized by the United States and its allies to continue the process of globalization with which they identify, while China, Russia, and other countries excluded from the American bloc will form their own blocs. Under the worst circumstances, due to security concerns and differences in values, there may be almost no communication between the two blocs. And if so, it is the Cold War model between the United States and the Soviet Union. Nevertheless, this view is not only untenable in theoretical logic, but also inconsistent with practical logic.

The United States excludes China mainly because the United States defines itself as "liberal capitalism", and China as "state capitalism". In other words, the United States excludes China or other countries because these countries do not accept American-style capitalism. But in reality, although the world today does not all accept American-style capitalism, yet compared with the era of the Cold War, the world is undoubtedly more capitalist. It is obvious that, with the exception of a few smaller countries, most countries, especially big countries, all accept the market economy and recognize the positive role of capital in the process of economic development. The United States uses the so-called ideology of freedom and democracy to suppress economies including China, but as long as these countries still adhere to the market economy and affirm the role of capital, these countries will continue to embrace globalization. In the meantime, the capital of the United States and Western countries, together with their technology, still will flow into non-Western countries. Capital is by nature is mobile, and once it stops flowing, it is not capital, while it is difficult for political forces and social forces to put capital into cages, or to regulate the flow of capital.

More importantly, as discussed above, China practices an inclusive and open international economy of multilateralism. Even if China and the United States themselves do not intersect, they are bound to intersect in other parts of the world. This is a "cross-regional model". In the process of globalization in the past few decades, countries around the world have developed economic and trade links with the United States and China. Although the United States wants to restructure the model of globalization by establishing a value-based trading bloc, yet it is difficult or even impossible for many countries to choose to stand with the United States due to their deep economic and trade links with China. For these countries, the maximization of their national interests requires them to continue to develop economic and trade relations with China. Under such circumstances, China and the United States will continue to intersect and interact with each other in different places. As a matter of fact, this model is already happening.

China's Belt and Road Initiative can be seen as a lever for China to advance its globalization. Since the launch of this Initiative, China has been upholding an open and inclusive attitude and policy, and hoping that more countries can participate in it. Countries such as the United States and Japan have been opposed, arguing that the Belt and Road Initiative is a grand strategy for China's geopolitical expansion. However, up to today,

China still remains open to all countries that oppose or are skeptical about the Belt and Road Initiative. In recent years, Western countries such as the United States or groups of countries (such as the Group of Seven) have begun to plan and start their own versions of the Belt and Road Initiative, directly competing with the Belt and Road Initiative of China. But in fact, the direct result of this competition is the intersection and interaction of countries such as China and the United States in different places. Although the initial intention of "planners" (such as US government) is the competition based on ideology, yet in the process of implementation, enterprises as executors must have the attitude of seeking truth from fact, and have relations and associations with enterprises in each country. In other words, though China and the United States compete in different places, yet there is no war between Chinese capital and American capital. China and the United States are parallel, but their capital is intersecting, even interacting.

This model of intersection and interaction occurs most prominently in the digital field. Although the world Internet has achieved rapid development since the 1990s, yet as far as China and the United States are concerned, it is difficult to say it is the Internet, but "not connected to each other". It has been found that as the geopolitical competition between the two superpowers in the world becomes more and more intense, the distance between them is getting farther and farther and their respective network environments have gradually become two completely different digital worlds. Most US Internet enterprises have failed in China, while the applications developed in China have not been a great success outside of their home country. Obviously, popular Western applications, including Google, Facebook, Amazon, Spotify, LinkedIn, Uber, and Airbnb, have been basically blocked by relevant departments in China, or eliminated by the Chinese market. There are only a handful of Western scientific and technological enterprises that can develop and thrive in China. Except for Apple, there may be no other enterprises. In the same way, China's "social media influencers" in the digital field are equally difficult to make progress in the United States or many other big countries. TikTok, owned by Chinese Internet giant ByteDance, is a rare exception.

However, the digital fields in the two global superpowers are not entirely independent of each other. Despite being subject to strict scientific and technological controls by the Chinese government, Didi, an online ride-hailing giant in China, has still successfully expanded to regions such as Latin America, which is also an unusually active place for US high-tech companies.

The interaction in different places is more frequent in the field of space. Although the common people in China do not have official access to Facebook or Google, yet these companies have sold billions of dollars in advertisements to Chinese enterprises. By doing so, these enterprises hope to reach out to Chinese citizens or Chinese-speaking people who are in other parts of the world.

Between China and the United States, business trends and business ideas will also flow within their respective Internet fields. For example, for a long time, new-model smartphones have always been smaller than the previous generation. Since then, however, large-screen smartphones have become popular among Chinese consumers, resulting in super-sized phones becoming the global mainstream. Due to the huge spending power of Chinese consumers, their consumption preferences can effectively influence the preferences of American consumers. Some trends in China are also changing the American experiences online. Until today, American Internet enterprises still continue to try to imitate China's entertainment-style livestreaming e-commerce, although none of them have been as successful as that in China. American enterprise executives and investors have high expectations for food delivery service in Europe and the United States, partly because takeaway service in China is everywhere.

And the replication of models is also two-way. Didi was originally a traditional application for car delivery service, but when Uber entered the Chinese market in 2014, and connected users with non-professional drivers, the business model for Didi has changed. Uber withdrew from China in 2016, but it still had a big impact on the transportation sector in China.

This shows that although the digital lives of the two countries are largely isolated from each other, yet their cyberspace is not entirely isolated from each other. The digital concepts of China and the United States are interwoven and permeated with each other, and there are various forms of interdependence. Such a situation shows that hard boundaries and political differences are not absolute obstacles to the Internet, and the Internet can still pull together this supposedly divided world.

4. Above all else, globalization will not end, because globalization is in line with human nature

Historically, whether it is globalization or modernization, its development process is not smooth sailing, and even not linear. Why do modernization and globalization encounter setbacks and resistance? Why can modernization and globalization overcome setbacks and resistance to start again? These two questions are the two sides of globalization and modernization. Any globalization and modernization in line with human nature will be accepted and supported by society; any globalization and modernization not in line with human nature will be opposed and resisted by society.

As far as modernization is concerned, the modernization that began in Western European countries has spread to all countries in the world, and the twists and turns in the process of spread reflect the needs of human nature. Although, as mentioned earlier, modernization itself is a progressive concept, yet it is understood differently by different civilizations and cultures, and its realization is more constrained by the national conditions of a real country that embodies this civilization and culture, including material conditions and psychological conditions. How is the process of modernization in a country going? This still needs to return to the three levels of modernization discussed at the beginning of this book, namely, the material level, the institutional level, and the human level. With the exception of some extremely devout religious small groups (such as ascetics), there is no one who does not pursue wealth. An ancient saying in China "birds die for food and people die for money" is a universal phenomenon in the world. The pursuit of wealth is the manifestation of modernity. In fact, modernity begins from the pursuit of wealth. Although wealth is universally pursued, the distribution of wealth in different social groups is unequal. When the gap in the distribution of wealth exceeds the acceptable level of some social groups, these social groups will oppose modernization. Therefore, institution becomes important, because institution is to regulate the relationship between material and people, and the relationship between people. If institution has the capacity to regulate material modernization and human modernization, then not only is modernization sustainable, but institution itself has also realized modernization in the process of regulation. However, on the other hand, if institution does not have the capacity to regulate material modernization and human modernization, then modernization becomes unsustainable, and institution is also seen as failing to adapt to the needs of modernization.

The response of different countries to modernization is similar to the response of different social groups to modernization. A country is a community of many individuals, and when a country can reap benefits in the process of modernization, then the country will accept and support modernization. On the other hand, when a country suffers losses in the process of modernization, then the country will refuse and resist modernization. Because the country is not abstract, but is composed of different social groups composed of different individuals. Whether modernization can be sustainable in a country depends on the ability of institution to regulate material modernization and human modernization.

The interaction and competition between the three levels of modernization constitute the overall picture since modern times. Modernization diffused from the Western world to the non-Western world at the earliest. During this process, some countries succeeded, and others rejected modernization because they were uncomfortable with modernization, while more countries went back and forward in the process of modernization. The Middle East manifested as religious civilization and East Asia manifested as secular civilization, are two typical examples.

Iran's radical Western-style modernization eventually led to the "counter-revolutionary" movement, that is, the Iranian Revolution. Previously, the modernization carried out by the Shah of Iran was aimed at Western-style modernization from all aspects of material, institution, and people. Although people accept material modernization, yet the material modernization which is particularly embodied at the individual level, is in direct contradiction to the religion that the Iranian people have accepted. Meanwhile, the nascent institution has no capacity to reconcile the contradiction between the two, and this makes "counter-revolution" become inevitable. The modernization in Turkey in modern times has been carried out around secularization, and great progress has also been made in all aspects. However, although Turkey has experienced modernization for more than one century, yet all aspects of modernization and its traditional religious civilization are still out of tune, or even out of place. Therefore, the current president, Erdogan, has gone the opposite way since he came to power, pushing for re-religionization. But re-religionization does not mean a complete return to the past. On the contrary, Turkey is still diligent in material modernization. Up to this day, more Middle Eastern countries are still lost in the concept of "modernization". If modernization means the Western-style secularization, then it will be in direct conflict with the religious civilization in the Middle East, and thus conflict with the believers of the religion, namely the people of the nation. But if they cannot pursue material modernization, then the country cannot avoid the situation of falling behind and being beaten. The discomfort of Middle Eastern countries with modernization is manifested as two extremes: Some social groups are obsessed with modernization, even the Western-style modernization, while other social groups cling to radical religions and oppose all forms of modernization.

In comparison with the Middle East, East Asia belongs to the Confucian cultural circle, or secular civilization. Because an important feature of modernization that began from Europe has been secularization, East Asian civilization and modernization are consistent in this respect. At the material level, the civilized countries in East Asia have never had any difficulty or resistance in pursuing material civilization. Several rises in Chinese history were all based on the rise of material civilization, including the Qin and Han dynasties, the Tang and Song dynasties, and the Ming and Qing dynasties. Since modern times, the fact that China was defeated by Western powers more strengthened people's willingness to pursue material civilization. Although China itself, as the core of East Asian civilization, did not succeed, or even failed one after another in the modernization of material civilization at the early stage, yet the fact that China was defeated greatly stimulated the motivations of other countries in East Asia to pursue modernization. Japan was the first economy to realize modernization in Asia, followed by the "Four Asian Tigers". In 1949, the founding of the People's Republic of China eventually ended the wars and revolutions in China, and China began its modernization. Before the reform and opening-up, China also proposed the "Four Modernizations", namely in the fields of industry, agriculture, national defense, and science and technology. China experienced the first wave of modernization with the goal of "catching up with Britain and the United States" at that time. However, although China was not much different from other countries and regions in East Asia in terms of material modernization, yet it was subject to many constraints in terms of institutional modernization and human modernization, which made the modernization in China lag behind that in other countries and regions in Asia at that time. The success of Japan and the "Four Asian Tigers" has undoubtedly provided a model for the modernization in China. Since reform and opening-up, the second wave of modernization that China has undergone is, in essence, not much different from the modernization in Japan and the "Four Asian Tigers". If there is any difference, it is only the difference in degree.

But even the modernization in Asia has not been smooth sailing. In many countries, the modernization in the three levels of material, institution, and people has from time to time shown incongruous and incompatible situation. At the level of material modernization, all countries do not have disagreement, but at the levels of institution and people, all countries behave differently. Some countries tend to understand institutional modernization as developing Western-style political systems, but these efforts have not always been successful. In the 1950s, Burma and Sri Lanka have been seen by the West as the most likely countries to successfully realize modernization after Japan in Asia. In the 1960s, two more countries, Philippines and Thailand, have been seen by the West as the most likely countries to successfully realize modernization in Asia. The reason why the West thought this way is that these countries began their Western-style political development while carrying out economic modernization. By far, however, not so many people have thought so, because these four countries have been caught in the "Middle Income Trap" for a long time, and even in the state of low development for a long time, and some countries even have been in the state of political instability for a long time. They have not yet solved the problem of the model for political development. The Western-style political development does not conform to their own civilization, culture and national conditions, but what is the political development model that conforms to their own civilization, culture, and national conditions?

Predictably, this question is one that all Asian countries must answer. Japan, South Korea, and Singapore can be said to be Asian countries disguised as Western countries. In other words, the manifestations of their political systems are Western-style, but the spirit that their political systems operate is Asian-style. Although more countries and regions in Asia have realized their material modernization, yet they have lost their independence in many aspects, even the independence in politics. In fact, even for those countries that have realized economic modernization, such as Japan, South Korea, and Singapore, their political independence can also be questioned, because the diplomacy for these countries is deeply influenced by the United States. Only China has achieved development and independence at the same time. As put forward by the 19th CPC

National Congress, China offers "an alternative"—a non-Western alternative—to modernization for those countries that want to both achieve development and maintain independence.

Whether it is in the Middle East or East Asia, the modernization course has shown that modernization is not a straight line, and that when modernization encounters difficulties or resistance at a certain time, it does not mean that people no longer pursue modernization. Although modernization presents a complicated situation in various countries, yet one point is clear, that is, by far more and more countries and regions believe that modernization is not a total Westernization, but the modernization of their own civilization and culture. In other words, if the modernization at the material level is universal in the world, then the institutional and human modernization needs to find a model that conforms to their civilization, culture and national conditions.

The process of globalization is also similar to that of modernization with the same logic. At the material level, people can say that globalization is in line with human nature and caused by human nature. Adam Smith, the founder of modern Western political economy, believes that trade (i.e. transaction) is the manifestation of human nature, and that people based on the principle of the division of labor, produce their own products and trade, thus producing wealth, improving and enhancing welfare. As discussed above, except for some devout religious groups, no one is content with poverty. If the pursuit of wealth is human nature, then the biggest driving force for globalization is human nature. Another British political economist David Ricardo applied the theory of the division of labor from within a country to between countries. According to Ricardo's theory, each country has its own comparative advantage, produces from their own comparative advantage, and then trades between countries. Trade between countries is the origin of globalization, that is to say, globalization not only enables all countries to play their comparative advantage, but more importantly, it provides a broader platform for each individual to play their "comparative advantage (talents)". It is obvious that what countries trade is not only the goods and products produced by all countries, but, up to this day, it has extended to the movement of capital, technology, and all kinds of services, even the movement of talents.

The Modern French thinker Jean-Jacques Rousseau said, "man is born free, but is everywhere in chains". No one wants to be a slave, and everyone pursues freedom. If freedom is human nature, then it can be said that globalization gives people the freedom beyond national borders. In other words, globalization gives individuals the opportunity to develop their talents on a global scale. From this perspective, globalization has become the most effective grasping hand and means for a country to realize its modernization. The reason is quite simply. Globalization has led to intense competition between countries for high-quality capital, technology, services, and talents. Whichever country can compete for better capital, technology, services, and talents is likely to win in international competition. On the contrary, if a country has no competitive ability in these aspects, then it will be weakened, and even invaded by other countries. Just because of this, globalization has also led to the modernization of the institution for a country, because only a competitive institutional system can have the ability to compete for high-quality capital, technology, services and talents.

Although globalization can effectively contribute to the modernization of a country, yet globalization does not develop in a straight line, but moves forward in a tortuous way, with progress and retrogress. As with modernization, when globalization conforms to the needs of human nature, globalization will be accepted and supported. When the effects produced by globalization do not conform to the needs of human nature, globalization will be rejected and will be met with resistance.

Not to mention the more remote globalization, such as long-distance trade in the Age of Empires, we can take as examples the several major waves of globalization that human beings have experienced since they entered industrialization. Industrialization first took place in Britain, then diffused to European countries and North America, and finally spread to non-Western countries such as Asia. After that, between 1875 and 1914, the world has undergone a wave of hyper-globalization, and this wave of globalization is centered in Europe. Along with the rise of economic liberalism in Europe, the high degree of trade dependence occurred between European countries. International trade with Europe as its core has also spread to other regions of the world. However, the high degree of trade dependence did not contribute to the vision predicated by many people at that time, that is, human beings did not need violence and war to achieve wealth growth. Not only did the high degree of trade dependence not bring the so-called "permanent peace" as expected, but also the First World War happened among European countries. Globalization brings wealth, but the distribution of wealth among social strata within countries is unequal, and the distribution between countries is unequal. In other words, globalization has led to inequality among social strata within countries, and created inequality among countries. Some social groups within a country achieved a huge amount of wealth, but other social groups have not only lost their sense of gain, but also become poorer. In the meantime, Western Europe at that time has achieved rapid development due to globalization, but the Central and Eastern European countries were still in a backward state. Social differentiation within countries has led to the rise of populism, while inequality between countries has led to the rise of nationalism. The overlapping and intersection of internal populism and external nationalism ultimately led to the war. Between World War I and World War II, the world was not only free of globalization, but also full of violence and wars.

After the end of World War II, the world began to globalize again, but this globalization was bifurcate. Because of the Cold War between the United States and the Soviet Union, the world was divided into two parts, that is, there was an international system with the Soviet Union as the core and an international system with the United States as the core. One side was the Soviet Union-Eastern European bloc, and the other side was the Western bloc headed by the United States. At the same time, these two blocs tried to expand their own spheres of influence to the vast developing countries or the Third World. From the perspective of globalization, the Western bloc succeeded, while the Soviet bloc failed. The key to success and failure is still the differences between the role of the market and the role of the government. The Western bloc took the market route which conformed to the logic of globalization, while the Soviet bloc followed the route of the planned economy which did not conform to the logic of globalization.

Because these two blocs have the nature of competition, this wave of globalization made economic sovereign of various countries tend to be strengthened. Western countries, including the United States, began to implement Keynesian economic policies since the Great Depression in the 1930s. After World War II, they fully accepted and carried out Keynesian economic policies, and the welfare countries achieved great development. By the 1970s, the proportion of the middle class in Western countries generally reached 60%–70%. The large middle class is the foundation of social stability for Western societies.s Taking the United States as an example, the 1960 saw the Anti-Vietnam War Movement, the Civil Rights Movement led by Martin Luther King, Jr. Moreover, the assassination of a president occurred during this time. But all of these have not led to a major social upheaval in American society. This is mainly because there is a large middle class in the United States. At that time, the Republican Party leaned much to the right, the Democratic Party leaned much to the left, but both Parties had to look out for the middle class and would not go to extremes. After the 1980s, the West completely abandoned Keynesian economic policies.

Keynesian economic policy has the advantage of the expansion of welfare society under government intervention, but it also has its disadvantage, that is, the dramatic expansion of bureaucratic economy. The vast welfare society, run by government bureaucrats, leads to big government. At the same time, welfare societies have also led to general high taxes in the West. These do not fit the logic of capital development. Therefore, in the early 1980s, Thatcher in Britain and Reagan in the United States launched the neoliberal economic revolution. The neoliberal economic revolution took privatization and financial deregulation as its grasping hand, and quickly spread from Britain and the United States to Western countries. When the neoliberal economic revolution was going on in the West, China also began to reform and open up. The combination of the two soon created a wave of unprecedented globalization or hyper-globalization. This wave of globalization created unprecedented opportunities for the flow of capital, technology, and talents on a global scale, thus effectively contributing to the effective allocation of production factors on a global scale, and greatly liberating labor productivity and creating a huge amount of wealth for human beings.

But this wave of hyper-globalization has also led to almost the same result as the wave of globalization from 1875 to 1914, that is, the rich-poor polarization among social groups within countries and between countries. In the Western world, the middle class was generally shrinking, especially in Britain and the United States where neoliberal economic policies prevail. The United States has transformed from the previous middle-class society to today's plutocratic society. The huge amount of wealth created by globalization has fallen into the hands of a small number of people, while most people not only have no sense of gain, but also become the victims of globalization. In the meantime, the developing countries involved in this wave of globalization, including China and India, have all achieved their corresponding development, though on the whole the developing countries are still far behind the developed countries. The internal divisions in the West caused by globalization have led to the rise of populism. Brexit and the rise of "Trumpism" in the United

States are the direct reflection of populism. What is reflected in the international community is the rise of US trade protectionism and economic nationalism, that is, anti-globalization.

However, anti-globalization does not mean the end of globalization. Globalization has been profoundly affected by the rise of unilateralism and trade protectionism, but just as the experiences in the previous waves of globalization have shown, economic globalization will not disappear. Globalization will start again after human beings digest and solve the problems caused by this wave of globalization. Globalization is in line with human nature, but these problems caused by globalization have indeed posed a severe challenge to human society. If human beings cannot solve these problems, then globalization will lose its original meanings. From this perspective, countries around the world must adjust the contents and ways of globalization. These adjustments are also in line with the needs of human nature.

CHAPTER 10

China's Resolve and Persistence

If anti-globalization is inevitable, China's goal should be clear, that is, instead of moving with the tide of anti-globalization, China will continue to do its best to advance globalization and lead a new wave of globalization. In other words, in the face of the wave of anti-globalization in the United States and some Western countries, China needs to show its own resolve and persistence. Specifically, China needs to adhere to the two most important aspects that have enabled China to benefit from the process of globalization in the past: First, continue to adhere to the concept of peace and development; second, continue globalization and continue modernization.

China's success in globalization and modernization over the past 40 years or so has been premised on the correct judgment of the theme of the times, "peace and development". The theme of the times is an ideological basis for a country to conceive its development strategy and determine the direction of social progress. During the Cold War between the United States and the Soviet Union, given the objective geopolitical environment of the country at that time, the main challenges China faced were national security and ideological struggle. Mao Zedong made a judgment of "war and revolution" on the theme of the times at that time, while China's international strategy was mainly aimed

Z. Yongnian, *The Great Convergence VS. The Great Divergence*, https://doi.org/10.1007/978-981-96-7846-4_10

at "holding high the banner of nationalism at home, exporting revolution abroad". After 1978, China entered the new stage of reform and opening-up. During this stage, Deng Xiaoping's judgment on the theme of the times was "peace and development". It should be emphasized that Deng Xiaoping did not make this judgment because he believed that the world was already in the state of peace and development. In fact, on the contrary, the world at that time was still in the period of the Cold War between the United States and the Soviet Union, and China's self-defense counterattack against Vietnam had just ended. This judgment by Deng Xiaoping reflected more China's aspiration, that is, China needed peace and development, and the world needed peace and development. Moreover, according to the general development trend of world politics at that time, Deng Xiaoping also believed that this was a goal that can be achieved. In accordance with this judgment, in the following time, China will no longer "export revolution", but will establish normal and friendly diplomatic relations with other countries in the world. And the national strategy will be aimed at developing the economy internally and connecting with the world externally. Through its long-term adherence to a peaceful foreign policy and its active integration into the world economic system, China not only caught every opportunity generated by globalization, but also became the major driving force to promote globalization with the rapid development of the country.

Today, the world landscape has been changing, and the changes are getting more and more rapid and violent. With the world entering the momentous changes unseen in a century, our judgment on the theme of the times and our conception of national development strategy should also be adjusted accordingly. Obviously, what kind of adjustment China makes needs to take into account not only our own needs, but also the views of other countries, especially other major countries, on the world situation. China is an important link of the world order, and the world order is the result of the interaction of countries, especially major countries.

The United States believes that the important theme in today's world is great power competition and the clash of values. The Trump administration has constantly adjusted the domestic and foreign policies of the United States, in particular, changed the strategy of "engagement and prevention" toward China that has continued in the past few decades, and turned to a competitive strategy. Its main symbol is that in December 2017, Trump released the first National Security Strategy of the United

States of America (NSS) during his term, which proposed that the United States is facing the new era of "great power competition" and clearly defined China as a "revisionist power" and a strategic competitor. In May 2020, the Trump administration issued United States Strategic Approach to the People's Republic of China, and once again clearly characterized Sino-US relationship as a strategic competition. The Biden administration maintains the judgment of great power strategic competition. In March 2022, Biden in his first State of the Union address after taking office, pointed out that the United States is currently facing a battle between "democracy" and "autocracy", and a strategic competition with China. Earlier, in December 2021, the United States hosted the so-called "World Summit for Democracy", which invited representatives from more than 110 countries and regions to attend, and focused on the so-called "media freedom", "fair elections", "preventing and countering corruption", and other issues. In September 2021, Biden in his remarks at the 76th session of the United Nations General Assembly, said that the United States would compete vigorously, and lead with its values and its strength. In November 2021, Biden said in his speech before the video meeting with President Xi Jinping that the United States and China were engaged in simple, straightforward competition. Shortly after the conflict between Russia and Ukraine, the United States and Western countries began to shape the narrative of the so-called "China-Russia axis", bound China and Russia together and defined this conflict as a war between "democracy and autocracy" and between "civilization and barbarism". On March 26, 2022, Biden delivered an impassioned speech at the Royal Castle in Warsaw, the capital of Poland, saying that this was "a battle between 'democracy' and 'autocracy', between 'liberty' and 'repression', between 'a rules-based order' and 'one governed by brute force'. In this battle, we need to be clear-eyed. This battle will not be won in days or months either. We need to steel ourselves for the long fight ahead".

Russia believes that the important theme in contemporary world is turbulence, inequality and crisis. The Annual Meeting of the Valdai International Discussion Club is an important annual political exchange event in Russia, and Putin usually makes a speech on the last day of the Annual Meeting, which is regarded as the important basis by all circles for predicting the direction of Russian domestic and foreign affairs in the coming period. At the Valdai Annual Meeting in 2020, Putin said that many acute problems and controversies have accumulated in modern international affairs, and we live in an era of palpable international shocks and crises. The theme of the Valdai Annual Meeting in 2021 is "Global Shake-Up in the 21st century: The Individual, Values, and the State". In his speech, Putin said that the capitalist model has come to an end, "even in the richest countries and regions, the uneven distribution of material wealth has exacerbated inequality, primarily, inequality of opportunities both within individual societies and at the international level". To a large extent, the Russia-Ukraine conflict is a continuation of this judgment by Putin.

The European Union believes that the important theme in contemporary world is the reorganization of power. French President Emmanuel Macron said in a speech at the conference of French ambassadors in August 2019 that "Western hegemony may be coming to an end", and "the international order is being subverted and transformed, and this is not only a geopolitical integration, but also a strategic reorganization". In February 2022, in response to the conflict between Russia and Ukraine, Macron said that the Russia-Ukraine conflict is a turning point in the history of France and Europe, it will have a far-reaching consequence and it will have an impact on the geopolitics of the European continent. The 58th Munich Security Conference (MSC) was held in February 2022 under the theme of "Turning the Tide: Unlearning Helplessness", and the Munich Security Report 2022 was released, arguing that all these challenges such as the COVID-19 pandemic, the threat of climate change and geopolitical tensions contribute to a feeling of a loss of control. In March 2022, Lars-Hendrik Röller, a senior economic advisor to former German Chancellor Angela Merkel, said that after the Russia-Ukraine conflict, the trend of deglobalization has been further strengthened, and there is a risk of splitting into two camps, and a new world order is taking shape.

The question we need to answer is: In such an international context, do we still need to continue to adhere to the theme of peace and development?

This question is not difficult to answer if we view it from the perspective of continuing globalization and modernization. The reason is simple. Continuing to adhere to the theme of peace and development is not only important for ourselves, but also has more world significance. As mentioned above, peace and development are not only our judgment on the international situation at that time, but also the goal we pursued. We have adhered to this theme for several decades, and have benefited from it. Although today's world has become unpeaceful and unstable, yet development is still the theme for the next phase in China. The per capita

GDP in Chinese mainland region has just reached $12,000 in 2021. This is still far away from the developed countries in the West, and is also far away from the last one of the "Four Asian Tigers" economies, that is, nearly $30,000 in China's Taiwan. Although our coastal areas can be said to have escaped the "Middle Income Trap", yet the country on a whole is still on the edge of the "Middle Income Trap". If we can break through the "Middle Income Trap", there is tremendous space for further development in China. More importantly, for more than 40 years since reform and opening-up, China has accumulated various problems in social, economic, and environmental aspects. If any of these problems are not properly handled, they will become the flash point of economic stagnation and social instability. However, there are too many stock problems, and coupled with the continuous deterioration of external environment today, China does not have enough time and space to solve these stock problems one by one. Therefore, only by continuing to develop, even if it will exacerbate certain problems to a certain extent, can the stock problems be transformed into the problems in development by making big increment. As long as these social, economic, and environmental problems are not be paid attention to statically with a magnifying grass, these problems will not become the cause of the events that influence the overall situation. This is actually a matter of exchanging time for space, enhancing China's comprehensive national strength through further development, and increasing China's own bargaining chips and confidence in the face of further encirclement from the West in the future. The internal development, on the other hand, needs a relatively peaceful international environment. In the past several decades, we have had such an environment. Today this environment is changing, but we still need to strive for such an environment.

Furthermore, whether China can persevere in the pursuit of the goal of "peace and development" determines whether its modernization will be interrupted. Since modern times, Chinese modernization has been interrupted several times. Today, the core of China Policy of Western countries, led by the United States, is also to stop Chinese modernization once again. In the past few decades, we have caught the opportunities presented to us by the changes in the international environment. Today's China is no longer a country that the United States can encircle at will. A rising China can create opportunities for itself by proactively reshaping and even rebuilding the world order.

What is more important is at the international level. Our pursuit of peace and development has become our core soft power in the international arena. For a long period of time, peace and development are not only emphasized by our country, but also the common vision for the international community. Once this insistence is revised, it means that we have given up this core soft power.

It is not difficult for us to understand the ideological encirclement toward China by the United States, and we can also respond to it calmly and rationally. So long as we do not repeat the ideological confrontations between the United States and the Soviet Union during the Cold War, it is not impossible to dissipate the ideological pressure from the United States. Although China in the era of Deng Xiaoping has successfully integrated into the world economy, formed economic interdependence with the Western world, and participated comprehensively and actively in the management and construction of major international institutions. But ideologically, the differences between China and the West are obvious: China is a socialist country with its unique historical experience, development model, political system and civilization paradigm. It also determines that China will interact with the world order in a way that is difficult for the West to accept. Now the deterioration of Sino-US relationship is also mainly reflected in ideological issues. Owing to economic interdependence, the United States lacks the means to counterbalance China. Under these circumstances, as previously discussed, the United States began to continuously carry out value diplomacy around the binary opposition of "autocracy-democracy", demonized China's political system, and asked all countries in the world to follow the United States in counterbalancing "authoritarian" China on the grounds of ideological differences. As a result, China is regarded as a "revisionist state" by the American authorities, that is, a regime attempting to subvert the liberal international order.

But we must distinguish between America's intentions and its ability to achieve the intentions. We should realize that the United States itself is facing a deep crisis in its own system of governance. After the collapse of the Soviet Union, there was a lot of optimism in American society that liberal democracy was the best and the last form of government in the world, but now few people in the United States think so. Today many Americans are worried about the future of American democracy. Some people within the United States contribute the root cause of the crises faced by American democracy to the so-called "authoritarian" challenges from China and Russia. This is tragedy in itself, indicating that American democracy has lost its ability to reflect on itself.

More importantly, the ideology of freedom and democracy advocated by the United States has gradually lost its appeal in the non-Western world. Since the end of the Cold War, the United States has spent a huge manpower, financial resources and material resources to promote its democracy around the world, and has even not hesitated to take advantage of violence and war to achieve its goals. However, the United States has only failed cases, but there are no successful cases. The US military actions in Iraq, Afghanistan, Libya and other countries and regions have long made the international community seriously question American-style democracy. The tide of refugees caused by the disintegration of Libya's regime has a severe social crisis in Europe. To a great extent, it is the irresponsibility of the United States to the world order that ultimately created the ideological vacuum of the world order. Under such circumstances, it is difficult for the United States to have a practical effect in its ideological encirclement toward China.

If more and more countries (including some Western countries) have profound doubts about whether Western liberal democratic system has the ability to cope with the crises facing the world, then peace and development are what all countries need. At the international level, peace and development are interrelated and mutually reinforcing. Peace creates a stable environment for development, and the achievements made by development further consolidate peace under the guarantee of good governance, forming a virtuous circle of common prosperity and sustainability. Peace is needed in times of ease, and even more so in times of turmoil. It is precisely because today's world is unstable and restless that peace and development have become the goals pursued by all countries in the world.

In other words, at the international level, China's adherence to the concept of peace and development also determines the ultimate rise of China on the international political stage. The turbulence in the international situation means that the concept of building a community with a shared future for mankind, which we advocate, is facing severe challenges. Therefore, how to help human community with a shared future tide over difficulties is a question that China as a major country must consider. China's continued advocacy and promotion of the concept of peace and development will help China, with the image of a responsible major country, unite the mainstream forces in safeguarding the world peace on a global scale, and jointly contribute to the stability and tranquility of mankind. Whether "peace and development" as an international public good can achieve sustainability depends on the degree to which the collective actions from the international community can be achieved, while playing the role of a responsible major country is an important condition for solving the difficult problem of the collective actions. As a result, the responsibility of China as a major country is manifested not only in its duty-bound support for the themes of the times, peace and development, but also in its persistent pursuit of this theme.

CHAPTER 11

Opening up to the Outside World and Continuing Globalization

As previously discussed, globalization and modernization are a pair of complex relationship. In some cases, they move toward the same directions, while in other cases they run counter to each other. Globalization is the product of mutual openness among countries. Without openness, there can be no globalization. The modernization of a country can be carried out both in an open state and in a closed state. If it is the former, then globalization and modernization are in the same directions; if it is the latter, then globalization and modernization are in the opposite directions. In the past several decades, China's globalization and modernization are a supplementary and complementary process, because China has realized its modernization under the background of globalization. Likewise, if we hope that continued globalization and modernization in the future will continue to supplement and complement each other, then our modernization need to continue to be carried out in the state of openness. The way to modernization should also be to continue to open up to the outside world and reform at home. In other words, if globalization and modernization are to be mutually reinforcing, then two requirements need to be met: First, China's foreign policy and globalization are in the same directions; second, China's domestic reform and the policy of opening up to the outside world are in the same directions. In a word, "peace and development" is the value and goal China has been

Z. Yongnian, *The Great Convergence VS. The Great Divergence*,
https://doi.org/10.1007/978-981-96-7846-4_11

pursuing, but what can enable China to achieve this pursuit is opening up to the outside world and reforming at home.

Continuing globalization is based on the premise that we continue to have a relatively peaceful international environment. As mentioned above, in the midst of the momentous changes in the world, all major countries are constantly competing each other in the world order that is being rebuilt, and striving for more rights to voice for themselves. In this regard, we should also find our own ways to respond to the three major factors that have affected the international order in recent years—the Russia-Ukraine conflict, the major-country competition and the Sino-US relationship. Among these factors, some need to be dealt with in the short term, while others need to be dealt with in the long term. We have developed to this day, and no longer been shallow and ignorant as before. So long as we deal with them calmly, we can overcome the difficulties of this kind or another, and move forward.

1. How to recognize and deal with the Russia-Ukraine conflict

As mentioned earlier, we have a very clear attitude toward the conflict between Russia and Ukraine. We are opposed to both the conflict and the root cause of the conflict, which is the NATO. The United States uses the Russia-Ukraine conflict to put pressure on China and bipolarize the world order, but its efforts are hard to realize. It is difficult for the United Stated to get out of Europe in a short time. The war may drag on for a long period of time, but if the United States fails to help European countries, its reputation among European countries will collapse. However, we do not need to take a policy with excessive opposition to the United States, and we still need to be rational. We do not need to regard the United States as a single interest group, because the United States is a country composed of many interest groups. The attitude of Wall Street toward China is different from that of the Cold War faction and anti-China forces. Wall Street hope that our market will be more open, mainly for the sake of its investment, so that its interest can be more guaranteed. Some political forces hope that China will gradually turn into a Western-style country through opening up. Of course, there are still some American anti-China political forces that want to isolate China. We need to analyze the different sorts of American vested interest groups in a practical and realistic way, so that we can make scientific decisions.

We need to come into contact with Europe. During this Russia-Ukraine conflict, European countries have been actually kidnapped by the United States to a large extent. There is no geopolitical dispute between China and European countries, but mainly commercial interests. Commercial interests are very important to European countries. Whether it is a democratic system or an authoritarian system, the sustainable development and growth of the economy are important to any kind of political system. When the economy develops well, everyone will lead a better life; when the economy is in crisis, all political bodies will have big problems. This is a general rule. China and European countries have many common interests, so we hope that European countries can be independent, instead of always following the United States.

Our relationship with Russia is not an ally in the eyes of the West. The China-Russia relations are not such alliance as that between the United States and Japan, and between the United States and South Korea, but a partnership. It is true that we have some influence on Russia, and it is also ok for us to communicate with Russia. We can do things similar to what Turkey has done in the Russia-Ukraine conflict. The international political crisis is also an opportunity for us. If by dealing with this crisis can our own Kissinger be produced, then it is also a blessing, and will be what our country needs for the rise of its diplomacy.

2. **How to respond to major-country competition**

As far as major-country competition is concerned, how do we deal with our relations with India, Turkey, Russia and Indonesia? Since the reform and opening-up, our views on other countries—views on India, Turkey, Russia—have been too influenced by our views on the United States, that is, we lack independent views on these countries.

In particular, in the study of international relations, everyone has put a lot of energy into studying Sino-US relationship. Sino-US relationship is important, but Sino-US relationship is not the whole international relations. China's international relations have much broader and deeper meanings. At present, there are several types of attitudes toward the United States in China: The first type is those who are hating the United States. It is very hostile to the United States and believes that whatever the United States does is aimed at China and that there is a conspiracy.

The second type is those who are fearing the United States, which is basically capitulationism. The third type is those who are "taking the United States lightly", that is, it looks down upon the United States and thinks that the United States has declined and is nothing remarkable. The fourth type is those who are pro-American, that is, it is inclined to the United States. After the outbreak of the conflict between Russia and Ukraine, some people also put forward that the United States was the biggest winner in this Russia-Ukraine conflict, so we should stand with the winner and cut relations with Russia. Many of us have the illusion that if we are good to the United States, the United States will accept us. This is not the actual case. As already discussed before, Gorbachev in the Soviet Union, Yeltsin in Russia, including Putin himself, were once all pro-American, but why didn't the United States accept it?

Politics is very realistic. The United States cannot accept a country that challenges it from within the system—even its allies. No matter which ally challenges the United States, the United States still suppresses it, so we see in the 1980s the United States suppressed Germany and Japan, because the technology of Germany and Japan posed a challenge to the United States. It is easier for the United States to deal with Germany and Japan, because Germany and Japan have no army and their security relies entirely on the United States, so these two countries are very dependent on the United States. What the United States means by alliance is not an equal partner, but an alliance that accepts the leadership of the United States and listens to the United States. Among the American alliances, the United States suppressed France the most, because France has both an economy and an independent army.

Our relations with major countries cannot be overly influenced by the United States. For example, in our relation to India, we are too influenced by the United States. Some people are always worried about that India will throw itself into the arms of the United States to deal with China, but this is actually a simplification of India. China has a border dispute with India, but we need to have our own position on India. And we also need to have own stance on Turkey. The United States cannot represent the entire diplomatic relations of China, and the entire diplomatic relations of China cannot be dominated by the relationship between China and the United States. The Sino-US relationship is important, but it cannot represent everything. We must be very clear about this point.

3. How to deal with Sino-US relationship

So, how will the Sino-US relationship be dealt with? The Biden administration has defined the relationship between China and the United States simply as a battle between "democracy" and "autocracy", which is an ideological statement. According to the classification of the United States, the Sino-US relationship can be divided into four areas, namely cooperation, competition, confrontation, conflict or even war. The emphasis of the United States is on cooperation, competition, and confrontation. But in fact, confrontation can be divided into controllable confrontation and uncontrollable confrontation. Controllable confrontation is confrontation and uncontrollable confrontation is conflict or even war. If all these aspects are unavoidable, then we should be more active, that is, strengthening cooperation, healthy competition, managing and controlling confrontation, and avoiding war.

There are certainly many areas of cooperation, including climate issues, nuclear proliferation issues, and public health issues. If China and the United States do not cooperate with each other on these issues, no one can do well, especially the climate issues. In addition, there are other places for cooperation, such as in the aspect of our space technology. As our space technology has improved, we have found a point of cooperation with the United States. There has never been cooperation between a weak country and a strong country. Only when you have the ability can you hold the tickets to cooperation. What kind of nuclear cooperation will a country with nuclear weapons talk about with a country without nuclear weapons? This is the relationship between China and the United States. Why do we emphasize that development is important? Because only through development can we be strong and have a foundation of cooperation with the United States. You do not have to worry too much about whether China and the United States will cooperate, because without cooperation, they will destroy each other. Therefore, we should advocate strengthening cooperation.

In respect of competition, though we do not want to define the Sino-US relationship by "competition", yet if the United States wants to compete with China, China has no choice either. As a matter of fact, competition has become inevitable, but we should not be afraid. Between China and the United Stated, there will be competition in all fields, and it will be all-round competition. In terms of science and technology, the United States is stuck in our neck on the chip, and we have to compete even if we do not want to compete. And do we have to compete in system? We have to compete, too. Nevertheless, healthy competition should be advocated here to avoid and reduce vicious competition. We must avoid the military competition between the United States and the Soviet Union in those years. We should carry out our modernization in national defense and military affairs in accordance with our own established guidelines, but it is for national defense, not for competition with the United States. Once it is caught into vicious military competition with the United States, then the Asia-Pacific region will easily evolve into a "powder keg". Over these years, we have paid attention to economy and trade, and most of our relations with other countries are in the aspects of economy and trade, which has forced the United States to put its attention on economy and trade as well. The "Belt and Road Initiative" is a good case. In recent years, the United States and other Western countries have also begun to commit to infrastructure construction in other countries and regions. If the United States and Western countries really implement it, this is undoubtedly a good trend. We should welcome all measures that are beneficial to the economic development and social stability of other countries. Military competition is a zero-sum game, but economic competition is often a win–win situation.

There are also many areas of confrontation between China and the United States. As has occurred for these years, there have been confrontations between China and the United States in areas including what the United States call human rights issues in Xinjiang, Tibet and Hong Kong. Although these confrontations have had some negative impacts on all aspects of China, in particular, on the business environment in China, yet these confrontations are generally under our control. If confrontation is controllable, there is no problem. What should be confronted still can be confronted. Nevertheless, it should be emphasized that it should not confront for the sake of confrontation, but should safeguard our national interests through confrontation. Aimless confrontation should be avoided and reduced. When compromise is needed, it should also be compromised, especially when compromise is more in line with national interests or can enhance national interests more.

There are areas between China and the United States that can lead to direct conflicts, but there are not many, mainly in the South China Sea issue and the Taiwan question. The experience of interaction between China and the United States over these years shows that there will be no major conflict in the South China Sea. For the South China Sea issue, we can not only manage it well, but also find a way to reconcile it.

The main area of conflict is on the Taiwan question. Taiwan is at the heart of our core interests, and we have no room for concession. The United States believes that China's solution to the Taiwan question is to dominate the Western Pacific and drive the US forces out of the Western Pacific. However, this is not the case for China. The Taiwan question is a matter of our sovereignty and national reunification. This conflict between Russia and Ukraine has also taught the Taiwan authorities and the United States a lesson. If Taiwan becomes independent, not only will our sovereignty be incomplete, but our national security will not be guaranteed. Therefore, the Taiwan question is not only a question of sovereignty, but also a question of national security. But, on the whole, the time to solve the Taiwan question is on our side. The United States has been anxious to push Taiwan to move toward the direction of independence by means of "cutting sausages" in recent years. This is mainly because our economic growth and military modernization are providing us with material conditions for a peaceful settlement of the Taiwan question. To a large extent, the Taiwan question has entered the stage of confrontation between China and the United States in recent years. As China continues its modernization, once it goes beyond this stage, then China will have the power to "neutralize" the United States, and at that time there will be more options for resolving the Taiwan question. In other words, at the stage of confrontation between China and the United States, we need to handle the Taiwan question with rare rationality. Around the world, the question of sovereignty is mostly likely to generate nationalist sentiments. Such emotions are inevitable, and emotion cannot replace reason.

In other words, although the world is in chaos, yet we have the ability to pursue a relatively peaceful international environment by using our material strength and rationality. While ensuring a relatively peaceful international environment, we are committed to pursuing and promoting globalization, and opening up to the outside is at the core of our continued globalization.

Whether it is the backwardness caused by the closure since the Ming and Qing dynasties, or the world economic miracle created by the opening-up policy in the past few decades, they all have proved the importance of opening up. Under the condition that the three pillars of the world order are in crisis today, and under the theme of the times of peace and development, we should clearly put forward the vision with peaceful coexistence as the main theme. Peaceful coexistence includes three aspects: economic coexistence, institutional coexistence, and value coexistence. Different from the peaceful coexistence between the United States and the Soviet Union during the Cold War, the "peaceful coexistence" advocated here is the coexistence under the condition of openness or even unilateral openness. Its essence is to promote others' openness with one's own openness, and realize the mutual openness and mutual integration.

1. **In economy, China continues to maintain a high degree of openness, even unilateral openness**

To a great extent, when Western countries such as the United States have given up the banner of free trade that they once have adhered to, China can take over this banner, do addition on the basic principles of this banner, and add in some of our own principles suitable for the new era.

The world landscape has entered multi-polarization. This means that the situation of the United States as "one hegemonic superpower" has officially come to an end. The United States is not aging as some American scholars or Chinese scholars have claimed. On the contrary, the United States is far from declining, and in many ways is still developing, but it is true that the United States is no longer the United States whose gross national product (GNP) accounted for half of the world after the end of World War II. The United States will lose its special position as a "buyer of last resort" more and more in the future. This requires China to improve its own degree of opening up. China not only need to provide productivity for the world economy, but also provide purchasing power for the world economy. For the global economy, China's opening up is one of the most important international public goods. Today, when the United States and some Western countries are engaged in anti-globalization, opening up itself has become the most important international public good. As the second largest world economy, China's opening up and the degree of its opening up will have a substantial impact on the opening up process of the whole world. To a great extent, we even have the ability to redefine globalization, though we will not use this right of definition unilaterally. Although in economy the competition between us and the United States is inevitable, yet we need to emphasize that economic competition is not a zero-sum game, but a win–win situation. Even if the United States and the developed countries in the West decouple from us in some fields, or even block us, we also need to implement an opening up policy to their capital. Decoupling is not in line with the interest of China, nor is it in line with the interest of Western capital. Moreover, for China, opening up is not only to continue to attract Western capital and prevent decoupling, but also the driving force for technological progress.

As far as continuing globalization is concerned, we need to develop technology-industrial cooperation with non-American Western countries as much as possible to break through the blockade by differentiation. The technological blockade of the United States against China is an important obstacle and driving force for China's independent scientific and technological innovation. It is difficult to break through the American technological blockade by relying entirely on independent research and development. However, not all Western countries want to blockade China in all technologies. Those countries most likely to develop the alternatives to the American technology tend to be some non-American Western countries (For example, Japan still has some catch-up potential in chip technology), and they are also not willing to be kidnapped by the United States and lose the Chinese market. In developing alternative technologies, cooperation with non-American Western countries may be one way to break through the blockade. China should provide funding incentives for the research and development of relevant technology to the world, protect its intellectual property rights, open its market, and provide investment convenience. This may be more promising than relying entirely on domestic research and development to break through the American technological blockade.

As for developing countries, we need to continue to implement and promote open and inclusive multilateralism, including important projects, and organizations such as the "Belt and Road initiative", the BRICKS, the Asian Infrastructure Investment Bank. These projects and organization can not only promote the economic development of local countries, but also open up new markets for China's commodities. It is mutually beneficial and win–win.

Unilateral opening up also means that China will have to make structural adjustments to its own economic development model and fiscal policy, including tax reform, revitalization of small and medium-sized enterprises, improvement of welfare, and advancement of the internationalization of the Chinese Renminbi (RMB). The development state has indeed made remarkable achievements in the past, but it has also caused a series of disadvantages such as uneven distribution of wealth, squeezed living space of private enterprises, loss of economic vitality in non-coastal areas, insufficient purchasing power of the people, anxieties in the middle class, and low fertility rates. More importantly, the state-dominated economic system is difficult to integrate with the international economy. We must vigorously develop private economy, and promote the integration of private economy with the international system. In fact, since Trump came to power, various efforts to decouple China and the United States have failed, which shows the resilience of China's private enterprises in the international economy. If China is to transform itself from a "world factory" to a "world market", it should summarize its past experiences, reflect on and rectify its existing development model.

2. **In international security, we must do something useful**

International security includes traditional security and non-traditional security. International security in these two domains is deteriorating rapidly. As mentioned earlier, in the field of nuclear non-proliferation, because of the Russia-Ukraine conflict, the world is facing the threat of a new wave of nuclear proliferation. As the COVID-19 pandemic has shown, the crisis in the field of public health is extremely profound, but international cooperation has become extremely difficult. This is even more true to the field of climate, where countries, big or small, are all in the same boat. In all these fields, international cooperation can all be regarded as an international public good. As a major country, China has the responsibility and obligation to provide more of such public goods.

In the meantime, China must play a more active role in regional security. Multi-polarization means that the United States has lost its position as "one hegemonic superpower", and it means that the military forces in various regions have begun to act in their own ways. This situation is very prominent in the surrounding regions of China. To begin with, whether it is in West Asia, the South China Sea, or East Asia, the arms race between countries has become a "common practice". Among them, terrorism in West Asia will pose a serious threat to the provinces in western China in the case of the rise of Turkey's power. South Korea and Japan in East

Asia are likely to increase their military spending, and even try to possess nuclear weapons due to the North Korean nuclear crisis. The disputes in the South China Sea, involving six countries, have also made the situation more unstable. Moreover, the main forces in East Asia and the South China Sea are actually the military allies of the United States. The encirclement network they have formed against China has directly hindered China's march toward a maritime country. China will not and also have no need to stir up troubles, but it must play a much bigger role in neighborhood diplomacy and collective security. China can take the governance in the Mekong River and the mediation of the Korean Peninsula nuclear crisis as the starting point, the Shanghai Cooperation Organization as a platform, to provide strong solutions to the security concerns and governance needs for neighboring countries and regions. China will from these security arrangements gain the agenda-setting power to lead regional security affairs, so as to better avoid possible military conflicts, and even nuclear proliferation issues between China and its neighboring countries.

On the issue of regional security, two points must be emphasized. First, the main way for the United States to deeply intervene and get involved in regional security in Asia is to confront China by forcing some regional countries to "take side" (stand on the side of the United States). While the United States is doing so, China must avoid doing the same. If China also forces some countries to "take side", then it will help the United States with its intention of world bipolarization. Second, when the United States engages in exclusive and closed gangs in this region, China needs to adhere to open and inclusive multilateralism. Only open and inclusive multilateralism can move toward the same direction with globalization.

3. **In values, China should draw experiences and nourishments from its thousands of years of civilizational tradition to provide new references for solving the crisis of modernity**

Chinese civilization has been developing for thousands of years and has never been interrupted, showing its strong resilience to survive. The "this-worldly secularism" of traditional Chinese culture—the concern of the Chinese culture for man and nature, pragmaticism, and the compatibility of Chinese civilization with different ideas and values—stands in stark contrast to the "other-worldly cosmopolitanism" of Western Christian civilization and Islamic civilization. If globalization in the past 500 years has developed along the ideological thread of the other-worldly doctrine in the West, then it is necessary for China to inject new ideas into the development of the world order with its "this-worldly secularism", and make contributions to human coexistence under crisis.

CHAPTER 12

Domestic Reform and Continued Modernization

Opening up is for the sake of development, and reform is also for the sake of development. But to advance and deepen the reform, China needs a "new stability". As far as the world order is concerned, we have entered a phase of chaos and crisis arising from the transformation of the old and new powers. This is also the phenomenon and challenge pointed out by General Secretary Xi Jinping's judgment that "the world today is undergoing the momentous changes unseen in a century, and the world has entered a period of turbulence and change". It should be realized that chaos and crisis are not just a simple confrontation between China and the West, but a global structural turmoil. Climate crisis, public health crisis, food crisis, energy crisis and nuclear proliferation crisis, have profoundly affected the whole mankind including developed countries, energy-producing countries, traditional powers, emerging economies, and poor countries.

At a time of turbulence and change in the world, stability is China's core interest and also the interest of the international community. Only when China itself is stable can it become the foundation of world stability. However, this stability cannot be the self-isolating and survival-oriented stability like Russia's fortress economy, but the "new stability" achieved through continued opening up and reform, because China has grown up and developed in the state of reform and opening-up. The new stability

Z. Yongnian, *The Great Convergence VS. The Great Divergence*,
https://doi.org/10.1007/978-981-96-7846-4_12

needs to meet the dual goals of "fending off short-term shocks" and "laying the long-term groundwork for China's rise in the new world order".

The new stability needs new responses. Specifically, it is a prepared and positive response. Since the reform and opening-up in more than 40 years, although our development has also faced various external pressures, yet on the whole, China's development is not only conductive to the development of hyper-globalization led by the West, but also can be said to be a key factor for the realization of hyper-globalization. However, with the development of industrialization and the enhancement of comprehensive national strength, China now has become the biggest competitor in the eyes of the United States, and the development space "given by the West" in the past has no longer existed. In the future, the further development of China in all respects will have to face the suppression and restrictions by Western countries, which has never been encountered in China's development experience in the past 40 years or so. Therefore, whether it is the international economic and financial system or the international geopolitics in the future, the further containment of China by the West will greatly exceed our control and prediction. As a result, making adequate preparations and plans for various changes beyond expectations will become a key for China's success in coping with various "black swan" and "grey rhino" events in the future. Centering on the new theme, China needs to do a good job emphatically in several main aspects in the next decade:

1. **Investing in soft infrastructure, replacing the engine of economic growth, and stabilizing economic development**

Many of the problems that have accumulated in China's reform and opening-up over the past 40 years or so are structural and institutional. The fundamental solutions to these problems all mean "breaking the bones", and will undoubtedly have to lead to the emergence of new problems. Therefore, we need to have a new understanding of the problems themselves, and no longer regard them as the obstacles to further development and reform, but as the driving forces to further advance modernization. We can view the importance of stability and maintaining economic development from two aspects. First, from the perspective of national social and economic governance, only when the economy achieves sustainable development, can governments at all levels have much more financial resources to solve the most prominent problems, and have the ability to pay attention to social equity and common prosperity in the process of development. At the same time, the establishment of strategic guidelines of the Party and the country should fully take into account the limitations of the governance capacity of local governments at all levels. And the clear and focused policy direction by the Party and the country should be more conducive to the implementation of the strategic guidelines at the local levels. Next, from the perspective of people's life and social development, only when emerging industries continue to emerge, the potential for career development continues to improve, and social lifestyles continue to innovate, can people's work and life have a continuous stream of motivation, and society can have a sustained vitality. Therefore, it is essential to maintain economic development and social progress.

From the perspective of maintaining the sustainable development of China's economy, the most important question that we need to answer at present is how to replace the engine of China's economic growth. Investment, consumption and net exports are the constant troika driving economic growth, but the relative proportions of the three are in dynamic balance and constantly changing, and the adjustment of their proportions will affect their driving forces for economic growth. For quite a long time in the past, real estate has occupied a very important position in investment and domestic demand. Real estate and land finance can be considered as a big engine that drives China's economic growth in recent 30 years. However, under the general trend of aging population, real estate has been unable to support the sustainable development of China's economy in the long term. In addition to the debt problem, the real estate sector is currently facing the crisis of excessive supply. Under such a background, the land finance based on the rapid development of the real estate industry will not be sustainable. For many local governments that rely heavily on land finance, to take what as their main sources of sustainable fiscal revenue is an urgent problem to be solved.

We should consider solving the problems in housing, education, medical services and elderly care fundamentally through large-scale investment in soft infrastructure, so that the majority of middle-income groups and low-income groups can be relieved of worries, and the middle class can obtain institutional guarantee. By upgrading soft infrastructure in an all-round way, for example, building public rental housing on a large scale in the first-tier cities and second-tier cities with high housing prices, the new-type urbanization will develop in the direction of building a city that is livable, conductive to doing business and suitable for nurture and education. In doing so, it can directly enhance the people's sense of gain, narrow the gap between the rich and the poor, promote social stability and contribute to the realization of common prosperity. This also can reduce the level of precautionary savings of Chinese residents, fully release the people's consumption potential, thereby greatly expanding domestic demands and promoting consumption. What's more, increasing investment in soft infrastructure itself can directly facilitate economic growth, because it is itself a part of investment demands and is an effective investment that will yield long-term returns in economy.

The media in Western countries often say that the rapid development for China's economy is a free ride on the West. However, the actual situation is that Western capital is a big beneficiary of China's economic development. Through their keen sense of business, they often take the free ride on the counter-cyclical adjustment by the Chinese government. In the aftermath of 1997 Asian financial crisis, the Chinese government's timely economic intervention, in terms of domestic economic policy, was mainly reflected in launching a round of large-scale investment in transportation infrastructure. After the dot-com bubble burst in the United States in 2001, international capital rushed to find new growth points and flocked to China to invest. The previous infrastructure construction led by the Chinese government and state-owned enterprises has greatly improved the efficiency of their investment in factory building, production and operation in China, which is equivalent to providing subsidies for these international capitals in advance. What's more, China's economy is also the winner during this process. From 2002 to 2012, China has maintained a dazzling economic growth rate and these ten years have been known as the golden decade for China's economy. At present, the transportation infrastructure construction in China has achieved the world-class level, while the soft infrastructure construction that is related to the livelihood and well-being of the people, is still relatively backward, which is our shortcoming. If we launch a wave of large-scale investment in soft infrastructure construction under the current situation of the strong downward pressure on economic growth, it can lay a foundation for fully releasing domestic demand, thereby consolidating China's position as one of the most important consumer markets in the world. At the same time, China will continue to promote high-level opening up to the outside world and expand market access for foreign enterprises, which will have a great attraction to foreign capital and boost the confidence of domestic private enterprises. From here, this is expected to promote another wave of medium–high-speed economic development brought about by the boom of foreign investment and private enterprises investment, and bring China's economy into another golden decade. In the meantime, it will defeat the attempts of the United States and some Western countries to isolate and blockade China economically and technologically. By then, China can be expected to completely cross the "Middle Income Trap" and realize its goal of becoming a developed country.

2. **Making up for security shortcomings, adhering to worst-case scenario thinking, and deploying ahead to prevent any possible irrational actions by US-led Western world**

National security involves all aspects, and we need to sort it out in the form of checklist. Let's take energy security as an example. The full-scale outbreak of the Russia-Ukraine conflict has completely exposed the energy security issues of the European Union. First, the European Union is too dependent on the energy of Russia alone. Next, the European Union has not made adequate preparations and plans for possible energy security issues. Again, the European Union has not systematically and comprehensively assessed the relationship between energy security and national security issues such as military security, economic security and food security, resulting in prematurely being kidnapped by the United States and imposing maximum sanctions on Russia. In the end, it could only passively face and bear the devastating blows of energy shortage to economy and society. The lessons of the European Union, especially Germany, in this conflict are very profound. We need to take them seriously. Similar to Germany, China is also a country with a high degree of external dependence on energy, in particular, on oil. Accordingly, we need to make it a priority to make up for the shortcomings of energy security in the next few years, which mainly involves the following aspects. To begin with, on the supply side, we need to ensure diversified sources of oil supply and ensure the security of energy payment, that is, negotiate the possibility of settling oil in RMB with more oil-supplying countries. The next, on the transportation side, we need to ensure the security of the channels for oil transportation, and at the same time increase the pipeline oil supply, even if it is not the best choice economically. Once more, on the demand side, while continuing to promote energy conservation and emission reduction, we need to more aggressively push forward the process of electrification in the transportation sector. The exposure of the energy security issues of the European Union reminds us that when it comes to energy security, we cannot solely deal with it with economic logic, and political logic is very necessary. In this regard, China also has an inherent advantage, because energy industry in China is mainly in the hands of central state-owned enterprises, and the specific implementation after clarifying the strategy of energy security is highly operable.

3. **Science and Technology are the primary productive forces**

First, it is necessary to realize technological upgrading in an open state. In East Asia, since the 1970s, Japan and the "Four Asian Tigers" economies have been able to achieve industrial upgrading almost every decade, and each industrial upgrading has been achieved in an open state, either by improving old technologies, or introducing new technologies (including their own original technologies and those from the West). Today, in the context of Sino-US competition, the government, state-owned enterprises, and private enterprises all attach their great importance to the investment in technology research and development. Empirically, if a country does not invest heavily in its technology research and development, not only can its high-quality development goals not be realized, but also in the long run, its economy will also fall into decline.

But it should be pointed out that even in the field of technology we are also facing the situation of rising nationalist and populist sentiments. At the social level, some people really believe that we have caught up with the West. These sentiments also extend to the government, where some officials have also begun to hold popular views in society as a result of the decline in technocratic officials who know technology.

It is not wrong for us to mention the whole-nation system, but we should not forget that this is a new-type whole-nation system. The traditional whole-nation system is the Soviet-style system, that is, "innovation behind closed door". This system of the Soviet Union has also made some achievements in its early years, but it could not realize the goal of sustainable development. There are two reasons. The first is that in the closed situation, technological innovation lacks new ideas, and over time there is no competitive pressure. The second is that innovation is not sustainable without the international market. The investment in technology is very huge, and it needs to be rewarded in the market. Without the market, it also means that there is no sustainability. China has also experienced the similar process before its reform and opening-up. Nevertheless, some people today still miss the "two Bombs, one Satellite" model. It should be clearly recognized that the "two Bombs, one Satellite" is also related to the West. What would have happened if the generation of patriotic intellectuals had not made painstaking efforts to study in the West and returned to China from the West at that time? It cannot be said that we will not be able to develop the "two bombs, one satellite" in the end, but this process will be certainly much longer. We should admit that although there have been many major technological inventions in Chinese history, mainly the Four Great Inventions, which have also had a huge impact on the West, yet most of the original technologies in modern times have come from the West. We are now catching up, but it still needs to take a long time to catch up with the West.

Therefore, the new-type whole-nation system must focus on innovation in the state of openness. So long as we are open to the outside world, Western capital still will not give up the markets in China, and those civilian technologies in the West can still spread to China. While discussing technology, we should not regard technology as a "single individual", but should put technology within a system of technology. If we compare with the West, the strength of Western technology lies in its systematization. Although our technology has caught up with or even surpassed the West in some areas from the perspective of a "single individual", we still lack systematization. In other words, the strength of the West is systematic, and our strength is regional. But so long as we open up to the outside world, we can use the foundational technologies in the West, that is, those technologies that are not seen by the West as a threat to the West. We do not need to start everything once again. Furthermore, as long as it is open, we can also keep track of the current state of technological development in the West at any time, so as to formulate the right policies to catch up.

Second, we need to aim at the frontier of science and technology, clarify the "national division of labor" ("national" refers to state-owned enterprises and private enterprises), promote "national integration", and provide a favorable environment for the cutting-edge scientific research and the transformation of scientific and technological achievements in various fields—there are not only the financial support without considering returns from the central government, but also the orderly, free and open environment of scientific research and business.

Although it is the most difficult work to realize "national integration", its practical effect is the greatest. It enables us to grasp the lifeblood of our country's modernization development, and fundamentally change the relationship between our country and the Western world and our country's role in the world economy. Whether it is in industrial circles or in academic circles, criticisms of state-owned enterprises have been going on for decades. Correspondingly, the reform of state-owned enterprises has been carried out for several rounds. However, it seems that a good balance has not been found between state-owned enterprises and private enterprises and scientific and technological innovation. The core question is that whether state-owned enterprises can play an active role in scientific and technological innovation, or what role should they play? From solar photovoltaic to electric vehicles, what we see more is wave after wave of technological innovation and product development led by private enterprises, but we tend to ignore the decisive role played by state-owned enterprises and state-owned capital in the early development of these technologies. Therefore, under the existing mixed ownership economy, we should not criticize blindly the destruction of innovation by state-owned enterprises and state-owned capital, but should think about what kind of "national relations" are conductive to scientific and technological innovation and the transformation of scientifical and technological achievements. One of the most crucial points is the issue of "national division of labor", that is, the issue of the boundary of state-owned enterprises. This boundary should not be the boundary of industries, that is, what industries state-owned enterprises should not participate in, because it will eventually lead to the "one-size-fits-all" problem. Instead, it should be discussed from the perspective of innovation process, that is, in the technological innovation process of "basic research—applied research—development research—productization and commercialization—production—sale", the boundary of state-owned enterprises and the exit mechanism of state-owned enterprises should be discussed, so as to truly realize the "national integration" of scientific and technological innovation and the development of emerging industries.

Third, we need to improve the mechanism of "creating the market" and "maintaining the market" of emerging industries. For the development of emerging technology industries, it is very important to obtain and maintain the first-mover advantage. Because many emerging technology industries have the network effect, the sooner the industrial scale areas (production network) are reached, the easier it is to attract the aggregation of production factors and the optimization and integration of the industrial line, form the scale cost advantage, and accumulate the know-how for mass production, thus inhibiting the emergence of competitors, further expanding the scale and forming the kinetic energy of development like a snowball. The size of China's domestic market and the whole-nation system with concentrated efforts for major undertakings means that by way of state-owned department procurement and policy adjustment, can China quickly provide a large-scale domestic market for new technology creation, or boost the market when industrial development is stalling. This is China's advantage in developing emerging technology industries, and it needs to be adhered to. In terms of government's support for emerging industries, China has accumulated a lot of experiences and lessons, and in general, some competitive industries have been formed. The tortuous rise of China's solar panel industry is a case in point. By carefully analyzing past experiences, policymakers can find the policy models that can help technology industrialization while controlling the risk of overcapacity, and continue to support the rapid development of China's emerging technology industries. Relevant investment in emerging industries is also an important way to stabilize the economy. After the rise of industry is on the right track, it is much more important to "maintain the market". Policymakers need to focus on and encourage policies such as standard setting, continuous research and development, and restraining vicious circles to help emerging industries maintain competitiveness and health development.

Fourth, we need to implement the policy of "two rewards and one penalty" and "leveling supervision" for large scientific and technological enterprises. The influence of large scientific and technological enterprises on innovation has two sides. On the one hand, large scientific and technological enterprises have sufficient financial resources, technical knowledge, business experience, and marketing capabilities. The venture capital of large scientific and technological enterprises is extremely important to the development in the field of new technology, and their own internationalization behavior is also of great help to enhance the influence of

China's technology. On the other hand, large scientific and technological enterprises also have the incentives for monopoly, using their own platform advantages to stifle emerging competitors and hinder innovation. Policymakers need to seek advantages and avoid disadvantages, encouraging the venture capital and "going out" behavior of large scientific and technological enterprises, while punishing their monopoly behavior at home. In terms of the regulation of large scientific and technological enterprises, the European Union and the United States will issue important domestic market supervision laws in the coming period. China needs to pay a close attention to these key legislations, and consider introducing similar regulatory measures to level out its domestic and foreign regulations. This is not because these regulatory measures are certainly correct, but rather because they can help China's enterprises find business models that adapt to these regulatory measures in a relatively well-intentioned domestic market environment. This will encourage large scientific and technological enterprises to go international.

4. **Internationalization of rules**

In rules, we need to continue to keep in line with international standards, and promote the internationalization of rules. In April 2022, the CPC Central Committee and the State Council jointly issued the Guideline on Establishing Unified Domestic Market. The Guideline emphasizes formulating rules, grasping overall planning, and fostering the construction of a unified national market. This is very correct. If there is no unified national market based on unified rules, the domestic circulation is difficult to realize. This is also the essence for the rise of Western countries in modern times. Modern countries are stronger than traditional countries. The reason is that modern countries have unified rules and unified market, while traditional countries are feudal, decentralized and operate separately.

In this regard, if there are difficulties in the national rules at this stage, then we can start from the large regions. Let's take Guangdong-Hong Kong-Macao Greater Bay Area as an example. We should align the rules within the Greater Bay Area and realize the integration of the Greater Bay Area rules. The present situation is that the rules among the nine mainland cities, Hong Kong and Macao have not been unified, even if the rules among the nine mainland cities are not unified. In terms of attracting investment, these cities do not have unified rules in taxation, land, social security and so on. In the past the rules in environmental protection were also not unified. Since the 18th CPC National Congress, the central government has attached great importance to environmental protection, localism in the field of environmental protection has gradually decreased, and the rules in environmental protection have begun to be unified. However, there are still no unified rules in other fields. Without unified rules, it will create a situation of being big but not strong.

In September 2021, the CPC Central Committee and the State Council jointly released the outline of the development plan for Hengqin and Qianhai, and in June 2022, they released the plan for the development of Nanshan in Guangzhou. Therefore, can we unify the rules of the Greater Bay Area through Hengqin, Qianhai, and Nansha with point-to-area in view? Actually, it is not difficult. This requires that the rules of Hengqin, Qianhai and Nansha should be unified first, instead of having their own set of rules. Then, how can we unify the rules of these three "points"? We should emancipate our minds and directly introduce the business rules of Hong Kong into the Greater Bay Area. Many rules in Hong Kong are very international and accepted by the international community. Under the system condition of "one country, two systems", we can make addition on the basis of the rules in Hong Kong, and add to some good rules from the mainland, such as high technology and new energy. With the passage of the Hong Kong National Security Law, the use of the Hong Kong Commercial Law in the Greater Bay Area will not pose a threat to national security. And the difference in rules between Hong Kong and Macao is not very large, and it is relatively easy to be unified in rules. At the same time, in doing so, we also have realized the internationalization of China rules.

5. Talents in the first resource

We need to create a systematic environment of cultivating, attracting, and retaining talents. Cities are gathering places and activity platforms for high-quality capital, advanced technology and high-end talents. Talent indicator is more important than all the other indicators. When capital comes, but talents do not come, then capital may come for arbitrage. When technology comes, but talents do not come, then the industries with low-cost labor may be brought out. When high-end talents come, there must be high-quality capital and technology behind them. Talents "vote with their feet". In recent years, although the United States is experiencing the crisis of political governance and the COVID-19 pandemic continues, talents all over the world have still fled to the United States. This is because the United States has the geographically embedded, world-class economic platforms like the San Francisco Bay Area and the New York Bay Area. They concentrate high-quality capital, advanced technology, and high-end talents in the world, and continue to attract high-quality capital, advanced technology, and high-end talents. No matter what happens in the social economy of the United States, these platforms will not be greatly affected. So, what is the scale of foreign talents for these platforms? Foreign talents in the San Francisco Bay Area and the New York Bay Ares account for about 40%, and the proportion in Silicon Valley, is even higher, reaching 60%. In Asian countries, Japan is the most conservative on the issue of immigration, but even so, the Tokyo Bay Area has attracted a large number of foreign talents. But we are still far behind in attracting foreign talents. The proportion of foreign professionals in urban population is almost negligible. What is more serious is that in recent years the United States has begun to systematically decouple talents, especially high technology talents. We can argue that the consequents of talent decoupling between China and the United States are more severe than decoupling in economy and trade and decoupling in technology.

In terms of cultivating and attracting talents, we cannot say that we do not work hard. In fact, we have worked very hard. Over these years, we have launched the national-level talent programs including "Thousand Talents Program" and "Chang Jiang Scholars Program", and there are countless talent programs in various places. However, compared with the developed Western countries, especially the United States, we still have a big gap. The private sector in the developed countries attracts a large number of talents by virtue of its developed economy (financial resources), high-quality universities, research institutes and enterprise laboratories, and the government has been adopting unilateral opening-up policy to attract talents. In this respect, the United States is the most typical. Theoretically, the opening-up policy of the United States has emphasized reciprocity, but on the issue of talents, the United States has always implemented unilateral opening-up policy. In a word, the talent system in the Western developed countries such as the United States has systematic advantages. In contrast, China's talent policy shows two main characteristics. The first is partial. It has advantages in some aspects, while in others it is reflected in disadvantages. And it is unbalanced and unsystematic among various elements that attract talents. The second is political. The introduction of talents is regarded as a national and political task to grasp. The United States and other Western countries do it through the immigration policy of the Immigration Bureau, that is, in a non-political way. We do it through political methods, and its advantage lies in that so long as the leaders pay attention to it, some difficulties faced by talents can always be solved. The disadvantage is that it varies from people to people, and people are treated differently. And because of political methods, it is easy to be politicized by Western countries, thus affecting the flow of talents. Over these years, the suppression of our "Thousand Talents Program" by the United States has illustrated the problem.

6. **Confronting the population issue**

We need to actively build cities "suitable for nurture and education" to cope with the crisis of zero population growth and negative population growth. A city is a place where people live and population is the foundation of a city. Anywhere, once population shrinks, big cities will definitely shrink. Today, worldwide, a contradiction has developed between city size and fertility rate. It is not difficult to find that the bigger the city is, the lower the fertility rate is. If we look at it from the perspective of GDP growth, the bigger the city is, the higher the GDP is. It is easy to calculate GDP, and GDP is the production of transactions. The more the transaction is, the higher the GDP is. The bigger the city is, the more and denser the transaction is. But from the demographic perspective, the city size is inversely proportional to the fertility rate. In the long run, there is no way out for Asian-style urbanization. Tokyo has gathered one-third of Japan's population, and Seoul has gathered about half of South Korea's population. Not to mention that in the event of war, these cities will face the devastating results (of course it also means the destruction of the country). Only from the perspective of demography, this model is also unsustainable. By contrast, the urban development model in Europe and the United States is more feasible. Don't Europe and the United States have the ability to make big cities? Of course not. Germany is a highly urbanized country in Europe, but about 80% of the German population lives in small towns with less than 20,000 people.

Both Guangzhou and Shenzhen in the Guangdong-Hong Kong-Macao Greater Bay Area have become megacities with a population of more than 20 million. Today, many cities have put forward the goal of building a city "suitable for living, working and travelling", but we should emphasize the construction of a city "suitable for nurture and education" to create physical and material conditions for the young people to increase their fertility rate. The current (mega) urbanization runs counter to the improvement of fertility rate. From a long-term economic goal of the country, the existing urban development model is unsustainable. It concentrates all high-quality things in the big cities, especially the first-tier cities, and attracts more people to these cities. On the surface, these big cities are winners, but the whole country may be losers. Our urbanization is in the hands of GDP-only economists and structural engineers. They tend to lack social and humanistic awareness. If this trend cannot be changed, then cities may become the "graveyard" for population.

Appendix 1: Status Quo, Trends, and Prospects of Sino-US Relationship: How to Escape the "Thucydides Trap"[1]

Introduction

After the Communist Party of China (CPC) successfully convened the 20th National Congress and elected a new core of the central leadership, China has embarked on a new round of intensive diplomacy. At the G20 Summit held in November 2022, President Xi Jinping and US President Joe Biden held a bilateral meeting, which has attracted worldwide attention and produced fruitful results, making a positive effort for peace in Asia and even the world. In recent years, the direction of Sino-US relationship has attracted global attention and concern. The relationship between China and the United States is not a simple bilateral relationship. China and the United States are two pillars of the international order, and neither of them can be missing. Since the United States launched the trade war during the Trump era, China and the United States has begun to show a trend of conflict, and this unstable development is also regarded

[1] This article is based on the author's lecture "How to Escape the 'Thucydides Trap': Status Quo, Trends and Prospects of Sino-US Relationship", held at the Institute for International Affairs (IIA), Qianhai, at the Chinese University of Hong Kong (Shenzhen) on October 26, 2022. Thanks to the IIA academic editorial team for their assistance.

Z. Yongnian, *The Great Convergence VS. The Great Divergence*,
https://doi.org/10.1007/978-981-96-7846-4

by many scholars as a structural contradiction between "established countries" and "rising countries". In the context of the increasingly changeable international environment and increasingly fierce Sino-US conflict, how can China, as the world's biggest developing countries and the second largest economy, escape the so-called "Thucydides Trap", strengthen cooperation, and actively participate in the construction of global governance and the reshaping of the international order? How should the future of the Sino-US relationship be defined? Chinese modernization is not only a contribution to the international community, but also needs a peaceful international environment, and a peaceful international environment cannot be separated from a stable Sino-US relationship. Therefore, these problems are also the problems faced by Chinese modernization.

The midterm elections in the United States are approaching. How to view the development of Sino-US relationship in recent years and what kind of uncertainty the relationship between the two countries is facing today have become urgent questions to be answered. Today I want to discuss Sino-US relationship around the "Thucydides Trap", a concept proposed by professor Graham Allison, the Founding Dean of the Kennedy School of Government at Harvard University. Thucydides was a historian in the ancient Greece, and he wrote a famous book called *The History of the Peloponnesian War*. In this book he puts forward a proposition: Why is there a war between the two countries, Athens and Sparta? He argues that Sparta is an existing power, while Athens is an emerging power, and it is the rise of Athens and the fear of Sparta that ultimately leads to the inevitability of war.

Allison and his research team revolved around such a proposition. By counting all kinds of major wars and conflicts that have occurred in mankind over the past 500 years, they found that there have been a total of 16 conflicts and power shifts between the emerging powers and the existing powers. Among them, 12 have been the wars and only 4 have not been wars. Therefore, he concluded that there must be a war between China and the United States.

Since this point of view was put forward, there have been many debates in academic circles. Personally, I do not think it is appropriate for Allison to compare the relationship between Athens and Sparta with the current relationship between China and the United States. This is equivalent to going back to the Spring and Autumn Period and the Warring States Period in the history of China, and analyzing contemporary international relations according to the relationships between countries 2000 years ago.

The wars between Athens and Sparta were wars between two small countries. Today, China and the United States are two big countries, and they are also two nuclear powers. By far, for human beings, there has never been a war between the two nuclear powers. The current conflict between Russia and Ukraine is on the verge of the nuclear war—although Ukraine does not have nuclear weapons, yet because this conflict is actually between Russia and the NATO, both sides actually have nuclear weapons directly or indirectly. If Russia really uses strategic nuclear weapons, as some countries in the West say, then the nature of things will change, because the NATO and the United States will be most likely to react. In like manner, the same is true of the relationship between China and the United States, so the relationship between Athens and Sparta cannot be simply applied to the relationship between China and the United States.

However, we also cannot completely ignore this proposition, because wars really occurred over and over again throughout history. Although no one likes war, yet why do wars still happen? General Secretary Xi Jinping has also specially emphasized that we should avoid two traps, the "Middle Income Trap" internally and the "Thucydides Trap" externally. In other words, it is emphasized that it is necessary to properly handle the major-country relationship between China and the United States. The 20th CPC National Congress just passed was held under the circumstance of great changes in the international environment, but we still continue to emphasize the pursuit of peace and development. The pursuit of peace and development shows that we need to avoid the conflict between China and the United States, that is, to escape the "Thucydides Trap".

Going back to the concept of "Thucydides Trap", the first question we need to answer is why the United States is afraid of China, and where does this kind of fear come from?

The Status Quo of Sino-US Relationship: Where Does the Fear of the United States Come From?

There are several reasons why the United States is afraid of China.

Firstly, the gap in GDP between China and the United States is narrowing. The economic gap between China and the United States indeed is narrowing. In 2021, the total GDP of the United States is $ 23 trillion, and the total GDP of China is $17.7 trillion. China's GDP is equivalent to 77% of that of the United States. For China, this is really a remarkable progress. In fact, if it is calculated in terms of PPP, that is, Purchase Power Parity, China's economic aggregate has already exceeded that of the United Sates in 2014.

And, of course, we ourselves should be aware that we should not pay too much attention to the total GDP, and should not talk only about the total GDP. The total GDP has practical significance, but it cannot be overestimated, because our per capita GDP is still far from the per capita GDP of the United States. In 2021, the per capita GDP of the United States is already close to $70,000, while our per capita GDP is only $12,000. From the perspective of development, when I was studying at Peking University in the early 1980s, China's per capita GDP was less than $300, and it reached $12,000 in 2021, which is an obvious improvement. In 1820, China's GDP accounted for one-third of the world's GDP. At that time, India's GDP only accounted for almost 30% of the world's GDP, while the seven countries in Western Europe, including Britain, only accounted for 7% of the world's GDP. But by 1840, China was defeated by Britain in the Opium War and again in 1860. China's total GDP is much larger than that of Britain, but it was defeated by Britain. It was even worse for India, and the country that was so big all has become a British colony. Therefore, the total GDP cannot determine everything.

Secondly, China has the comparative military advantages in the region. As far as military expenditure is concerned, the military expenditure of China is actually far less than that of the United States. In 2021, the military expenditure of the United States was $801 billion, and China's military expenditure was only $293 billion, just reaching one-third of the military expenditure of the United Sates. However, it does not mean that it does not matter if it is only one-third, because the use of military expenditure between China and the United States is very asymmetric. The United States wants to maintain global hegemony, while China is only a regional defense.

What the United States is now very worried about is China's navy. China has 355 ships, while the United States has only 305 ships. The 60% of the US ships are deployed in our Indio-Pacific region, that is, the United States has just over 180 ships that can be used to counter China. If the United States wants to maintain a global hegemony, then it will aim to maintain its absolute superiority anywhere. Therefore, it is uneasy for the United States about the enhancement of China's military strength.

Thirdly, the profound internal problems in the United States cannot be solved, which makes its institutional system with freedom and democracy as its core and the ideology based on it continuously weaken. After the collapse of the Soviet Union in the early 1990s, there has been a wave of optimism in the United States and Western countries. Francis Fukuyama wrote a book called *The End of History and the Last Man*. In this book, he argued that the American-style liberal democracy was the best system in the world, and it was also the last system that human beings could have. Within few years, however, problems occurred in the Western world itself. Today's West has completely lost its confidence that it had then, mainly because Western democracy has been evolving, and it has become difficult to govern. American democracy was an elite democracy in its early days, but later it was a middle-class democracy. After World War II, the middle class in the United States reached 60% or even 70% of the total population, and the middle class was the stable force for democracy. The middle class in the United States has been shrinking since the 1980s, shrinking to less than 50% now. American Middle-class democracy thus has evolved into populist democracy.

This phenomenon not only exists in the United States, but also occurs in other democratic countries. Populist democracy in the era of social media has led to the rise of many "political outsiders" who do not have political experiences. For example, Trump is a typical figure, and so is the Ukrainian President Zelensky. These people are democratically elected, but many of them really have no experiences in politics, which will lead to the frequent problems in domestic and foreign affairs. The problem for the West now is, in fact, a lack of an effective government. Any country needs an effective government, because social economy is changing and developing, there will inevitably be problems, even serious problems. Once problems arise, there must be an effective government to solve them. However, in the era of populist democracy, party politics in the West has been difficult to produce an effective government.

On the aspect of political parties, there is traditionally a word called "loyal opposition" in Britain, but now there has not been loyal opposition anymore, and the opposition parties are all opposition for the sake of opposition. Therefore, Fukuyama said that the opposition parties now are vetoing each other, and they are the vetoing parties. For example, if the Democratic Party and the Republican Party in the United States veto each other, Congress and Parliament will be a quarrelling place, and this is difficult to have an effective government. Under the condition that there is no effective government, it will be difficult to solve many problems. When there are internal problems in the United States, they want to turn their attention to diplomacy, but in so doing, it not only does not solve the internal problems in the United States, but also often worsen the internal problems.

Fourthly, from the external point of view, the implementation of Western-style democracy has also encountered huge problems, mainly reflected in two levels: ideology and institution. After 1945, the United States promoted the system of freedom and democracy everywhere, but in fact none of the democratic systems it promoted overseas for decades were successful. Nominally, the two most successful democratic countries promoted by the United States after World War II were Germany and Japan, but many scholars believe that Germany and Japan would have become the democratic countries even if they had not been occupied by the United States—because there has been a democratic movement in Japan long before World War II, not to mention that Germany was originally a part of the West. The occupation of these two countries by the United States has accelerated the democratic process in these two countries, and made these two countries, especially Japan, more Western.

In recent decades, there have been no successful examples in the promotion of democracy by the United Sates, in particular, the complete failure of democracy plan in the Greater Middle East for the United States. The United States used counter-terrorism as an opportunity to promote its democratic system in the Middle East, but none of them were successful. In 2021, the withdrawal of the US troops from Afghanistan has totally changed people's perceptions of American-style democracy.

The internal problems in the United States and the failure to promote democracy more highlight the rise of China's institution. In fact, the United States is not afraid of China's economic development. What they are most afraid of is the rise of a different set of institutional system in China. China's institutional system is regarded as a challenge to Western democratic system.

The Major Trend of Sino-US Relationship: The United States Promotes Bipolarization in the World

Since Trump, great changes have taken place in the relationship between China and the United States. Trump launched a trade war. As a businessman, he mainly focused on the trade deficit between China and the

United States. If the problems between countries can be solved in US dollars or currencies, it is still possible to solve them, but once they rise to the level of ideology, many problems will not be solved. The relationship between China and the United States has evolved in this way in recent years.

During the Trump era, the United States formulated a "four divisions" strategy toward China. The first is to distinguish the Communist Party of China from the Chinese people; the second is to separate the Communist Party of China from its leadership group; the third is to separate the Han nationality from the ethnic minorities, mainly the ethnic minorities in Xinjiang, Tibet and other places; the fourth is to distinguish between the Chinese on the mainland China and the overseas Chinese.

If Trump wanted to get a little more money, then Biden focused more on the ideological battles. Since Biden took office, the strategy of the United States is to bipolarize the world, that is, the so-called "one world, two centers", namely a center with the United States as the core, a center with China as the core and some people also say it is a center with China and Russia as the core. Also, there is the so-called "one world, two markets", one market with the United States as the core and the other market with China as the core.

The Cold War faction in the United States hopes to lead Sino-US relationship to the same relationship as that between the United States and the Soviet Union in the past, and to ideologically divide the United States and China into two camps. Specifically, it is manifested in the ban on high technology, especially in the ban on chips. Nevertheless, this ban is still slight, and the serious thing is that the United States has begun to turn to systematic decoupling.

Why do we say so? If we compare science and technology in modern times to a mountain, then this mountain is the accumulation of human civilization for thousands of years. All countries, including our Four Great Inventions in China, have made contributions to this mountain. However, since modern times, first, the European countries in the West dominated this mountain, and later, the United States dominated the mountain. After China's reform and opening-up, our integration with the West means that we also have climbed up this mountain. Systematic decoupling means that they are going to drive us off this mountain. This is a much more serious problem than getting stuck in the neck, because getting stuck in the neck only means that the United States will not let China continue climbing up this mountain. As a matter of fact, the systematic decoupling by the United States has caused a constant competition between China and the United States in many fields.

Therefore, in the field of high technology, we are facing huge challenges. Many of the software we use today is developed by the United States and other Western countries. What if they do not let us use it? For example, in 2021, the United States banned Harbin Institute of Technology from using Matlab software, and this had a negative influence on our research. As for engineers, if the United States does not allow them to use tools for drawing drawings, they are likely to turn to the era of drawing drawings by hand in a short time. For another example, our mobile phones generally have two operating systems, but they both are Western inventions. Of course, we can say that HUAWEI can create the HarmonyOS system, but if the HarmonyOS system cannot match the Western system or is not allowed to be matched, I am afraid that it can only be used in China and cannot be used abroad. In any case, systematic decoupling poses a greater challenge to us than getting stuck in the neck.

The United States is also engaging in alliance while engaging in bipolarization. For example, the "chip alliance" wants to bring South Korea, Japan and China's Taiwan, together. The United States still want to establish a so-called "democratic Internet alliance". Our current Internet is actually not open to the West, because we have a "firewall". The reason why it is still called the Internet is that the West is still open to us now. If Western countries also have a "firewall", people may not be able to call it the Internet, but "intranet". Some agencies in the United States are also planning the intranet, and it is not difficult to do technically. If it is really implemented, the loss for both sides will be heavy. This also will be a field of competition.

In Asia, the United States is trying to establish its dominant Asian version of NATO. Strategically, the United States has shifted its focus from other parts of the world to the Indo-Pacific region. Why did the United States give up Afghanistan, and why did it give up Europe and shift its focus to the Indo-Pacific region? It is just to target China. During Trump's period, the National Security Strategy of the United States of America still took China and Russia as the main competitors, but after Biden took office, he removed the rival Russia, believing that China is the only competitor who have ability and willingness to challenge the United States. The newly released National Security Strategy of the United States of America in 2022 made some changes again. It defines Russia as the most direct and immediate threat, and China as the only competitor who have willingness and ability to pose a challenge to the United States on a global scale. In any case, the main enemy defined by the United States is still China. In addition, the United States is still looking for an opportunity to clash with China and formalize the Asian version of NATO. This kind of willingness is especially manifested on the Taiwan question.

Of course, the United States mentioned here is not the entire US government, but many political figures in the United States, including Democrats and Republicans. The economic gap between China and the United States is narrowing, and the gap in military strength between China and the United States is narrowing. Therefore, they believe that the United States as one country does not have the ability to target China alone. If NATO is used to deal with Russia, then they also need such an organization to deal with China and contain China.

The key problem facing the United States is how to formalize the Asian version of NATO. The current Asian version of NATO has begun to take shape and can be summarized as "two, three, four, five, and six plus". The "two" is the bilateral allies of the United States in the Asia-Pacific region, such as the United States and Japan, the United States and South Korea, and the United States and Australia. The "three" is "AUKUS", that is, the trilateral alliance of the United States, Britain and Australia. The "four" is the Quadrilateral Security Dialogue (QUAD) between the United States, Japan, Australia, and India. The "five" is the "Five Eyes Alliance". The "six" means adding Singapore, Vietnam and other countries on the basis of the four Indo-Pacific countries. The United States can still expand indefinitely to make it become "six plus", and the number can be increased all the time.

But so long as there is no direct conflict between China and the United States, it is difficult to form the Asian version of NATO. Because Asian countries, especially Southeast Asian countries, have very deep relations with China and the United States, if there is a real conflict between China and the United States, then these countries will have to consider choosing a sideline. This will be a big loss for them. Once there is a major conflict or even war between China and the United States, just like this conflict between Russia and Ukraine, ASEAN will have to be like European countries, and even the originally neutral countries will have to consider choosing a side station. However, although some political figures in the United States have been looking for opportunities to create conflicts on the Taiwan question, yet the United States cannot succeed, and it can even be said that it has failed by far.

The Frustration of the US Strategic Shift

In dealing with China, the United States is ambitious. But our evaluation of the United States should not base on what it wants to do or what it says it will do, but on its actual effect. In fact, from almost all the aspects, the ambition of the United States has been hit hard, and the United States has a great sense of frustration.

First, on the issue of the Middle East, the United States completely gave up Afghanistan. Now the influence of the United States in the Middle East has dropped dramatically, and there are consequences for this. Today's Organization of the Petroleum Exporting Countries (OPEC) member countries, especially Saudi Arabia, which used to listen to the United States very much, now do not listen to the United States anymore. Recently, there has been a tense situation between Saudi Arabia and the United States. Some officials and scholars in Saudi Arabia have made it clear that the United States will have no influence after leaving the Middle East. Why should we still listen to the United States? The United States is not the only buyer of oil. A similar situation is also reflected in issues such as Iran and Israel.

Second, on the European issue, the United States has also suffered a heavy setback. Europe used to be the most stable ally of the United States. The United States believed that Europe would maintain a stable situation after its strategic shift to Asia, but the United States did not expect Russia to launch such a war. At the very beginning of the Russia-Ukraine conflict, the United States was very optimistic, and believed that this conflict had achieved at least two "unity". One was the unity between European countries; one was the unity between Europe and the United States. Of course, there is another unity that is "being united". China and Russia are "being united" together. But now, it seems that three "unity" have not become a reality.

European countries are more and more divided. Britain has left the European Union, but the country's leadership has not been stable since the Brexit, and the vicious consequences are unfolding. The conflict between Russia and Ukraine has led to the energy crisis in Europe, and the European energy crisis has not led to the unity in Europe, but to the opposite. The current situation is that Germany's energy dependence on

Russia is more than 60%, and the general energy dependence of European countries on Russia is more than 40%, so it is difficult for Europe to break away from Russia in energy supply in the short term. If there is a five-year plan or a ten-year plan or even longer, such a separation will still be feasible, but it is impossible to decouple immediately. Decoupling is only the wishful thinking on the part of political figures. At the beginning of the Russia-Ukraine conflict, the United States and European countries together condemned China's attitude toward the Russia-Ukraine conflict, but this joint condemnation did not last. German Chancellor Scholz will visit China in November. In order to govern the country, political figures, no matter how idealistic they are, must face the reality.

The unity between Europe and the United States has not been realized either. Most of the damages caused by the Russia-Ukraine conflict are borne by Europeans, not by Americans, so now Europe has many complaints about the United States. In Asia, Japan and South Korea basically follow the lead of the United States. However, now the United States is engaging in quantitative easing (QE) and excessive currency issuance. This has had a great negative impact on the economies of these two countries, so they are also complaining about the United States right now. There is no unity between the United States and Europe, and there is no unity among European countries. After the Russia-Ukraine conflict, Europe will be in a more divided state. For example, Germany took advantage of this conflict as an opportunity to increase its military expenditure to 2% of its GDP in an attempt to become a normal military country. In East Asia, Japan has been trying to amend its Constitution for many years, to increase its military expenditure and to become a normal military country. Asian countries such as China, South Korea, and North Korea reacted to this strongly. Germany used this conflict as an opportunity to become a normal military country, leaving Europe unable to blame. But after this conflict, what does a "re-militarized" Germany mean to France? What does it mean for other countries? This is worth pondering.

The problems facing Europe are actually very big. Britain has left the European Union and populism in Italy has also risen. Many people think that after the end of the Cold War there will be no more wars between European countries. Huntington has written a book entitled *The Clash of Civilizations and the Remaking of World Order*, arguing that future wars would happen between different civilizations such as between the Islamic civilization in the Middle East and the Christian civilization in the

West, or between the Confucian civilization in China and the Christian civilization in the West. This point of view is too influenced by ideology and is not reliable. Let's not forget that World War I and World War II took place under the same civilization. European countries have the same God, the same civilization, the same culture, and even almost the same political system, but they can all be so divided and even at war with each other. Many people are fantasizing that so long as China turns into a "democratic" country, there will be no conflict between the United States and China. This is obviously wrong. Gorbachev in the Soviet Union was pro-Western, Yeltsin in Russia was also pro-Western, and even Putin was pro-Western in his early days, but in the end national interests prevailed over ideology, Russia was not accepted by the West, and Russia itself did not transform into a democratic country recognized and identified by the West.

The United States wants to tie China and Russia together, but China and Russia handle the relationship between them comparatively rationally. As a matter of fact, there is no alliance between the two countries as the West thinks.

Third, America's Indo-Pacific strategy is even less satisfactory, and it has also encountered major setbacks. The United States shifted its focus from Europe to the Indo-Pacific, and from the Middle East to the Indo-Pacific, just to target China. However, in promoting the Indo-Pacific strategy, it first encountered problems here in India, which is the most critical one. India has common interests with the United States, because China has border conflicts with India, and from this perspective, India needs to help the United States. However, India, as a big civilized country, will not completely at the beck and call of the United States. Like China, India also pursues an independent foreign policy in the world. Meanwhile, India is too big for the United States to digest. In this Russia-Ukraine conflict, China has taken almost all the international pressures, while India hid behind China, openly purchased Russian energy and then sold it to European Union countries. Western countries have a better attitude toward India than toward China.

ASEAN is not so cooperative with the United States. If ASEAN does not cooperate, it will be basically difficult for America's Indo-Pacific strategy to become successful. The current situation for cooperation between China and ASEAN is the result of China's reform and opening-up. Before the reform and opening-up, our relationship with ASEAN was very ordinary. At that time, we promoted communism to Southeast Asia.

It was not until Mr. Deng Xiaoping visited Singapore that China stopped its ideological propaganda of communism for ASEAN countries. In the 1990s, Premier Zhu Rongji vigorously pushed the development of a free trade area between China and ASEAN, so China's relations with ASEAN countries have developed very well over the past 40 years.

During the Cold War, ASEAN has developed a very deep security relationship with the United States. For example, Philippines and Thailand are both the allies of the United States, and many military officers in Malaysia and Indonesia were trained by the United States. But after the reform and opening-up, these countries have developed very deep economic relations with China. If there is no conflict between China and the United States, they can get the benefits from the two sides. They can both have security, and make money in China. If there is a conflict between China and the United States, these countries will have to choose the United States, because their security completely depends on the United States, and this choice will undoubtedly make them suffer huge economic losses. Therefore, this platform of ASEAN countries, is very important to China. If the United States forces these ASEAN countries to choose the sides, but China does not force these countries to choose the sides, China will be able to gain the trust of ASEAN countries.

Among ASEAN countries, the position of the Indonesian government is very important. At the Shangri-La Dialogue in 2022, Indonesian government representatives said that they should get along with China in an Asian way rather than in an American way. Former Malaysian Prime Minister Mahathir Mohamad said very well before that China and Malaysia have been neighbors for thousands of years, and China has not conquered Malaysia. The Chinese nation is a still relatively peace-loving, but within a few years of Western contact with Malaysia, Malaysia has become a colony. In fact, many aggressive thinking in modern Asia came from the West. There is no root of aggressive thinking in China's own culture, nor can it find the genes of aggressiveness. Many Western scholars think that there is no nationalism in China, but only culturalism. This is a profound understanding. Of course, China's nationalism has grown stronger now, but it is mostly a reaction to the West, a reactive nationalism.

Japan and South Korea are also allies of the United States, but so long as China handles it properly, they will not easily lean entirely toward the United States, because in terms of economy and geopolitics, China is also of great significance to Japan and South Korea.

Fourth, changes in Sino-US relationship have led to a crisis in the international order. Because the relationship between China and the United States is not good, the international order is now facing a huge crisis and the international order established after World War II with the United Nations as its core is crumbling. The essence of the crisis is the crisis of international public goods. What we are facing now is that we have too few good international public goods and too many international public bads. Public bads are just like extreme climate, nuclear proliferation, public health crisis, marine crisis, and so on. Because the United States is the largest economy in the world, it needs to provide the largest share of international public goods for the survival and development of the international order. In the academic circles, Robert Gilpin called this "hegemonic stability". The concept of "Kindleberger Trap" put forward by Professor Joseph Nye at Harvard University in recent years, also means this. It argues that the maintenance and stability of the international order requires sufficient international public goods. Once the international public goods are insufficient or missing, the international order will be in a big trouble. So, who will provide international public goods? Big countries need to provide more, but small countries are unable to do so. As a result, small countries can only choose to be "free riders" in the face of international public goods.

If China and the United States do not cooperate with each other, good public goods will certainly be not enough, and public bads will certainly increase. Good public goods such as the United Nations system, if China and the United States do not cooperate, the United Nations system will be paralyzed. The same is true of the World Trade Organization, and the same is true of the International Monetary Fund. In any international system, China and the United States will achieve nothing without cooperation. Therefore, Sino-US relationship are not simply bilateral ties. China and the United States are two pillars of the international order. Neither of them can fall and both of them need to cooperate with each other.

In terms of total carbon emissions, now China ranks first and the United States ranks second. Two countries together account for about 50% of the world's total carbon emissions. If these two countries do not cooperate, many island countries will face a crisis. The current Pacific Island countries are facing the crisis of being submerged by the ocean. After all, there are still a few people who, like Trump, thinks that climate crisis is a conspiracy theory. The climate crises in various forms are all happening around us, and tackling these crises needs cooperation between countries.

Fifth, the internal affairs of the United States continue to deteriorate. There have been so many problems in the internal affairs of the United States, and they are getting worse. Around the inflation issue and the upcoming midterm elections, there is a continuing great division in American society. After World War II, from 1945 to the early 1970s, the middle class in the United States became very large, reaching about 70% of the total population. Although the Republican Party was a little to the right and the Democratic Party was a little to the left at that time, yet both political parties had to take care of the interests of the 70% of the middle class. So, the two political parties would not take extreme routes and do extreme things.

From the 1980s to the present, the middle class in the United States has shrunk to less than 50% of the total population, resulting in a very divided American society. Take the question of voter turnout as an example, is it better for a democratic country to have a low voter turnout or a high voter turnout? We often criticize the low voter turnout in democratic countries, even less than 50%, which is a democracy for the minority and a fake democracy. So, is the voter turnout 20% or 100% better? This is a simple and profound question. From an empirical point of view, 20%–30% is enough for democratic countries. In the 1960s, there was a crisis in Western democracy, that is, the crisis of excessive political participation. The United States, Europe, and Japan formed a tripartite community, including the famous professor Huntington. They wrote a book named *The Crisis of Democracy*. At that time, the voter turnout was less than 50%–60%, and everyone already felt that there was a crisis. What is the voter turnout in the United States right now? It has reached 80%–90%. This seems to be a good democracy, but it is actually not a good democracy.

The reason is simple. Why is it good to have a low voter turnout? It can be explained by the logic of collective action. Voting has a cost. Assuming all of us in this room are the middle class and our political intentions are similar, if the principal and the vice principal go to vote, then we do not have to vote, because we trust them. If everyone trusts each other, the social voting rate will be low. Only in a society of mutual distrust each other can the turnout be high. The current problem in the United States is that people do not trust each other, and everyone only believes in their own votes. Let's look at the percentage of the base voters of all political parties in the United States. The base voters for the Republican Party accounted for about 30%, the base voters for the Democratic Party accounted for about 30%, and the middle voters with uncertain intentions accounted for 40%. Such a proportion will be very stable, because neither the Republican Party nor the Democratic Party can go to extremes and must win the support of these 40% voters. Now the voter turnout in the United States is so high that the middle voters have all but disappeared. They either support the Republican Party or the Democratic Party, which will lead to polarization for the whole country.

Our neighbor Thailand is also like this. For example, this kind of political figures who represent farmers like Thaksin are not be recognized by the urban middle class. So, some people say that the prime minister elected by the farmers is not recognized by the urban residents, and the prime minister elected by the urban residents is also not recognized by the farmers as well. The same is also true for Taiwan region today. Therefore, there are many "conclusions" on political issues that need to be reexamined. Many of the knowledge that we have learned before is wrong, and we need to proceed from the reality and re-recognize.

Biden was already a president with very weak influence, and it could get even weaker after the midterm elections. What if Trump comes back two years later? Trump has said that he has to come back for the good of the American people. These days he has also already expressed such a wish. Every political figure will say that he is for the interests of his own nation and people, and will not say that he is for his personal interests. This is the political situation in the United States.

The Prospects of Sino-US Relationship: China's Approach Is "Fighting Without Breaking" and "Fighting Without Warring"

Under such circumstances, what will be the prospects of Sino-US relationship? During the Deng Xiaoping era, the relationship between China and the United States was called "fighting without breaking". It is easy to understand that we "fight", but do not "break". After the reform and opening-up, we joined the world system, and in this system, we got along with the United States. We "fight", but do not "break" in one system. Even if we fight, we will not leave this system. We hope that Sino-US relationship should "fight without warring" on the basis of "fighting without breaking" in the future. "Fighting" is possible and inevitable, but we should not "war". As long as we treat Sino-US relationship rationally, it is actually not difficult to do so.

First, we need to learn the lessons of closing our doors to the outside world. To begin with, we are not the Soviet Union. The United States and the Soviet Union originally have no substantive connections, so these two countries became two camps as soon as World War II ended. China grew up in this world system, so it cannot break away from this system, nor does it want to break away from this system. We do not create two system like the Soviet Union, or "start a new stove". I think that even if the United States wants to drive us off this mountain, we also should tell the Americans that this mountain is only temporarily controlled by you, but this mountain is not yours and we have also contributed to it. Therefore, in recent years, we have been advocating deep opening up, and even unilateral opening up. Even if the United Stated and Europe do not open up to us, we also open up to them.

The United States is not one single entity, but an entity that is composed of many interest groups. The Cold War factions and the Anti-China forces have a completely different interest demands from those of Wall Street. China has a middle class with 400 million people and it is the largest single market in the world. Which capital will give up such a large single market? Why did German Chancellor Scholz visit China? When he first came to power, he also showed the attitude that he was determined to decouple from China, but once he saw the number of Germany's Mercedes-Benz and BWW cars sold in the market of China, he would not advocate decoupling. If the Chinese people do not consume, the car companies in Germany will not be competitive. Opening up is good for everyone.

Wall Street put pressure on China to make China "truly open up", and did not want to isolate China. Recently, German Chamber of Commerce in China, American Chamber of Commerce in China and American Chamber of commerce in Hong Kong, indicated that their enterprises did not want to leave China. However, we ourselves should be sober-minded. What General Secretary Xi Jinping emphasizes is the "new-type whole-nation system". It is not to innovate behind closed doors, but to innovate in an open state. Empirically, innovation behind closed doors is difficult to achieve sustainability.

History has already taught us many lessons. Let's not forget how developed China's science and technology were during the Tang and

Song dynasties, but how the West defeated us after the closure of the Ming and Qing dynasties. The British thinker Bacon said that it was China's "three great inventions"—printing, compass, and gunpowder, that opened the history of the modern world. The combination of compass and gunpowder created a powerful British navy. Although gunpowder was discovered by the Chinese, yet it was only after it was spread to Europe that gunpowder science has formed, while in China, gunpowder has remained in application. Some people joke that we entertained the high technology of the time in a closed state, used gunpowder to set off firecrackers, and used compass to watch Feng Shui. There is a very thick book named *The Gunpowder Age* and it is well-written. The author is the American historian Tonio Andrade. He explained why the emergence of gunpowder has made the rise of Europe, and why China, the inventor of gunpowder, was defeated in the Opium War. This is worth thinking about.

There is another lesson from the Soviet Union. In the early days of the Soviet Union, there was the most powerful whole-nation system since the modern time, and great achievements were made in its early development. However, the Soviet Union, in a closed state, innovated on its own behind closed doors. It showed two characteristics: One was that after closing its doors for a long time there would be no markets for ideas. Without the markets for ideas, this means that there is no source of ideas for innovation; the other was that there were no markets for commodities, so development would be unsustainable. Some arms made by the Soviet Union were only sold to the Warsaw Pact countries or other developing countries. For example, Vietnam bought a little and India bought a little, but the markets were too small. Innovation requires a lot of investment and needs to get rich returns from the markets. Without the markets for ideas and commodities, the development of the Soviet Union became unsustainable. Therefore, the Soviet Union was defeated not by the United States, but by itself.

Second, we need to attach importance to talents, and introduce talents into China from all over the world. The United States has stressed reciprocal openness in all aspects, but it is always unilaterally open in terms of talents. The United States is an immigrant country. How many European scientists came to the United States before and after World War I and World War II? During the Cold War, the United States fought against the Soviet Union, using talents from all over the world, including those from the Soviet Union and Eastern Europe who went to the United States, to fight against the Soviet Union and eventually defeated the Soviet Union. Today, we are faced with a severe task. The United States used talents all over the world, including those from China who immigrated to the United States, to compete with China. Unless we have the ability to compete with the United States for world talents, it is difficult to respond to the United States.

We need to retain talents, just as we need to retain wealth. The current problem is that we can create wealth, but we cannot keep it; we can cultivate talents, but we cannot retain them. Wealth and talents for a country have the greatest mobility and can go everywhere. But there are two other things that cannot move: poverty and power. Without wealth and talents, but only poverty and power, what kind of country would it be? Therefore, we need to be open, especially open to talents.

Third, in the reconstruction of the international order, China and the United States should strengthen cooperation, promote healthy competition, and avoid war. The US Secretary of State Antony Blinken advocated that US relationship with China would be collaborative when it can be, competitive when it should be, and adversarial when it must be. But we should guide them in the right direction. We should strengthen cooperation, advocate healthy competition, and avoid war at the same time.

We need to avoid falling into the "Thucydides Trap". In terms of cooperation, such as extreme climate, nuclear proliferation, public health crisis, marine crisis and so on, we can cooperate. Many developing countries hope that China and the United States can cooperate. As mentioned earlier, if China and the United States do not cooperate on the aspect of climate, there will be a catastrophe. Moreover, this disaster is approaching, and everyone is in the same boat.

Healthy competition also includes institutional competition and scientific and technological competition. We are not afraid of institutional competition. China and the United States have their own rights to develop their own systems. In technological competition, if the United States wants to block us, we can only compete and we cannot avoid competition. Our massive investment in scientific research will eventually yield results over time. Our "Belt and Road Initiative" is a good international public good, and we do not need to be afraid of the competition from the United States in this respect. At the US-EU Summit in 2021, the United States and Europe proposed to invest more than \$1000 billion to compete with China in infrastructure, while at the Summit in

2022, there was only $600 billion left. We are not afraid to compete with the United States and Europe in infrastructure investment, and we can be more generous. So long as it can promote the economic and social development of developing countries, there is nothing wrong with it. We can all welcome it. If China does a little, the United States does a little, and Japan does a little, the economies of other countries will develop. Therefore, we should welcome competition. We should not always be afraid when the United States engages in competition, and think that the United States is containing China. Such a point of view is wrong.

To avoid war is to "fight without warring". In recent years, China's model in coping with the South China Sea issue has been good. China and the United States have managed and controlled the conflicts on the South China Sea issue very well, and there have been no major conflicts for many years. You're here and I'll hide. I'm here and you'll hide. On the South China Sea issue, as long as the militaries on both sides maintain rationality and restraint, war can be avoided.

During the Cold War, there is also no formal conflict between the United States and the Soviet Union. All that happened were proxy wars. The most troublesome issue in Sino-US relationship is the Taiwan question. On the Taiwan question, Pelosi's visit to Taiwan aroused the anger of the people, but it should be affirmed that our official is still very rational. If we had followed the opinions of populism, there would have been a war long before. Since the United States has pushed toward Taiwan's "independence" by way of "cutting sausages", we should also "take down" Taiwan step by step by way of "cutting sausages". We should also realize that the Taiwanese are also Chinese, and the "Taiwan Independence" elements are still in the minority. With the military modernization of China, it is more and more possible for China to resolve the Taiwan question peacefully instead of resolving the Taiwan question by force.

We need to change our view of the United States. We are not handling the relationship with the United States with the aim to defeat the United States. If we solve the problem from the perspective of defeating the United States, then all the problems will never be solved. The United States cannot defeat China, and China cannot defeat the United States. If the United States fails, then it defeats itself. If China fails, then it defeats itself as well, just as the Soviet Union defeated itself.

Our goal is not to defeat the United States, but to rebuild the international order. From the perspective of rebuilding the international order,

China and the United States have too much to cooperate with each other. There are the hardliners in the United States, but we should not be dragged by them. We scholars still have a responsibility. Is it inevitable for Japan to launch World War II? No! It was the hardliners in the military who seized the whole regime. There is no inevitability in history, and there are many accidents in history.

For another example, is openness inevitable? There is also no inevitability. Some time ago, someone wrote that it was also a good thing to close the doors to the outside world. It delayed the process of imperialists' invasion of China. I don't think so. When the Ming Dynasty closed its doors to the outside world, Zheng He's fleet was very strong. American scholars say that Zheng He's fleet at that time was equivalent to the current aircraft carrier group of the US army. In the meantime, during the Ming Dynasty, our folk businessmen were also very strong. At that time, the so-called "pirates" referred to the Japanese, but the main body still was the maritime merchants in Fujian and Zhejiang, and the leaders of the Japanese pirates were still Fujianese.

At that time, if the normal development had continued, and the country had not been closed to the outside world, there would have been no such thing as Western imperialism. Portugal and Spain were still very weak at that time, and their Age of Discovery only began as adventurous activities by a group of pirates. Zheng He's fleet in the Ming Dynasty represented the power of the country, while pirates such as the Japanese pirates represented the power of the people from the folk. After we closed our doors to the outside world, we stopped developing toward the ocean.

Fourth, we need to adhere to open and inclusive multilateralism. What China needs to do now is to embrace multilateralism with inclusiveness, and China has done a good job in this regard. Both China and the United States are engaged in multilateralism, but the multilateralism pursued by the United States is aimed at the third countries. We call it "group gangs", and such multilateralism is not good multilateralism. As mentioned earlier, American-style multilateralism has not achieved much success, and its frustration is very obvious. What China is practicing is true multilateralism. But it is not very standard to use the word "true" in academic research. China's multilateralism should be defined as open and inclusive multilateralism that is not aimed at the third countries, but aimed at the common problems faced by these member countries. We should adhere to this multilateralism.

The future world order can be understood in terms of the traditional Chinese concept of "harmony". It is necessary to admit that the world is harmonious but different. Peace and order are built on the basis of "difference". This is not difficult to understand. Although we are not all the same, yet we all live on the same planet earth. In the era of globalization, the earth is getting smaller and smaller, and the fate of human beings is shared.

I am still relatively optimistic about Sino-US relationship. So long as we make good use of the power of reason, and do not get swayed by emotions, in particular, we scholars need to be vigilant. Emotion is very simple and everyone has emotions, but everyone must be calm after expressing their emotions. When reason triumphs over emotion, there is a hope for peace.

Appendix 2: The Prospects of Chinese Path to Modernization[2]

In the Report to the 20th National Congress of the Communist Party of China (CPC), General Secretary Xi Jinping clearly put forward the concept of "Chinese modernization". This has had a wide response in the international community. China is a global power. Compared with the modernization of a small country, the modernization of a big country has very different international significance. Singapore is a small country. The realization of modernization in Singapore is certainly very important to its own people, but it cannot exert much influential power in the international community. But the modernization of a big country, in particular, the modernization of China with a population of 1.4 billion, has a huge spillover effect, and it is not difficult to understand that it has been deeply concerned by the international community.

Chinese Modernization and the World

"Modernization" used to be called "*jindaihua*" in Chinese, namely "modernization" in English. Because modernization began in the West, it is not difficult to understand that modernization is Westernization in

[2] This article was compiled by Xu Lanmeng based on the author's keynote speeches at Shanghai Jiao Tong University and the People's Procuratorate of Zhejiang Province.

Z. Yongnian, *The Great Convergence VS. The Great Divergence*,
https://doi.org/10.1007/978-981-96-7846-4

the eyes of Western countries. When China emphasizes Chinese modernization, Western countries are thinking about what impact Chinese modernization will have on the Western world. At the same time, developing countries are also paying attention to Chinese modernization. Most of the modernization in developing countries began after World War II. In the early years, developing countries (Asian, African and Latin American countries) basically followed the Western model to carry out their own modernization. However, with the rise of contemporary China, especially today, China has put forward Chinese modernization, which is very popular among developing countries, because they used to follow the Western model of modernization, and after more than half a century, it did not produce much effect. Now the Chinese modernization proposed by China is of reference significance to them. Of course, the reference significance of Chinese modernization to developing countries is also a concern for some Western countries, because the West has always regarded its own modernization model as the universal. Five years ago, at the 19th CPC National Congress, the "modernization of China" was proposed, believing that China's modernization has offered "an alternative" for those countries that want both development and independence—a modernization model other than the Western model.

Three Dimensions of Chinese Modernization

The definition of Chinese modernization proposed by the Report to the 20th CPC National Congress is all-round, compound and three-dimensional. So, it can be understood from many angles. This paper mainly understands Chinese modernization from an academic perspective. The first question to be answered here is: What is modernization?

From the perspective of history and experience, modernization can be divided into three levels, that is, modernization at the material level, modernization at the human level and modernization at the institutional level.

For modernization in the material sense, all countries in the world have a considerable consensus. High-rise buildings, high-speed rails, expressways and advanced science and technology, and so on, are all modernization at the material level. As far as this level of modernization is concerned, there is no big controversy, and it is just that different countries have different ways of expressions. For example, China's architecture has Chinese characteristics and Western architecture has Western characteristics. At the same time, there is also a consensus for the measurement standard of material modernization in the international community. For example, the top speed of a car produced in country A is only 100 kilometers per hour, while the top speed of a car produced in country B is 200 kilometers per hour, then country B will definitely be considered as more modern than country A. Although there are a few social groups, such as ascetic monks in Nepal and some religious groups in India, who oppose material modernization, yet for most countries, material modernization is what everyone pursues together.

Modernization at the human level is very important. In fact, whether it is in the East or in the West, modernization is ultimately to realize human modernization. Modernization is what people pursue, and without people, modernization is meaningless. Human modernization is actually divided into material level and spiritual level as well. As mentioned above, there is no big controversy about the modernization of material level, but there is a big controversy about the modernization of spiritual level. Human existence is not abstract, and people are cultural people, such as Chinese and Americans, both representing their own civilization and culture. Therefore, human modernization mainly focuses on the modernization of spiritual level.

The core of modernization is people. The concept of modernization was first put forward in the West during the Renaissance. Before the Renaissance, European countries were all in the era of religious theocracy, also known as the Medieval Dark Age. God was the basis for judging everything, and everything was based on God. The Renaissance shifted the focus and center of society from God to man himself, which was an epoch-making great change. From the Renaissance to the Enlightenment in Europe, humanism was gradually established, which started the process of modernization. However, because commerce and capital are the main bodies that start the modernization in the West, the modernization of Western countries is too capital-led, which makes the modernization that originally served people led to human alienation. Or, the Western-led modernization produced what Marx called the alienation of people. Originally, capital is supposed to serve people, but in the West, it has become people at the service of capital. Humanism is not unique to the West. Humanism has always been rooted in the tradition of China. The Confucian culture with Confucius and Mencius as its core in China, in essence, emphasizes a people-centered approach.

To sum up, people are the product of culture. The modernization of people is related to the modernization of culture. People are not abstract, because the modernization of people is not only manifested in people's pursuit of material modernization, but also in the modernization at the spiritual level.

In addition to material modernization and human modernization, there is another important variable between the two, that is, the modernization of institution. If we regard material modernization as the vertical axis of the coordinate, and human modernization as the horizontal axis of the coordinate, then institutional modernization is an important variable between the two, regulating material modernization and human modernization. An important indicator of the realization of institutional modernization is which institution is more capable of promoting and ensuring the realization of the modernization of material and people. In recent years, around economic development and economic modernization, the discussions on the comparison of the institution between China and the West, have become more and more popular in academic circles. Everyone is debating which institution can realize material modernization and human modernization faster. In the West's point of views, the democratic system they believe in is more capable of achieving the modernization of material and people, while Chinese scholars also believe that our system has advantages and is more capable of promoting the modernization of material and people.

Another important indicator to measure institutional modernization is whether it can meet the needs of the majority of the people in a society, not just the needs of the minority. Because modernization is, in the final analysis, to serve people, and the goal of modernization is to provide a foundation for the all-round development of the majority, so what people should pursue is the modernization of realizing common prosperity, not the modernization of the prosperity of the minority. When discussing the institution to promote the modernization of material and people, we should also discuss the modernization of the institution itself. Judging whether one institution is good or not, we should see whether it has strong ability of governance and whether it can keep pace with the times to adjust itself. In traditional Chinese culture, the general purpose of the institution is to maintain social order and manage society. In modern times, the function of realizing modernization has been added to the purpose of the institution. Institutional modernization means that our institution should not only play the role of governing society and maintaining social order, but also play the role of guiding material modernization and human modernization.

In short, no matter how it is defined, modernization can be basically divided into three levels of modernization: material modernization, human modernization and institutional modernization.

Socialism and Chinese Modernization

The Report to the 20th CPC National Congress defined Chinese modernization as the modernization under the guidance of the thought on socialism with Chinese characteristics. I think there are three main reasons why there is such a definition. The first is that the socialism emphasized in Chinese modernization is a universal value. The second is that Chinese modernization has drawn profound lessons from Western modernization. The third is that Chinese modernization comes from China's own historical experience.

To begin with, the socialism in Chinese modernization is a universal value. If we do not say the term "universal", we can also say a "general" value. In fact, when we observe different civilizations and different countries, we can find that every civilization has the idea of a fair society, and every religion has the idea of fairness. In the early days of Europe, there was the idea of Utopian socialism, and Marxism transformed Utopian socialism into scientific socialism, that is, realized the transformation of socialism from Utopian socialism to reality. In China, the ancient society put forward the notion of Datong Society, and Datong Society is a typical socialist thought. The ideal of Datong Society is highly consistent with the ideal of modern European socialism. In the late Qing Dynasty in modern times, the book *Datong Shu* written by Mr. Kang Youwei once again proposed the Datong Society. During the period of the Republic of China, before and after the May Fourth Movement, all kinds of the doctrines in the West spread to China, such as nationalism, liberalism, democracy, socialism and anarchism, and so on. We had what the West had, which can be described as "a hundred flowers bloom and a hundred schools of thought contend". But there is a question that needs to be answered here. Why, up to now, no other doctrines can remain, and only socialism has remained and has been accepted by the Communist Party of China? In fact, before the Communist Party of China, Dr. Sun Yat-sen has also accepted socialism, and the Principle of People's Livelihood in the Three Principles of the People he put forward was an important part of socialism. The development economics we talk about now in our economics is actually copying and pasting the development economics of the West. However, in fact, Dr. Sun Yat-sen is often regarded in the West as the first person who put forward development economics. Development economics, as a branch in economics, was developed only after World War II, while Dr. Sun Yat-sen has already proposed the Three Principles of the People at the beginning of the twentieth century, including nationalism, democracy and people's livelihood. From ancient times to modern times, the shadow of socialism can always be seen in the social thoughts of China's governors. Therefore, the Communist Party of China has its own background of civilization and culture in its acceptance of socialism. The idea of socialism has a high degree of coincidence and consistency with the traditional Datong Society in China, and they are manifested as the same kind of value.

Why is the concept of socialism accepted and preserved? The fundamental reason lies in the fact that socialism is in line with human nature. In the early 1990s, after the collapse of the Soviet Union-Eastern European bloc, Francis Fukuyama of the United States wrote a book called *The End of History and the Last Man*. In this book, he argued that the system of democracy and freedom in the West was the best system that human beings could have, and it was also the last system, because this system was the one that was the most in line with human nature. Now the liberal and democratic system in the West has so many drawbacks, Fukuyama does not see it this way anymore and he is constantly revising his views. In my point of view, the pursuit of fairness and justice in socialism is the most in line with human nature. On the one hand, as has been said before, except for a few religious groups, no one wants to be poor, and everyone wishes to live a rich life, while socialism is to pursue material prosperity. As Mr. Deng Xiaoping emphasized, poverty should not be the feature of socialism and socialism is to make people's lives better. On the other hand, the pursuit of fairness in socialism is also in line with human nature. People do not wish to be poor, and do not wish to be rich but unfair. If a society achieves prosperity for only a small number of people, and a large number of people still remain in poverty, then such a society will not be liked by its people. If we say that the pursuit of prosperity is a part of human nature, then the pursuit of fairness is also a part of human nature. Socialism precisely respects the material interest demands from different groups, attaches much importance to the cohesion of various social resources and social forces, and seeks the common development for most people. Just as Mr. Deng Xiaoping emphasized, the nature of socialism is to release and develop the productive forces, eliminate exploitation and bipolarization, and ultimately achieve common prosperity. In the process of seeking development for the society and enabling everyone to live a rich life, socialism pursues both prosperity and fairness, but it should avoid wealth but unfairness, which embodies the characteristics of human nature.

Second, Chinese modernization has learned profound lessons from Western modernization. There is no argument about the fact that modernization originated in the West. As mentioned above, the values of modernization were established from the Renaissance to the Enlightenment, while the real modernization, that is, the modernization that can enable everyone to live a rich life, began after the Industrial Revolution in Britain. Industrialization first began in Western Europe, diffused from Britain to European countries such as France and Germany, then diffused to Northern America, and finally diffused to other countries and regions in the world. Japan was the first country in Asia to realize modernization. After Japan, the "Asian Four Tigers" economies also realized their own modernization one after another, and then China and other Asian countries and regions. China, in particular, is seeking to realize the modernization of the country on a large scale.

The modernization model in the West is mainly capital-driven modernization, but too much capital dominance has led to the emergence of unfair social phenomenon in the process of realizing modernization through industrialization, and the phenomenon of people exploiting people, which is what Marx called primitive capitalism. The tragic world described by the British writer Charles Dickens and the French writer Victor Hugo in their works was the product of early capitalism. The modernization led by capitalism has brought about great social instability, which is the economic background of the massive socialist movements that broke out from the nineteenth century to the early twentieth century. The socialist movement is the product of capitalism, and Marx also acknowledged this. From today's view, the socialist movements at that time were highly populism and very violent, especially the European revolution that broke out in 1848. The transformation from primitive capitalism to capitalism in the West does not conform to the logic of capital development itself, but is the product of socialist movement. Later, after the Great Depression in the 1930s, Keynesianism appeared in the West, advocating that the government should intervene in the economy when the market could not play an effective role and failed. For a long time, the economics community often debated about economic liberalism and Keynesianism. Although Keynesianism is less talked about nowadays, yet it is not deniable that it has played an important role for the stability of Western society. Starting from the 1930s, Keynesianism has been embraced and adopted by most of Western countries including the United States after 1945. From 1945 to the 1980s, the Western world was divided into two parts: One half was the Warsaw Pact led by the Soviet Union and the other half was the Western world. The world led by the Soviet Union also advanced modernization, but the Soviet Union and the Warsaw Pact carried out modernization behind closed doors, while the Western camp opened their doors to carry out modernization. Keynesianism not only can promote the government to play its role, but also can play the role of capital. Therefore, before the energy crisis in the West from 1945 to the 1970s, the welfare society in the Western world achieved great development. The development of the welfare society is contributed to Keynesianism, and its greatest achievement is to expand the middle class in the West. From 1945 to the early 1970s, the proportion of the middle class in the West reached 60%, or even 70%, which ensured the stability of Western society. However, since the 1980s, the West abandoned Keynesianism and began to promote neoliberalism. On the one hand, capital, technology, labor, and talents flowed around the world, which caused what many economists called hyper-globalization, and created a huge amount of wealth for human beings. On the other hand, it also made Western society unstable, especially in the United States. The United States used to be called a middle-class society because it had a middle class with a population of 70%, but now the United States has become a rich society, that is, a very few people have mastered the huge amount of wealth, and most people have no sense of gain, which has led to the rise of populism. The proportion of the middle class in the United States has been declining all the way since the 1980s, from about 70% in the past to less than 50% nowadays. The middle class in China now accounts for about 30%, a relatively small proportion. But for the people, everyone is still in the process of developing from poverty to prosperity, so they can wait patiently. But, the proportion of the middle class in the United States has been falling from 70% to 50% and this means that many people have gone from wealth to poverty, which is unacceptable. The shrinking of the middle class in the United States has led to the rise of "Trumpism" and the rise of populism. After Musk bought the

Twitter, he unsealed the Twitter account of Trump. Within just a few days, Trump's fans rose to nearly 100 million, which shows that Trump is still influential. Trump's election as president of the United States is the manifestation of the rise of populism in the United States. His election is regarded by the American media as a "referendum of white Americans". This also makes sense, too, because white Americans all live in small cities or rural areas, and globalization has led to the decline of small cities and rural areas, which brought out dissatisfaction among white Americans. Populism has made American society very unstable today. Britain is also facing social instability caused by the rise of populism.

The social instability in Britain and the United States is an inevitable result of the wealth but injustice in Western society, and it is also the manifestation of social dissatisfaction brought about by the decline of social welfare level. The United States has the lowest welfare level among Western countries. Britain was also a welfare society before the Thatcher Revolution, but a wave of privatization brought about by the Thatcher Revolution has led to the decline of social welfare level. Different from Britain and the United States, Germany and Nordic countries have a higher welfare level, which constitutes the foundation of social stability. Germany is a "social market economy", which is two Chinese characters less than China's "socialism market economy". Its economy that realizes social market is relatively stable.

The first wave of problem of wealth but injustice in the West was solved by the social welfare system. So, can the current problem of wealth but injustice in the United States and other countries be solved by the social welfare system? My judgment is that it cannot solve the problem. The United States does not have a deep-rooted idea of the welfare society. As a matter of fact, the capital in the United States has been working hard to resist the welfare society. In addition, the United States also has so large population that it does not dare to mention the problem of welfare society at all. The proportion of the middle class in the United States has fallen the fastest when Barack Obama was president in the United States. During his eight years in office, the proportion of the middle class in the United States has declined at a rate of 1 percentage point per year. Even Obama, with a background of the Democratic Party, also is inclined to capital. In the global financial crisis triggered by Wall Street in 2007–2008, the Obama administration had to use taxpayers' money to rescue Wall Street, but when Wall Street was rescued, there was a phenomenon of indiscriminate payment of hundreds of millions of dollars in bonuses.

The Nordic countries in the West promote the welfare society and the government bears most of the expenditure on public welfare. The people do not need money to see a doctor, do not need money to go to school and do not need so much money for housing. The difference between the people is very simple. For example, the price of red wine is different. However, these societies developed early with small population size and single race, so it is relatively easier to realize welfare society. In contemporary times, these societies are experimenting with a one-person-one-salary principle, and the country gives a salary for each person regardless of whether they work or not. This principle can be practiced in small societies and small countries that originally has achieved the developed level, but it is not practicable to implement this principle in a populous country like the United States. How to solve this problem is the biggest headache in the United States now, and it is also a problem that many people are thinking.

Third, Chinese modernization comes from China's own historical experiences. Japan was the first country in Asia to realize its modernization. China was defeated by the West during the First Opium War (1840–1842) and the Second Opium War (1856–1860). However, after being defeated by the West, China's elites at that time still regarded the West as the barbaric one and did not attach much importance to the modernization in the West. It was not until Japan, which used to be regarded as the student of China, defeated China in Sino-Japanese War of 1894–1895 that China's elites woke up and pursued modernization in earnest. But China's understanding of modernization was not very clear at the very beginning. The modernization proposed by the earliest people was to "enrich the country, strengthen its army" (*fu guo qiang bing*) for the realization of military modernization, so the early generation made every effort to promote military modernization. Later, when military modernization failed, new voices appeared again. Some people said that we should "save the country through industry" (*yi gong jiu guo*) for the realization of industrial modernization. Some people said that we should "save the country through commerce" (*yi shang jiu guo*) for the realization of commercial modernization. There were also other people who put forward that we should "save the country through education" (*yi jiao jiu guo*) for the realization of educational modernization. There were many points of views. Therefore, for a long time since modern times, China has been trying on unilateral modernization, and has never wanted to promote comprehensive modernization as much as it does today.

After the founding of the People's Republic of China in 1949, China embarked on a wave of modernization dominated by the country in the era of Mao Zedong. Today's dual household registration system in urban and rural areas was the product at that time. The household registration system realized industrialization at the expense of rural areas. The agricultural products were purchased and sold in a unified way. The peasants had no right to eat the food they grew, and they had to hand it over to the country first, which is to supplement the work with agriculture. The modernization of China at that time was to a large extent influenced by changes in the international environment. Except for the "one-sided" foreign policy toward the Soviet Union at the beginning of the 1950s, when the Soviet Union gave us some assistance, China basically pushed ahead with modernization behind closed doors, mainly doing the modernization of some basic industries. At that time, to catch up with Britain and the United States was actually to catch up with the Soviet Union. Therefore, the modernization at that time can be defined as "catch-up modernization". From today's point of view, the "Four Modernizations" proposed by Premier Zhou Enlai, namely, the four modernizations in industry, agriculture, national defense, and science and technology, are actually all material modernization.

Whether it was subjective reasons or objective reasons, at that time we were engaged in modernization behind closed doors, which led to China gradually becoming a generally poor country. So, at the beginning of the reform and opening-up, Mr. Deng Xiaoping made a fundamental redefinition of modernization. He believed that poverty should not be linked with socialism, and the original intention of socialism was to pursue prosperity. The revolution in which the CPC members shed their blood and sacrificed their lives was not to build a poor society, but to build a rich society. Socialism is about the pursuit of prosperity, so Mr. Deng Xiaoping redefined socialism. The socialism in Deng's era can be defined as "developmental socialism" or "developmental modernization". In Deng's point of view, in order to achieve common prosperity, it is necessary to allow some people and some regions to get rich first, and then lead others and other regions to common prosperity together. Therefore, the common prosperity we are talking about today is actually not a completely new concept. Mr. Deng Xiaoping has said it long time ago, but at that time it was only that we focused on exploring how to "fight our way out" and realize the goal of development under the socialist condition of widespread poverty. And how to move toward common prosperity after development is a matter for future generations. Mr. Deng Xiaoping gave several instructions to the self-employed during his lifetime and it was of symbolic significance, because the self-employed at that time was the main body of the private economy we talk about today. The development of Zhejiang (especially Wenzhou's development in the 1980s) and the development of Shenzhen all emerged in heated debates. Without the political support of Deng Xiaoping and other statesmen, it would be difficult to have the development that people see today.

Since the 18th CPC National Congress, after realizing the rapid economic development, political stability and a certain degree of social prosperity, that is, after having a solid economic foundation, China has put forward an all-round, systematic and overall concept of modernization and summarized it into the "Five-Sphere Integrated" modernization, namely the "Five-Sphere Integrated" modernization in economic construction, political construction, cultural construction, social construction, and the construction of ecological civilization. Such a three-dimensional, holistic and composite modernization would not have been proposed and believed by anyone twenty years earlier or in the era of Deng Xiaoping. Now when conditions permit, it only can be proposed. Therefore, Chinese modernization should be put forward from the perspective of Chinese history, on the basis of materialism and in accordance with the characteristics in each era, instead of raising the goal to an extent that it is difficult to achieve all at once.

The Chinese modernization put forward at the 20th CPC National Congress, is not the modernization in which a few people are rich, but the modernization in which all people are rich together. China emphasizes the modernization of common prosperity for all people. This is the important difference between Chinese modernization and the rich but unfair modernization in countries such as Britain and the United States. However, people are not always clear about the issue of common prosperity.

What is the modernization of common prosperity? This question deserves our careful consideration. At present, most people do not understand the modernization of common prosperity. Even at the level of policymakers, the formulation about it has been improving all the time. Now the formulation about the modernization of common prosperity is gradually becoming clear. Common prosperity is not about robbing the rich to help the poor, nor is it about engaging in egalitarianism. But when common prosperity was just put forward, many people thought that common prosperity should pay attention to three distributions, namely primary distribution, second distribution, and tertiary distribution. However, the word "distribution" must be used with cautious, because in the Chinese context, the government is responsible for distribution. So, what role does the government play in the three distributions? The first is the primary distribution. The primary distribution is the income from labor and this is the most important. In the past, it was said that primary distribution was about efficiency, secondary distribution was about fairness and tertiary distribution was about supplementation. I think that it is a problematic statement. It is not right to talk about efficiency alone in the primary distribution. It is necessary to stress not only efficiency but also basic social fairness, because everyone's salary is the income of labor and is the most important income. If wages do not enable people to live a prosperous life, but are realized through secondary distribution or even tertiary distribution, then common prosperity will be a Utopian dream and there is a great possibility that people will remain poor. As a result, the primary distribution is very important and people must get enough income in the primary distribution. However, the primary distribution has little to do with the country, because the country cannot enforce how much the boss pays the employee, and the salary level is determined by the company according to market demands. Although many countries are generally implementing the minimum salary system stipulated by the law of the country now, yet the primary distribution is still mainly the behavior of enterprises. It is the distribution of the enterprise, not the distribution of the country. Only the second distribution is distributed by the country through fiscal taxation. The second distribution is not just about fairness, and many countries use the second distribution to promote sustainable economic development. For example, the Western Keynesianism is like this. The tertiary distribution is the conscious and voluntary behavior of donation by entrepreneurs, and cannot be called distribution. Many economists do not understand common prosperity, and some economists simply think that common prosperity is three distributions. This is undoubtedly an oversimplified thought, and a reflection of populist sentiment. Some entrepreneurs are influenced by this populist ideology and take the initiative to make large donations when the country is proposing common prosperity. This puts a lot of pressure on other enterprises. It is worth encouraging and advocating that entrepreneurs usually serve the society and support education through donations, but entrepreneurs should not donate because they are influenced by populism. This will play a bad role. We should have a correct understanding of common prosperity. General Secretary Xi Jinping has made it very clear that common prosperity is to divide the pie properly on the basis of continuing to make the pie bigger. In 2021, China's per capita GDP was only $12,000, while the per capital GDP of the United States was nearly $70,000. Don't Americans strive for fairness? They also pursue fairness, but the United States is too capital-led, and they cannot realize fairness. In Asian society, Singapore is a society characterized with a little common prosperity. Singapore's per capita GDP in 2021 also reached $ 70,000, but the society of common prosperity is not without poor people. Singapore also has 20% of the people at the bottom of society. Empirically, the policy in the society of common prosperity has three characteristics: The first is that it has no ceiling. It cannot be stipulated that a business owner can only own so much money; the second is to protect the bottom of the society and ensure the basic social fairness in a society; the third is to expand the middle class. Among them, "expanding the middle" is very important. Common prosperity does not mean that 100% of the people live the same life. If the middle class in a society can reach 60% or 70%, then this society can be said to be a society of common prosperity. Only we have a correct understanding of common prosperity can we move toward common prosperity. If we only divide the pie in a hurry and do not pay attention to make the pie bigger, then it will lead to the socialism of widespread poverty as described by Mr. Deng Xiaoping. Vigorously developing productive forces is still the most important. In the past, Deng Xiaoping said that "development is the absolute principle", and now General Secretary Xi Jinping says that "development is the first priority". In fact, they basically mean the same thing, that is, we must pay attention to development.

Leading Chinese Modernization with Institutional Modernization

The importance of institutional modernization has been elaborated above, that is, institutional modernization leads material modernization and human modernization. Under the background of China, it is mainly manifested in the modernization of system in governing the country.

After taking office, the US president Joe Biden called the competition between China and the United States the competition between the systems. He believed that the Sino-US competition is the competition between "American democracy" and "Chinese autocracy". In my opinion, the Sino-US competition is indeed the competition between the systems, but it is not the competition between the systems defined by the US president. Instead, it is to see which system can better guide the modernization of a country, including material modernization and human modernization.

Examining the modernization of China from the level of the institution, although many scholars have many criticisms and even doubts about China's institution, yet from the past experiences, there is a great advantage in China's institutional system, especially since the reform and opening-up, the achievements that we have made are inseparable from China's institutional advantages. Around the world, critics of institution in each country will find a lot of faults if they only focus on their own institutions, but if they look at it from the comparative perspective, they may be more confident in their own institutions. Since China's reform and opening-up for more than 40 years, China has achieved two sustainability at the same time: One is the sustainable economic development and the other is the sustainable social stability. It is not easy to achieve the two sustainability. In the past 40 years, both the West and China have done well in their economic developments and both have achieved the sustainable increase in national wealth. In other words, both China and the West have achieved sustainable economic development, but the West has not achieved sustainable social stability. On a global scale, there are societies that are very stable, but the whole society is dead, lacks the momentum for development and does not realize economic development. Also, there are societies that have developed economically, but the society has become unstable. China has achieved the two sustainability at the same time, the sustainable economic development and the sustainable social stability. The realization of the two sustainability cannot separate from the third sustainability of China, namely the sustainable institutional support and leadership. The three sustainability are indispensable, and their mutual support only can achieve social and economic development. The realization of sustainable institutional support and leadership in China, is related to China's basic economic system and political system.

How to examine our own basic economic system and political system is now a focus in academic circles. Today, we advocate the establishment of an independent knowledge system, but the construction of an independent knowledge system needs to be carried out around how to understand our basic economic system and political system.

Comparatively speaking, China is a mixed economy, while the West is completely dominated by capital. You can see a very interesting phenomenon. Since modern times, there have been two kinds of extreme thinking in the West. One thinking is that "private property is sacred and inviolable". From Adam Smith to classical liberalism and then to the current neoliberalism, they all have insisted on this point. In the capital-led economic system, people basically follow this thought. But the other thinking is completely opposite. From Rousseau in France to Marx in Germany, they all have believed that the root of all the problems in the world is private ownership. Therefore, only by eliminating private ownership can human beings solve the problems they face. Although the practice of the fully public ownership in the Soviet Union has gone bankrupt, yet so far there are many left-wing Marxist advocates who still analyze the problem from the perspective of private ownership and believe the key to solving the problem is to eliminate private ownership. In reality, however, there are few economies with fully public ownership. On the one hand, the Soviet Union is the most typical representative of eliminating private ownership. It took the road that considered public property was sacred and inviolable. Now it has failed and disintegrated. On the other hand, the economic system represented by Britain and the United States has also encountered great problems, which maintains the system that private property is sacred and inviolable.

China's basic economic system is a mixed economic system. Traditionally speaking, China actually has never gone to extremes. We have neither the concept that "private property is sacred and inviolable" nor the concept that "public property is sacred and inviolable". Chinese civilization is a civilization of moderation. It has long wanted to put public ownership and private ownership together to explore which kind of the division of labor is better between public ownership and private ownership. China's attempt to combine public ownership and private ownership can be traced back to the practice of the well-field system in the pre-Qin period. The basic meaning for the well-field system is to divide a farmland into nine equal parts according to the shape of the Chinese character " 井" (*well* in English). Among them, the middle part is the public land, and the surrounding eight parts are the private lands. Although this is the original combination mode of public ownership and private ownership, yet we can see one way of thinking for Chinese civilization from it, that is, we are looking for an institutional mode that can promote balanced economic development. Let's take the planned economy as an example. The same is also the planned economy, but the planned economy in China is completely different from that in the Soviet Union. The collapse of the Soviet Union marks the ultimate failure of the planned economy of the Soviet Union because it was difficult to lead to the reform, while the success of China's reform shows that the planned economy of Chinese model can be reformed. Looking at the planned economy of the Soviet Union from the perspective of the property rights system, the central bureaucracy of the Soviet Union mastered more than 90% of the means of production and the factors of production in the entire society, and the local governments in the Soviet Union had no substantive rights (property rights). However, in China, it is just the opposite. Most of the property rights in China's planned economy are in the hands of the localities, including the local governments at the levels of province, city, county and township, and the grassroot autonomous organizations at the level of village. The localities master more than 80% of the means of production and the factors of production in society. In other words, even the public ownership under the planned economy, in China, can be shared by the governments at the central, provincial, municipal, county, township and village levels, and the grassroot mass autonomous organizations. This is different from the Soviet Union. Generally speaking, the public ownership in the Soviet Union is the public ownership of the central government, so once the planned economy is disintegrated, it will easily develop into oligopolistic economy and oligarchy. Until today, this problem has not been solved in Russia. However, for China's public ownership, if we draw an arrow, the higher the level is, the more the public ownership components will be, and the lower the level is, when it goes down to the village level, it is actually closer to private ownership.

China's current model of economic system is actually a mixed economic system. Although the West is also a mixed economy, yet the mixed economy in China is completely different from the mixed economy in the West. China's mixed economic system is the mixture of state-owned enterprises and private enterprises. This is a kind of mixed economic system based on the division of labor. Many years ago, my collaborator and I spent more than ten years researching and writing a book. Now it has been translated and published in Chinese. The name of the book is the *Market in State: The Political Economy of Domination in*

China. This book writes that from the Han Dynasty to the modern times, China is basically the market composed of three layers of capital. The top layer is state-owned capital, the bottom is a large number of private capitals represented by micro, small and medium-sized enterprises, and the middle is the field where private capital interacts with state-owned capital. The modern people are smart and they classify the enterprises represented by these three layers of capital into three types, that is, "government-run" state-owned enterprises, "business-run" private enterprises and "government-supervised and business-run" state-owned and private cooperative enterprises. Up to now, China has basically had these three types of enterprises. There were also several periods in Chinese history that went to extremes. One was the period of Wang Mang's Reform between the Western Han Dynasty and the Eastern Han Dynasty. The second was the period of Wang Anshi's Reform during the Song Dynasty. The third was the period of Zhu Yuanzhang's Reform in the Ming Dynasty. The fourth was the period of the planned economy before the reform and opening-up. During these four periods, the market disappeared and the country occupied an absolute dominant position. From the perspective of Chinese history, when these three types of capital develop in a balanced way, the country will develop well. When these three types of capital are unbalanced, that is, they completely take the road of nationalism or the country does not play its role but only relies on the role of the market, there will be big problems.

Summing up our historical experiences, we can know that it is very important to do a good job in the division of labor between state-owned enterprises and private enterprises. State-owned enterprises should be responsible for large-scale infrastructure construction such as water conservancy projects, high-speed rails, roads and bridges, and those fields related to national security such as aerospace. However, a large number of fields in people's livelihood economy should be left to private enterprises. Confucianism has advocated that the country should not compete with the people for profit, and advocated the division of labor between state-owned enterprises and private enterprises. Today, if we observe the regional development of various regions in China, we can find those regions where the division of labor between state-owned enterprises and private enterprises, and between state-owned capital and private capital is well handled, and where the boundary between them is relatively clear, tend to have a better economic development, while those regions where state-owned enterprises and private enterprises are unbalanced, tend to encounter problems in their economic development. Zhejiang and Guangdong are two typical regions with developed private enterprises, so that they have a good economic foundation. In contrast, the Northeast region is dominated by state-owned enterprises. A large number of local state-owned enterprises with huge volume but low operational efficiency, have remained and squeezed the development space of private enterprise, thus lacking economic vitality and urban competitiveness, finally resulting in a large loss of population and now facing the crisis of talents and population. In the long run, the mixed market economy with the mixture of state-owned enterprises and private enterprises is unchangeable, but the division of labor between state-owned enterprises and private enterprises must be properly handled.

Some liberal economists believe that China's state-owned enterprises are the product of the planned economy and should be abolished. However, state-owned enterprises have survived thousands of years of Chinese history, not the product of modern China, nor the product of planned economy. On the other hand, some scholars believe that private ownership should be eliminated and public ownership should be implemented. The reality is that the one-sided idea that we can only choose public ownership or private ownership has experienced failures. We should not stand in the perspective of the West and use Western thinking to solve China's problems. In the Report to the 20th CPC National Congress, what is different from the past is that adapting Marxism in the Chinese context is discussed as an independent section. This change is of profound significance. We accept Marxism's concept of building a fair and just society, but Marxism's ideas of eliminating class, countries and private ownership were the product of European society at that time. These ideas can hardly reflect the reality of Chinese society. China cannot do it now, and it will be difficult to do it in the future. Western countries followed two lines in practicing Marxism. One was the line of the Soviet Union. This one completely copied and pasted Marxism, eliminated private ownership, and practiced complete state ownership, but the result was failure. The other is the Nordic line. The Northern Europe partly followed the Marxism's ideas of building a fair and just society, but in terms of methodology it realized Marxism in the "Nordic" context, that is, it realized social democracy or democratic socialism, which has achieved success. How to adapt Marxism to the Chinese context? It is very important to answer this question. The victory of Chinese Revolution was achieved by relying on Marxism in the Chinese context in Mao

Zedong's era. In the early days of Chinese Revolution, both urban riots and uprisings failed in accordance with the book-oriented Marxism. Mao Zedong realized China's problem was the rural problem, and proposed to take the road of encircling the city from the countryside, which started the process of Marxism in the Chinese context and led the CPC to victory in revolution. Similarly, we are now promoting socialist construction. In order to realize Chinese modernization, we need to continue to promote Marxism in the Chinese context, and it will be more thorough Marxism in the Chinese context. Some of the book-oriented Marxism that often appeared now is prone to problems in practice.

So, what is about China's basic political system? Some scholars believe that the system of separation of powers implemented in the West, that is, the system in which the legislative, executive and judicial powers are independently excised by three organs and check and balance each other, is what China should learn from, because China itself does not have such an institutional system. Actually, it is not. If we observe the history of China for more than thousands of years, we will find that the West has three powers, and China also has three powers. We can call it a Chinese-style system of division of labor and cooperation among the three powers, that is, the system of three powers of decision-making, executive and supervision. This system has existed for more than 2000 years from the Han Dynasty to the late Qing Dynasty. In the past, in the traditional society dominated by imperial power, all powers belonged to imperial power, but the exercise of imperial power was divided into three powers in accordance with the time when the power occurred, namely, the decision-making power, the executive power and the supervision power. After the Qing government was overthrown in modern times, this system was abolished. In his early days, Dr. Sun Yat-sen learned from the West and implemented the presidential system and the parliamentary system, but both of them failed. Later, Dr. Sun Yat-sen proposed the implementation of the "Five-Power Constitution" which integrated the three powers in the West, namely the legislative, executive and judicial powers with the two traditional Chinese powers. Dr. Sun Yat-sen believed that the three powers in the West are basic, but there are also some good powers in the Chinese tradition. He found out two of them, one is the examination power and the other is the supervision power. Therefore, he combined the three powers in the West with the two powers in China, and put forward a "Five-Power Constitution". When Dr. Sun Yat-sen was alive, he did not have enough time to test and practice his "Five-Power Constitution". However, Taiwan's experience shows that it is difficult to mix the power structure of the West and China. We should either choose the three powers in China, or implement the three powers in the West. The examination power and the supervision power have long lost their functions in Taiwan. Taiwan basically implements the three powers in the West. Empirically, this does not conform to the logic of Chinese civilization and culture. Nowadays, many scholars are keen to compare China's Taiwan and Singapore to see the impacts of different systems on the development of economy and society. In the 1990s, there was no big difference in per capita GDP between China's Taiwan and Singapore, but now the per capita GDP in Taiwan ranks the last among the "Asian Four Tigers", which is about $27,000. Although it is not bad, yet the per capita GDP in Singapore has reached $70,000. The changes in Taiwan came during the reign of Mr. Chiang Ching-kuo. During the administration of Mr. Chiang Ching-kuo, the development thinking in China's Taiwan was similar to that in Singapore. If we observe the political system in the two places, we can find the differences. China's Taiwan implements the three powers in the West, while the political system that Singapore practices is actually the "sage-king politics" in the Confucian tradition. In Singapore, the Western-style democratic election, namely the referendum, is actually just a form. The most important thing in the election is still the "sage-king politics" in the Confucian tradition, that is, selecting first and then electing. Mr. Lee Kuan Yew's philosophy is to make good selection before election. It is to select eight or ten good apples first and then give these good apples to the common people for election. Anyway, any one is a good apple. Unlike Singapore, China's Taiwan has no selection system. If both are rotten apples, then it will be not good for the common people to select anyone. Trump was a political amateur before he participated in the presidential election in the United States, and he had no experience of governance. After being elected the US president, he made a mess of the United States. Zelensky in Ukraine also lacks the experience of governance. In Western countries, people who lacks the experience of governance are frequently elected as presidents. In fact, there are problems with political systems.

Today, China has once again realized the system of the division of labor and cooperation among the three powers through institutional innovation. After the 18th CPC National Congress, the supervision power was piloted in several provinces such as Beijing, Zhejiang and Shanxi. After the 19th CPC National Congress, the status of the supervision power was officially restored to its traditional position in China. The current supervision power is different from the previous one. In the past, there were also supervision departments, but they belonged to the State Council, while the current supervision power is independent of the State Council, parallel to the State Council and is under the leadership of the National People's Congress. China's basic system of the division of labor and cooperation among the three powers operates in accordance with the time stages, that is, decision-making first, then execution, and then supervision. Of course, although this basic system has been formed, and it will produce long-term political influence, yet this power structure still needs to be constantly refined and improved. In particular, it is necessary to avoid the phenomenon of excessive use of the supervision power. In Han Dynasty, there was the abuse of the supervision power. If the only task of the people who have the supervision power is to find fault with others, any kinds of faults can be found, such as eating the wrong way, sleeping the wrong way, walking posture the wrong way. If these faults are magnified without limit and associated with political loyalty, resulting in many "unwarranted crimes". Later, the Han Dynasty carried out reforms, defined the six areas that needed to be supervised, and stipulated other areas that cannot be supervised except for these six areas, so as to realize the gradual improvement of the system. In modern times, it is also very important to improve the system, to recognize the boundary of the supervision power, and to avoid the excessive supervision. At the same time, it can also promote more democratic and scientific decision-making, so that it cannot influence the exercise of the execution power. Basically, it is a long-term task to improve the national political system of the division of labor and cooperation among the three powers. Considering the problems faced today by the separation of powers and checks and balances in the West, it is of more theoretical and practical significance for us to improve the system of the division of labor and cooperation among the three powers.

The Separation of Powers and Checks and Balances in the United State often leads to the failure of the President, Congress and the Supreme Court to cooperate with each other, each setting up their own rules, which causes frequent government paralysis. This political system undoubtedly has a big problem, but China's system of the division of labor and cooperation among the three powers will not only not cause the government paralysis, but also make its operation more scientific and effective. In addition, we are now proposing to realize "whole-process people's democracy". There is still a lot to explore in order to realize it. For example, it needs to classify where democracy should be and where centralization should be. If we compare it with the West, historically, I think at the top of the political level, the General Secretary and the Prime Minister should have the "power to form the cabinet" and form the governing team. Without the power to form the cabinet, it is difficult to form an effective administrative team, and it is difficult for the administration to be effective. The level of the Standing Committee of the Political Bureau of the Central Committee of the CPC is the governing team of the country, and it needs to stress efficiency. It should not be the parliament where everyone argues with each other. At this level, democracy cannot be practiced, but centralization should be practiced. On the contrary, democracy should be practiced at the level of "parliament", including the Central Committee, the National People's Congress, the National Committee of the Chinese People's Political Consultative Conference and other institutions in decision-making. However, once a policy has been decided, when it comes to the stage of implementation, power should be centralized. The democratic centralism that China practices is very good, but there is still a need for more exploration and practice on such issues as where democracy should be and where centralization should be.

To sum up, China's basic system of governing the country is the mixed economic system composed of three layers of capital economically, and the institutional system based on the division of labor and cooperation among the three powers politically. We cannot underestimate the effectiveness of this system. From an economic point of view, since the reform and opening-up, we have begun to embark on the mixed economic system. China has maintained long-term stability and development in the whole world economy. From the Asian financial crisis in 1997–1998, to the global financial crisis in 2007–2008, and then to the current COVID-19 pandemic crisis, China basically relied on the mutual cooperation of various economic components to overcome various problems, and did not let these crises affect the healthy development of our economy. From a political point of view, this is the same. Some American friends of mine often proudly say that although there are problems in the democratic system, yet democracy has an error correction mechanism. At the same time, they think that there is no error correction mechanism in China's political system. I said, from the experience, that is not the case. Let's compare several presidents in the United States since the 1980s, from

Reagan, George H.W. Bush, Clinton, George W. Bush, Obama, Trump to Biden. There have been seven presidents, but have they ever corrected their mistakes? Since George H.W. Bush launched the Gulf War, there is hardly one day when the United States is not at war. The War is wrong and the American people are also anti-war, but the mistakes have not been corrected. But on the other hand, in China, no major mistakes or what we call subversive mistakes occurred either in theory or in practice since the 1980s. The Communist Party of China has a strong error correction mechanism, while the United States has no error correction mechanism, because democracy does not have the ability to correct mistakes. With the development of social politics and economy, there will be a crisis. If a crisis occurs, it will not be possible to solve the problems by relying on enterprises, non-governmental organizations (NGOs) and various civil society organizations (CSOs) alone. At this time, there must be an effective government. Although the United States recognizes that the war is wrong, yet no political party has the ability to correct this mistake. It is very important that China now have an effective government. Of course, we should also pay attention to not to be arrogant. General Secretary Xi Jinping has emphasized that we should not make subversive mistakes. We need to keep this in mind at all times.

Leading the Modernization of the Country with the Modernization of the Governing Party

We must lead the modernity of the country with the modernity of the Party and lead the modernization of the country with the modernization of the Party. The Communist Party of China is a leading political party. It must lead our socialist construction and lead our Chinese modernization. If a party wants to lead the modernization of the country, it must realize modernization itself. If a party itself cannot realize modernization, then how can it lead the modernization of the country? This is an obvious fact. I studied in the United States in the early 1990s. At that time, the West predicated all day that the Communist Party of China would live for several days, several months, several years and so on. They believed that the Communist Party of China was a very feudal and backward party, and it was out of date. But the question is that, if the Communist Party of China is feudal and backward, then how can China be more advanced than the West in many respects. This cannot make sense. The

Communist Party of China is the governing party, and if the Communist Party of China is feudal, then China also moves toward feudalization. The West should look into the Communist Party of China realistically. Compared with the political parties in the West, the Communist Party of China is one of the few political parties in the world that can pursue modernity. Since modern times, the political parties in the West have been very advanced, because in the early days, the political parties in the West were ruled by elites, and elites were the vanguard and could make the country go toward the advanced nature. However, now the party politics in the West have moved toward populist politics, governing the country with the so-called public opinion. Public opinion is indeed very important, but if everything is based on public opinion, then this party will lose its leadership. In the past, Mr. Lee Kuan Yew said that a party should have a long-term vision. Even if some policies are implemented now, they will be regarded as not obeying public opinion, or even will be opposed by public opinion, thus encountering great social resistance. However, so long as this political party thinks it is beneficial to the future of the country and it is in line with the future interests of this country, even if ordinary people oppose it, it must be pursued. Because ordinary people cannot see the future, most of them only pursue immediate interests.

Then, in what way does the Communist Party of China realize its modernity and advanced nature? In what way does the Communist Party of China have the ability to lead the modernization of the country? I think there are mainly five points as follows:

First, the Communist Party of China is a mission-oriented political party. The Communist Party of China governs by fulfilling its mission. The mission is the promise made by the Communist Party of China to the Chinese people. Therefore, we not only have the Five-Year Plan and the Ten-Year Plan, but also have the "two-step" strategic plan proposed by the 19th CPC National Congress, that is, we will basically realize socialist modernization on the basis of building a moderately prosperous society in all respects from 2020 through 2035, and from 2035 through 2050, on the basis of basically realizing modernization, we will build our country into a great modern socialist country that is prosperous, democratic, civilized, harmonious and beautiful. In addition, we also have the First Centenary Goal and the Second Centenary Goal. However, the political parties in the West revolve around elections, and it is impossible for them to have a long-range planning. Because the Communist Party of China is a mission-oriented political party, it will have a long-range plan. For a political party, there are many tools and means to help it realize its mission. For the West, it is the politics of ballot. 51 out of 100 votes can be in power. So long as you win in the election, it does not matter whether the promise you made during the election can be fulfilled or not. If you cannot fulfil it, you have no responsibility. You can shift the responsibility to the opposition party and you have no responsibility. All the mistakes are from the opposition party. As a result, all political parties shirk their responsibilities to each other. The political parties in the West have evolved into "mutual veto parties".

Second, the Communist Party of China is an open political party. The West always thinks that China is a "one-party dictatorship", while we think that China implements the system of multiparty political participation under the leadership of the Communist Party of China. Because there is only one governing party, in this sense, we also can say China is a one-party system. However, the "one-party system" is not a "one-party dictatorship", because the Communist Party of China is an open one-party system. I call the Chinese system "internal pluralism" and the Western system "external pluralism". In the West, if you do not like the Republican Party, you can support the Democratic Party. If you do not like the Democratic Party, you can support the Republican Party. If you do not like both, then you can also form your own political party. This is external pluralism. There is only one governing party and only one political process in China, but this governing party is open and this political process is also open. All social and economic interests can access this political party, enter this political process, and make the interests develop in a balanced way through various democratic means such as consultation within the political party and within the political process. In addition, this party's recruitment of talents is also open to all social groups, which is related to China's previous meritocracy. In the Chinese system in the past, the society was divided into the four classes, that is, the *shi* (gentry scholars), the *nong* (peasant farmers), the *gong* (artisans and craftsmen) and the *shang* (merchants and traders). Anyone could enter the class of the political management through the imperial examination. In the past, although the imperial power belonged to the specific families, yet the power of the prime ministers was open to the society and many prime ministers in history were born of poverty. Since modern times, the party power replaced the imperial power, but the party power and the imperial power have different properties, because party power itself is open. Therefore, we have an open political system and our management class comes from all corners of the country and different places. As a result, the interests are diversified, and we can realize balanced development through coordination and consultation within the system.

Third, the Communist Party of China is a political party that places great emphasis on social participation. This is especially reflected in the "whole-process people's democracy" that we are emphasizing now. The realization of democracy in the West is mainly through the elections of presidents and prime ministers once every four years or once every five years. The people exercise their right to participate when voting, and it is usually difficult for the people to participate in the democratic process. There used to have media supervision in the West, and media supervision was regarded as the fourth independent power. However, in the previous times when the elites governed and when the proportion of the middle class was large, this could be achieved. At that time, the media supervision power did not lead to social division, but now this supervision has a big problem. In the case of social division, it is difficult for the media to implement supervision, and the media itself is also an important factor that cause social division. In the past, in the United States, even if the Republican Party was a little to the right and the Democratic Party was a little to the left, both parties needed to take into account the interests of the middle class which accounted for about 70% of the total population. Both parties disagreed with each other, but they did not go to extremes. Nowadays, the proportion of the middle class in the United States has shrunk to about 50%, the American society has become divided, and the political parties also has moved toward polarization. From the distribution of the votes in the United States, we can see the signs of division. When the middle class was large, 30% supported the Republican Party, 30% supported the Democratic Party, and the remaining 40% were not clear. The distribution of the political parties was not clear, but it was a stable force. Now is it a good phenomenon that the voter turnout of Trump and Biden is very high? When we were studying political science, we were told that a country with a higher voter turnout is more democratic. If the voter turnout is only 30%, this country is not democratic. Actually, it is not the case. The high voter turnout is a manifestation of low social trust and lack of social trust. In the past, only one people voted in a family, and a few people voted in a community. Everyone trusted each other and did not need to vote. Everyone believed that others could make the right choice instead of them, so the voter turnout was relatively low. However, the American society is very divided now. Everyone only believes in their own votes and people cannot trust each other, so the voter turnout is unusually high and the extremely high voter turnout actually shows social instability. Unlike the United States, viewing from the level of the formal system, China has the system for the election of deputies to the National People's Congress (NPC), and the system of the Chinese People's Political Consultative Conference (CPPCC), in which the NPC deputies and the CPPCC members at various levels, including townships, counties, cities, provinces and the whole country, are selected from the public to exercise the right to vote or contribute policy suggestions. In addition, there are also various organizations and societies, such as All-China Federation of Industry and Commerce (ACFIC), All-China Federation of Trade Unions (ACFTU), The Communist Youth League of China (CYLC), All-China Women's Federation (ACWF). In recent years, various types of think tanks have been added. Since entering the era of the Internet, social media has been added again. Now many top-level designs and policies collect public opinion through various channels.

I call the Communist Party of China a "party in society", that is, a party that exists in society. We have more than 96 million party members from a broad range of 1.4 billion people. In contrast to the United States, under the American electoral system, although the president can serve for two terms at most, yet the Congress of the United States can hold office for life if it has the ability. In China, on the other hand, among the party representatives, the Central Committee, the National People's Congress, the Chinese People's Political Consultative Conference all retire at the age of retirement in accordance with the regulations. The number of our political participation is actually far larger than that of the United States. It is only that people's understanding of democracy now is generally influenced by the West too much, and they lack their own definition of democracy. In recent years, we put forward the whole-process people's democracy. We need to make a careful study, find sufficient evidence and sort out which parts in our people's democracy are embodied in our systems, and what parts still need to be improved.

Fourth, the Communist Party of China is a learning political party. China has a system of party school and a system of administration academy. Both of them are the platforms to provide learning opportunities for party members and cadres again. The periodic learning of the Political Bureau of the Central Committee of the Communist Party of China has become a learning system at the top of the governing party. In particular, our party school system has attracted the attention of many countries now. Some developing countries have also paid attention to this system and some people have proposed to learn from the system of the party school in China. Many of our cadres have graduated from universities, but they cannot stop learning after they work. They must go through the system of party school to make further study and training, learn the latest scientific and technological development, learn the latest economic forms and update their scope of knowledge in real time. Why did Trump fail? Because he is a real estate businessman and does not have the way of governance that conforms to the current economic form in the United States at all. Although he became president, yet his thinking way still stays in the thinking way of a real estate businessman. China arranges the group study sessions of the Political Bureau of the Central Committee of the Communist Party of China many times every year to strengthen communication with high-end think tanks. This does not exist in the West. No matter it is discussed from any angle, the Communist Party of China is a learning organization that constantly seeks progress.

Fifth, the Communist Party of China is a self-revolutionary political party. The future of a political party is nothing more than two kinds: One is being revolutionized and the other is self-revolution. In other words, it is either being reformed or self-reform. Political parties in Western countries are the type of political parties that are revolutionized and reformed. If they do not govern well, they will be ousted by other political parties. If the Communist Party of China is to remain in power for a long time and to realize its effectiveness governance, then it must be self-revolutionary. Self-revolution is especially valued after the 18th CPC National Congress. The establishment of the supervision power, and regaining the supervision power, is just a kind of self-revolution. According to the data released by the CPC Central Commission for Discipline Inspection (CCDI), since the 18th CPC National Congress, the governing party has dealt with about 10% of its party members. About 10% of more than 96 million party members of the Communist Party of China have been dealt with. This is not a small number. Besides, during the decade from the 18th to 20th CPC National Congress, more than 500 central management officials have been punished or even punished by law, which shows the strong self-revolutionary courage of the Communist Party of China. The Report to the 20th CPC National Congress emphasized that the Communist Party of China has found the second answer, the self-revolution, to the question of how to jump out of the historical cycle of rise and fall. The first answer in the past was put forward by Mao Zedong in his "cave-dwelling conversation" with Huang Yanpei. He believed that democracy was the way to solve the problem of regime change. Now in addition to the first answer, the second answer has been found, that is, the self-revolution of the governing party. Even if the West slanders the self-revolution of the Communist Party of China as an internal power struggle, in the case that the Communist Party of China is the only governing party, both self-struggle and self-revolution are necessary. The key is not whether there is a struggle, but whether the struggle has rules and the rule of law.

Institutional Opening Up and Chinese Modernization

Whether we want to realize the modernization at the material level, the institutional level or the human level, the most important thing is development. Previously, it used to be said that "development is the absolute principle" and now it is said that "development is the first priority". They convey the same thing. The question is, under the current situation of the momentous world changes unseen in a century and in the context of the tense international situation, how should China develop in the next steps?

I think that the key is to open up, open up and open up again, and promote Chinese modernization through institutional opening up. In recent years, the central government has proposed the idea of dual circulation. It is necessary to "gradually form a new development pattern with domestic big circulation as the main body, and domestic and international dual circulation promoting each other". In fact, the Central level has always been adjusting the definition of the dual circulation. What do you mean by taking domestic big circulation as the main body? I have always advocated that these regions such as the Pearl River Delta and the Yangtze River Delta, which have developed through external circulation from the very beginning, will have the main task to promote external circulation in the future. If the Yangtze River Delta and the Pearl River Delta, which are dominated by export-oriented economy, turn to the development of internal circulation, then what other regions can develop external circulation? If these regions turn to internal circulation, then it will lead to a serious outcome, that is, China will decouple from the West. Personally, I am very worried about China's decoupling from the West. Because once it is really decoupled, it will be very difficult to go back again. We will very likely become like the Soviet Union back then. After choosing to decouple from the West, we can no longer be linked with the West. Russia has been linked with the West since modern times, but it completely decoupled from the West after the 1917 revolution. Gorbachev, the last leader of the Soviet Union, was pro-Western. Yeltsin, the first president of Russia, was pro-Western. Even Putin was also pro-Western in his early days, he even wanted to join the NATO and relinked with the West, but all failed. It is very important for China to integrate with the West and become one part of the world economy now. Various conditions at that time contributed to China's integration with the West. On the one hand, it was still in the Cold War between the United States and the Soviet Union, and the United States strategically needed China to counterbalance the Soviet Union at that time. In the meantime, the capital of the United States and the West wanted to open up a new battlefield. On the other hand, China has the willingness to open up and integrate with the international economic system established by the West. Various conditions contributed to China's integration into the stage of the world economy, and brought rapid economic development to China for decades.

Similarly, in order to realize Chinese modernization and to promote high-quality development, we still need to give priority to external circulation and still retain opening up. The Report to the 20th CPC National Congress pointed out that we should realize institutional opening up. What is institutional opening up? The rules, regulations, management and standards are the important contents of institutional opening up. Over these years, General Secretary Xi Jinping has been emphasizing the "three optimizations" of the business environment, that is, marketization, legalization and internationalization. In fact, these "three optimizations" are not only applicable to the business environment, but also applicable to various aspects of reform, and more applicable to China's promotion of institutional opening up.

The importance of opening up is almost self-evident. Historically, no economy can achieve sustainable development without opening up. The more open the economy is, the faster it will develop, because only in the case of openness can the flow of the factors of production be realized and the allocation of the factors of production can be realized. The essence of the market is opening up. Without opening up, there will be no market. The Soviet Union was the first typical country to implement the whole-nation system since modern times. The ultimate failure of the Soviet Union stemmed from its non-opening up and from its "closed door". First, the mind is not open. Without opening up, there would be no markets for ideas, and the progress in technology and scientific ideas cannot be achieved. Although the Soviet Union has made good achievements in its early years, yet the lack of the markets for ideas made its innovation capacity insufficient to sustain a country's long-term innovation and competitiveness. Second, the market is not open. Without opening up, there would be no markets. At that time, the Soviet Union implemented the planned economy. At most it only negotiated with the Warsaw Pact market in Eastern Europe or sold some arms to some third world countries such as Vietnam and India. Although the Soviet Union invested a lot in scientific research, yet because there were no large enough markets, scientific research cannot be transformed into production capacity and cannot be rewarded in the market. The economy cannot develop rapidly, and it is difficult to support innovation, which also made scientific and technological progress unsustainable. Therefore, the Soviet Union failed in its competition with the United States.

In recent years, we have emphasized that "the East is rising and the West is declining", believing that the United States is gradually weakening and is failing. This statement is over one-sided. We need to have a scientific and rational understanding. This judgment of "rising in the East and declining in the West" is partially correct. China and India in the East rose rapidly, but the statement of "declining in the West" is wrong. The West is not declining, but rising a little more slowly. It is undeniable that the United States is more advanced than us in many aspects. The core of America's strength lies not in its claimed democracy, but in its nature of opening up.

The United States has several key open systems. First, an open scientific and technological innovation system for enterprises; second, an open financial system; third, an open system for education and talents. These three open systems are interrelated and mutually reinforcing.

It must be realized that the principle of opening up in the United States is the principle of reciprocity, that is, "I will open to you only if you are open to me", but in many key areas, the United States has always practiced unilateral opening up according to its own needs. In particular, its openness in the system of education and talents cannot be compared with other countries. The United States was originally an immigrant country. During World War I and World War II, the United States attracted a large number of European scientists, and during the Cold War, the United States again attracted a large number of scientists who ran out of the Soviet Union and Eastern Europe. In a half-century-long competition between the United States and the Soviet Union, the Soviet Union only had the talents of the country itself, while the United States used the talents from all over the world, including those who ran out of the Soviet Union, to compete with the Soviet Union and finally defeated the Soviet Union. The same is true today. The United States is using the talents around the world, including the talents from China, to compete with China. Since the reform and opening-up, China has sent millions of talents to the United States, and most of them still chose to stay in the United States. I have always believed that if China wants to compete with the United States, it must share a slice of the international talent market with the United States.

Even in today's China, its openness is far from enough. Let's take Shenzhen as an example. It is very proud to be the first-tier city in the reform and opening-up, because Shenzhen is regarded as China's Silicon Valley. But as far as its degree of openness is concerned, Shenzhen is still difficult to compare with the Silicon Valley in the United States. The proportion of the foreign people in the Silicon Valley in the United States has reached 60%, while the proportion of the foreign people in Shenzhen is basically negligible. Looking at the two Bay Areas in San Francisco and New York again, the proportion of the foreign people there is about 40%, while what is the proportion of the foreign people in the Yangtze River Delta region? And what is the proportion of the foreign people in the Guangdong-Hong Kong-Macao Greater Bay Area? The number and proportion of foreign talents should be an important indicator to measure the degree of internationalization of a city. How many foreign professionals are there in Shanghai as an international metropolis? According to the statistics by the American Chamber of Commerce in Shanghai, in the past ten years, about 20% foreign people chose to leave Shanghai, and 40% foreign people chose to leave Beijing. There were not many international talents in China, and they were greatly reduced after the outbreak of the COVID-19 pandemic. Therefore, China still has a long way to go to realize internationalization at the level of talents. The internationalization mentioned by China is only the internationalization of commodities, because China is the world's largest country of trading in goods, and have realized the internationalization of commodities, but we are far from realizing the internationalization of talents.

We should realize that the problem was not serious when the United States did not regard China as its competitor in the past, but nowadays the United States has regarded China as the main competitor, not only blocking China in the field of high technology, but also seeking systematic decoupling from China. This is very serious. As a response, we still advocate institutional opening up, still continue to connect with the world rules and integrate with the world. Many people say that we are now close to the center of the world stage, and even have stood on the center of the world stage. If so, we need an international outlook even more. As a major country, we need to prevent from ignorant and fearless patriotism, not populist patriotism, but rational patriotism. Economic competition and technological competition depend on real ability, not on words. Entrepreneurs know about this point best. For example, although HUAWEI is suppressed by the United States, yet Mr. Ren Zhengfei has always been very modest, because he knows American technology is very advanced. It must be realized that since modern times, most of the original technologies came from the West. Before World War II it was Europe and after World War II it was the United States. This basic situation is difficult to be completely changed in the foreseeable future. What we are advocating is the "new-type whole-nation system" today. This is the whole-nation system in the state of openness, and is definitely not the Soviet-style innovation on its own and behind closed doors.

China should not only continue to open up, but also practice unilateral opening up. As mentioned above, the United States has emphasized reciprocal opening up in many fields, that is, "I will open to you only if you are open to me". However, the United States has always been practicing unilateral opening up in terms of its needs, especially in terms of talents. Today's China must also open up unilaterally, even if the United States and some Western countries blockade us and do not open up to us, we still open up to them. Our country now is in a very critical period. In the previous several decades, we were fortunate to seize every opportunity brought about by the reform and opening-up and realized rapid modernization. During these several decades, our modernization and globalization have moved toward the same direction, and realized the mutual promotion and reinforcement between globalization and modernization. Under the current circumstances that the West is promoting anti-globalization, we need to realize Chinese modernization and continue to open up to the outside world even more. We cannot follow the example of the Soviet Union or China before the reform and opening-up, and carry out modernization on our own behind closed doors.

The Report to the 20th CPC National Congress, made it clear that "Chinese modernization is socialist modernization under the leadership of the Communist Party of China. It has both the common characteristics of the modernization in all countries and the Chinese characteristics based on its own national conditions". Chinese modernization is based on the general characteristics of socialism, emphasizing the universal part of socialist modernization first, and then emphasizing our own characteristics in China, so as to achieve the balanced development in both aspects, instead of just emphasizing Chinese characteristics. Everything is a combination of universality and particularity. We should not overemphasize particularity, and more emphasize that we have generality, because only in this way can Chinese modernization has global significance. As a matter of fact, this is also the case.

Appendix 3: Traditional Chinese Economics and Chinese Modernization[3]

My topic today is how to combine traditional Chinese economics and Chinese modernization so as to discuss how traditional Chinese economics can contribute to the realization of Chinese modernization. The 20th National Congress of the Communist Party of China (CPC) clearly put forward the concept of "Chinese modernization". I think it is necessary to have ideological and theoretical guidance for the realization of Chinese modernization. So, what kind of theories and ideas do we use to guide Chinese modernization? For a long time after the May Fourth Movement, and even when I was in the University in the 1980s, many people still thought that modernization was Westernization. However, it is not the case. Today, we have made it clear that the modernization of China is not Westernization, so we put forward the concept of "Chinese modernization".

[3] This article is based on the keynote speech delivered by the author at the second China Business Ethics Conference (December 3, 2022), which was guided by China Association for Ethical Studies (CAES) and Zhejiang Federation of Humanities and Social Sciences (ZFHSS), and which was co-sponsored by the Research Center for Ethics and Moral Construction at Renmin University of China (a key research base of humanities and social science of the Ministry of Education) and Zhejiang Gongshang University.

Z. Yongnian, *The Great Convergence VS. The Great Divergence*,
https://doi.org/10.1007/978-981-96-7846-4

The modernization of any country has both similarities and dissimilarities with other countries. On a global scale, I think modernization actually can be divided into at least three levels: the modernization at the material level, the modernization at the human level and the institutional modernization between the material level and the human level.

Let's first look at modernization in the material sense. With regard to the modernization at the material level, there is not much disagreement between China and the West. Except for a few religious groups in the world, such as the ascetic groups in Nepal, the common people all seek prosperity and better life. At the same time, modernization in material sense is relatively easy to measure. If you build a car with a speed of 100 kilometers per hour, and he builds a car with a speed of 200 kilometers per hour, people will think that the car with a speed of 200 kilometers per hour is more modern than the car with a speed of 100 kilometers per hour. Of course, the manifestations of material modernization are different. Although there are all high-rise buildings in all countries, and these high-rise buildings reflect the civilization and culture of all countries to varying degrees, yet they are expressed in different forms.

In terms of human modernization, China and the West share some common values and they also have different or special values. People cannot choose the civilization and culture which they were born into, but everyone is a person with civilization and a person with culture. Therefore, human modernization does not mean that each of us becomes a Westerner and all accept Western values. Even if a person changes his or her previous long gown and white coat into a suit or vice versa, his or her thoughts and ways of thinking may still be Chinese-style or American-style.

Institutional modernization lies between material modernization and human modernization, and it is an important dimension to adjust material modernization and human modernization. In measuring institutional modernization, we should not only see which institution can promote material modernization and which institution can promote human modernization, but also see whether it can coordinate the relationship between human modernization and material modernization. If these two cannot be coordinated, there will be great problems in modernization. Although all countries pursue modernization, yet modernization may produce destructive forces. In some countries, the old social system has been destroyed, but the new social system cannot be established, so an effective institutional system is needed to adjust it. The previous revolution in Iran, the development of Turkey in modern times, and the modernization of many developing countries since World War II all have the lessons in this respect.

In my point of view, since we have put forward the proposition of "Chinese modernization", we should answer a key question, that is, what kind of approach should we choose to pursue Chinese modernization and what kind of theories should we use to guide Chinese modernization.

Therefore, I would like to combine traditional Chinese economics and Chinese modernization and share some of my views today.

Why do we say like that? Today our economy is facing very serious problems, and we need to solve these economic problems. So, what is the problem? What is the solution to the problem? This involves the question of Chinese economics. Does China have its own economics today? Generally speaking, we still do not have Chinese economics, and all we have are Western economics. Even if there is a little bit of it, it is very thin and not thick. By the end of 2021, the country has carried out the rectification of the three base camps of private enterprises, that is, education and training, the Internet and the real estate. This rectification of course is very important. In the long run, the purpose of the rectification is to provide a better institutional foundation for the development of private enterprises. However, because there are some problems in the way of rectification, mainly through administration means and movement means, so far, private enterprises are still sluggish. Whether it is in the Yangtze River Delta or in the Pearl River Delta, many private entrepreneurs are still in a state of "lying flat".

So, how can we solve China's problems? Solving problems requires thought. We have been talking about the "market of thought", but what thought in China's current markets of economic thought can be used to guide China's private enterprises out of their predicament? Or to help China's economy as a whole get out of its predicament? This question must be solved, because if the economy in China does not develop, how can we realize Chinese modernization? It is not difficult to observe that in the markets of economic thought in China, it mainly revolves around the doctrine or economic thought of the "three people". One is Marx, the other is Keynes, and the other is Hayek. There are also some others, but they are all related to these three great thinkers.

Marx's thought is certainly the guiding ideology of our Communist Party of China. Without the guidance of the thought of Marx, there would be no China that people see today. However, don't forget. From

Mao Zedong, to Deng Xiaoping, and then to Xi Jinping, the leaders have been emphasizing Marxism adapting to the Chinese context. This time, the Report to the 20th CPC National Congress, made a special exposition of Marxism adapting to the Chinese context, which shows its importance. However, this does not mean that our circles of economics have realized the Sinicization of Marxism. Although from any angle, today's China is the country that has the largest number of institutions, and also has the largest number of scholars for the research of Marxism. However, does our Sinicization of Marxism have a good job? Obviously, it has not been, or it is nearly not enough. This is especially manifested in our policy of deteriorating attitudes toward private enterprises.

It must be clearly realized that Marxism is the product under the background of capitalism in Western Europe. At 2021 China Business Ethics Conference, I also emphasized that in modern times, there have been two lines in Europe on the issue of property rights. One line is from Adam Smith's liberalism to contemporary neoliberalism, believing that "private property is sacred and inviolable", and the other line is from Rousseau to Marx, and down to the socialist model of the Soviet Union, and then to China's planned economic system before the reform and opening-up, believing that all problems are caused by private property. The first line advocates the protection of private ownership and the second line advocates the elimination of private property, the elimination of class, and even the elimination of the country itself in the future.

So, what does Marxism adapting to the Chinese context really mean? I personally think that we have accepted the Marxist concept of building a fair and just society. Today we are promoting the path to common prosperity in order to realize the Chinese modernization of common prosperity for all people. This is to practice the core part of Marxist economics. However, we need to realize that Marx put forward the methods of eliminating private ownership, eliminating class and eliminating country, and these methods were aimed at the European society of that time. If we today still view private enterprises or state-owned enterprises with the book-oriented Marxism, then it is not Marxism adapting to the Chinese context. The idea of eliminating private property advocated by the book-oriented Marxism has been experimented. The Soviet Union was the most typical model, and it was also such a model in China before its reform and opening-up. We have had so many painful historical experiences and we can accept the lessons from them. Now we must reconsider these problems once again. When Communism is realized in the future, it may be possible for the elimination of class and the elimination of country, but it is just a matter of the future. Since the reform and opening-up, beginning from the 1980s, we have been emphasizing that we are still in the primary stage of socialism and the primary stage of socialism will still be a long-term process. Therefore, it is not a realistic way to guide the economy of China with the book-oriented Marxism. From the empirical point of view, the book-oriented Marxism advocates the elimination of private property, which is not in line with the actual conditions in China. The Constitution has established that China is the socialist market economic system with public ownership as the mainstay and diverse forms of ownership economies developing together. From the practical point of view, blaming private enterprises once economic problems arise will not only bring out huge uncertainty for private enterprises, but it is also unfair.

The second is Keynesianism. A few years ago, there was a debate in domestic academic circles about which is better, Keynesianism or Liberalism. In my view, I think that there is not much point for such a controversy. To begin with, both are the products of Western economic development, and they are aimed at Western economic problem, so it is hard to say which one is closer to China's economic reality. Even if they are used to explain China's economy, the explanation is often superficial. Furthermore, in the words of Marx, economics is used to explain and transform the world. Any thought in economics is put forward in response to the problems of that time. This determines that economics is time-sensitive.

Keynesianism played a very large role in history, especially in the West after the Great Depression in the 1930s. After 1945, most Western countries, including the United States, all accepted Keynesianism. From 1945 to the 1970s, Western countries implemented Keynesian economics, mainly by the countries intervening in the economy in various ways. During that period, the Western welfare society achieved great achievements, and the size of the middle class expanded. But is Keynesianism effective for today's China? There is no problem for the government to intervene in the economy, but the question is how to intervene in the economy? If it is implemented in the specific policy level, Keynesianism emphasizes that the government should engage in public works and invest in infrastructure construction. But we must think that our large-scale infrastructure construction such as roads, bridges, and high-speed rail, has been basically completed, especially in the eastern coastal areas. Infrastructure construction has also injected great momentum into

China's economic growth in the past. Of course, there is still a lot of room for improvement now. However, if this kind of public construction investment is made on a large scale once again, it will cause great waste. In particular, for the western regions, we are now carrying out large-scale infrastructure construction in the western regions, but there are not many economic activities in the western regions. If you look at Japan, you will know that excessive infrastructure construction will cause great waste. Japan is a country with excessive investment in public infrastructure, but now with the shrinking population, many public facilities are being abandoned, resulting in great waste. We need public investment, but we cannot continue with these same public investments that we used to make. Now, when we go to the local places, the direct thing is these traditional public investments. Therefore, roads and bridges are repaired and dug up, dug up and repaired again. GDP is here, but it does not have much benefits to the people's livelihood economy. In today's China, Keynesianism-style investment is needed, but it should be placed on the area what we call soft infrastructure, including social security, medical care, education, public housing and so on. Hard infrastructure has been completed, but we are still reluctant to invest in soft infrastructure. Therefore, when we talk about Keynesianism, we should be careful and think about what kind of Keynesianism it is and which part of Keynesianism we can adopt. After World War II, in the West, soft infrastructure construction has been the most important part of Keynesianism. Considering the current realities in China, simply advocating Keynesianism is not beneficial to the recovery of private enterprises. As I will analyze below, a major problem encountered by private enterprises is the problem of investment space, which is caused by the continuous expansion of borders of state-owned enterprises.

The third is Hayek's liberalism. Hayek's *The Road to Serfdom* can be said to be the Bible of China's liberal economists. So, can Hayekism save China's economy? To start with, Hayek's thought is not in line with the reality of China. Hayek' s thought was based on the belief from Adam Smith that "private property is sacred and inviolable". China's reality is a mixed economic system that is composed of various ownership components such as state-owned enterprises and private enterprises. I have made an investigation before. For more than 2000 years, there have been state-owned enterprises in China, and the existence of state-owned enterprises in China are almost eternal. Whether it is "private property is sacred and inviolable", or it is "state-owned property is sacred and inviolable", they are all the products of the West. The former is represented by Britain and the United States, while the latter is represented by the Soviet Union. The former is having big problems now, because it is too capital dominated, while the latter has failed. These two models have not found their social and cultural roots in China. The Liberals want the government not to intervene in the economy, but in China's environment of civilization and culture, this is completely an illusion. The fully public ownership economy has failed in China, and it is not feasible, but the Liberal view that the country does not intervene in the economy also cannot work in China. The Eastern and Western economic philosophies and economic theories are not the same. During the period from ancient Greece to the Roman Empire in the West, their economic thought was similar to that in the East, and they all believed that economic management is one part of the government responsibility. Since modern times, with the rise of capitalism, politics and economy have been separated from each other, and the market was regarded as a self-sufficient and independent system. In other words, economy and society were originally embedded with each other, but now they are de-embedded. However, in our East, not only in China, but also in the whole Confucian Civilization circle (other civilizations are similar), all believe that economic management is one part of the government responsibility. Since modern times, promoting economic development is further regarded as one part of the government responsibility. To put it simply, Hayek's liberalism is not in line with the reality of China, nor can it solve the problems faced by China.

Of course, there are also some other schools of economics in the West, such as Neo- Institutional Economics and Monetarism. We have talked a lot about these schools, but these schools of economics are also the products of the Western economic environment and are branches of Western economics. For example, the premise of Neo-Institutional Economics is the theory of private property rights. There are too many Western economic theories in China now, but there is a lack of economics which is based on China's experience and practice, and which can explain China's economic practice. Therefore, in recent years, we have advocated the construction of our own independent knowledge system. I am very supportive of building an independent knowledge system, and I myself have been advocating it for more than ten years. When I was studying in the West, I found that Western theories are all based on the Western practical experiences and are used to explain Western economic phenomenon. We still have not yet constructed our own economic theories on the basis of our own practical experiences now. Of course, this does not mean that we should reject Western economics, but that we should construct our own theories in the process of dialogue with Western economics.

We are determined to construct an economic theory based on China's experiences and practices. This is entirely possible. The ancient Chinese texts such as *Guanzi* and *Yan Tie Lun* all contain very good Chinese economic theories. In traditional Chinese economic theories, most of those Western economic theories and concepts are involved. However, although the ancient people in China have observed these phenomena, yet they did not present or express them in the form of economics or social science in the West.

Compared with Western economics, many contents are very excellent in traditional Chinese economics. Here I want to talk about one point. In contrast to Western economics, traditional Chinese economics place more emphasis on the principle of balance and equilibrium (*junheng*), the principle of level and stability (*pingzhun*) as well as the light-heavy (*qingzhong*) principle. From *Guanzi* to *Yan Tie Lun*, to Mao Zedong's On the Ten Major Relationships and Jiang Zemin's On the Twelve Major Relationships, and then to today Xi Jinping's emphasis on the "Five-Sphere Integrated Plan" (that is, economy, politics, culture, society and ecology), the core thought of all these expositions is to be balanced, to be stabilized and to be weighed. Modern people are very interesting. Sometimes they translate Western "political economics" into "light-heavy economics". This translation version is very interesting.

So, how can we judge and solve the current economic problems in China according to the concepts in the light-heavy principle and the principle of level and stability? Here, I want to briefly mention a few points for your reference.

First, the most important thing is to maintain the neutrality of policy. Whether it is for light-heavy economics or for level-stability economics, the core point is the neutral policy of the government. This is very important for the Chinese culture which views the golden mean (*zhongyong*) as its core values. In the traditional culture of China, the Legalism tends to emphasize state monopoly and considers that private monopoly is toxic. Confucianism, on the contrary, opposes state monopoly and considers state monopoly is toxic. At the practical level, or at the level of economic practice, we combine Confucianism and Legalism. People view state-owned capital and private capital, state-owned enterprises and private enterprises in a relatively neutral and impartial approach, while people will not view state-owned capital and private capital, state-owned enterprises and private enterprises from an ideological and political standpoint. In this regard, tradition is much more advanced than we are now, because some of us now view state-owned capital and private capital, state-owned enterprises and private enterprises from ideological and political standpoints. What traditional economics emphasizes is balance and equilibrium. On the basis of the division of labor, it is necessary to see whether state-owned capital and private capital are developing in a balanced way. This is exactly what we need today and what we need is a balanced development of state-owned capital and private capital, state-owned enterprises and private enterprises on the basis of the division of labor.

Second, the structure of state-owned enterprises and private enterprises needs to be adjusted. Why are private enterprises now "lying flat"? Today the country's credit is very loose and some large private enterprises themselves still have funds, but the phenomenon of "lying flat" still exists in private enterprises. Some people think that this has something to do with the rectification in 2021. Although it is related to the rectification in 2021, yet it is mainly because private enterprises lack space, and cannot solve the problem of "what to do". To a large extent, this is related to the fact that state-owned enterprises occupy too much economic space. The spatial structure of state-owned enterprises and private enterprises, state-owned capital and private capital needs to be adjusted. After the reform in China was carried out during the periods of Jiang Zemin and Zhu Rongji in the 1990s, the state-owned enterprises and private enterprises have a more reasonable structure. In the reform at that time, after a large number of state-owned enterprises with non-efficiency and low efficiency are privatized, private enterprises developed rapidly. After that, the problem of "the state sector advances, the private sector retreats" that people often talked about appeared after the development of private enterprises, because there were no private enterprises with substantive significance before. However, in recent years, the phenomenon of "the state sector advances, the private sector retreats" has been discussed by people. There is basically no problem from the perspective of central state-owned enterprises, because the number of central state-owned enterprises is not large, and they are all in the areas that are of vital importance to the national economy. The main problem lies in the fact that local governments have developed too many local state-owned enterprises for these years. These enterprises occupied too much economic space, and their efficiency is very low, or even inefficient. For this part of state-owned enterprises, the further reform is still needed today, and the more effective way is similar to privatization in the 1990s. But if privatization is not feasible, it is also possible to implement what modern people called the "government-supervised and business-run", that is, state-owned capital can also be operated in the way of private enterprises and in the way of markets.

Third, it is necessary to create an open environment for large enterprises. Compared with the corporate system in the West, China's corporate system has a big difference, that is, whether it is state-owned enterprises or private enterprises, they are closed to each other and do not open up to each other. For state-owned enterprises in China, each enterprise is self-enclosed and does everything by itself. The relationship between our large private enterprises is also the same. This lack of opening up has two fatal weakness. On the one hand, if large enterprises do not open up, small enterprises cannot grow up, and at the same time, large enterprises themselves create monopoly. On the other hand, the lack of opening up hinders technological progress. In today's society, technological progress is based on the division of labor, and the more detailed the division of labor is, the faster technological progress is. If you go to the United States, there is a company that produces everything by itself and is self-sufficient? Let's take the Boeing Company as an example. There are tens of thousands of companies that serve Boeing, they provide different parts and components for Boeing, and different parts and components are produced by different companies. This means that there is a competition between different parts and components, and the improvement of one part and component will force the improvement of another part and component. Enterprises in China, especially state-owned enterprises, do not open up to each other, let alone private enterprises. Therefore, from the perspective of technological progress, the principle of the division of labor between large enterprises has not been established. This is a big problem. Large enterprise must open up. If state-owned enterprises, especially large state-owned enterprises, open up to private enterprises, then there is a lot of room for them to be released, and released to private enterprises. Moreover, we also need to advocate that large private enterprises should open up to small private enterprises, and that they should not do everything by themselves. It is a universal rule that technology will not make progress if you do everything yourself. And it is also the same in China. In fact, the mutual opening up between enterprises, especially between state-owned enterprises and private enterprises, will be much more effective than the PPT implemented in recent years. The PPT model, which facilitates the entry of state-owned capital into private enterprises, has produced a series of problems. First, it led to the "chaotic scurrying" of state-owned capital, squeezing the space of private enterprises and making the space between state-owned enterprise and private enterprises unbalanced. Second, it changed the logic of capital operation, resulting in low efficiency. State-owned capital and private capital each have their own operating logic. Once state-owned capital enters the field of private capital, private capital will change its original operating logic and gradually evolve into the operating logic of state-owned capital. Third, it is leading to the loss of state-owned capital. State-owned capital is not an abstract entity, but enters the field of private capital through the agents of the country. The agents of the country have their own interests, and are not necessarily represent the interests of the country. In the meantime, private capital allows the entry of state-owned capital, and also has its own purpose. This purpose is more private. Under such circumstances, when state-owned capital and private capital mix together, state-owned capital is easily lost.

Fourth, it is necessary to have a financial structure with level and stability. The country's credit is very loose, but small and medium-sized enterprises still cannot get the financial support that they need. Why is that? It is quite simply. It's because the financial structure is not level and stable enough. The natural service targets of large-scale state-owned banks are large-scale state-owned enterprises or large private enterprises. Although these state-owned banks also have loan service sectors for small and medium-sized enterprises, yet most of these sectors have been set up under administrative and political pressure, because economically, they often lack sufficient incentives to serve private enterprises, especially micro, small and medium-sized enterprises. Viewing from experiences, they either serve state-owned enterprises or large private enterprises. As a result, state-owned enterprises do not have incentives to develop, let alone create, because they can often get money with too low interest rates. And those large private enterprises themselves have money and do not need the money of the banks, but the banks still desperately give loans to them, which leads many large private enterprises to rashly invest and expand, and later to go to the road of death, because it is very easy for them to borrow money. Even more seriously, those small and medium-sized enterprises that really need money still cannot get money. Therefore, a large number of small and medium-sized state-owned banks or private banks need to be set up to specially serve small and medium-sized enterprises. Moreover, the assessment standards of small and medium-sized state-owned banks should be different from those of large state-owned banks. If they have the same assessment standards, it still cannot solve the problem. It should be realized that it was not the large banks on Wall Street that helped the United States out of the global financial crisis in 2007–2008, but those small and medium-sized banks, especially community banks. However, we do not have such a financial structure at all. The Chinese always hope the bigger the better, and the stronger the bigger. So, what about the small ones? Who will help small enterprises? The country needs to introduce a policy to build a large number of small and medium-sized financial institutions or state-owned banks to specially serve small and medium-sized enterprises. If the problem of financial structure cannot be solved, small and medium-sized enterprises in China will still not be able to develop. Over these years, the country has been advocating the "specialized and sophisticated" small and medium-sized private enterprises which produce "novel and unique" products, but have they received sufficient financial help? Many enterprises are struggling to survive.

Fifth, it is necessary to build a unified national market. The disadvantages due to the lack of a unified national market are also reflected in the management and control of this COVID-19 pandemic. As you can see, it goes without saying that unified rules have been established throughout the whole country, even if the rules cannot be unified within each province. In Guangdong province, COVID-19 nucleic acid test results in Shenzhen and Guangzhou do not recognize each other. How much does this add to the economic cost? This phenomenon is not only manifested in the mutual recognition of nucleic acid test results, but also in various aspects including environmental protection, land, labor, medical care and education. All these aspects do not have uniform standards. Without uniform rules and uniform standards, a unified national market cannot be formed. Therefore, the Report to the 20th CPC National Congress, especially emphasized that these respects such as rules, regulations, management and standards should be unified. Without uniform rules and standards, it will be difficult to release productive forces. In recent years, we have discussed internal circulation and hoped to develop internal economy through internal circulation, but there are many obstacles in this regard. For example, we could have gained new impetus for development through the east–west circulation. The eastern coastal provinces have advantages in capital, manufacturing and technology, while the western provinces have advantages in labor, land and resources. If these two are combined together, the two sides can get new development impetus. But now if the eastern provinces go to invest in the western provinces, the negotiation between an eastern province and a western province may be more difficult than that between two countries. In fact, international institutions such as the World Bank have long found that enterprises in China tend to do business with foreign (Western) enterprises, and they do not like to do business with other enterprises in China. Provinces in China tend to deal with foreign countries, and they do not like to deal with other provinces in China. Why is this happening so? It's simple. It is because we do not have uniform rules. When China's enterprises deal with foreign enterprises, at least everyone has a contract that can be fulfilled. But if an eastern enterprise goes to the northeast or the northwest part in China, it will be difficult to have this guarantee. Therefore, building a unified national market can greatly release labor productivity. People are increasingly aware that the next reform that can release productive forces is to build a unified national market. This point of view has its rich historical evidence. What is a modern country? Modern countries expanded into all the corners of the world since they came into being in Europe, and now they are still expanding. Why is that? It is because modern countries are the most effective than all other forms of countries. The reason why it is effective lies in the fact that modern countries have uniform rules and uniform laws. In this sense, the importance of the rule of law is self-evident. However, our country still has not yet had a unified national market up to now. Our unification happens only at the political level and at the administrative level, not at the level of rules, regulations, and laws. The construction of a country under the rule of law has long become our target for our political development. Literally, our laws are also unified. However, the implementation is different from one place to another place. Just like all other places in the world, a unified national market cannot be formed naturally as a result of economic development, but requires many profound reforms.

Sixth, it is necessary to realize institutional opening up. This point is also very important, because opening up is the essential feature of market economy. Without opening up, there will be no market economy. It is quite simply. If Zhejiang province does not open up to the outside world, how can it develop a market economy? How can a city develop a market economy if it does not open up to the outside world? In the past, we emphasized opening up, but now we emphasize institutional opening up and have made great progress in our discourse. Although in recent years, we have been emphasizing greater opening up, yet at the practical level, people's perceptions and feelings are not the same, and even the opposite. This is because our opening up encounters institutional bottlenecks. Therefore, we are now advocating institutional opening up to overcome institutional bottleneck. But the main resistance for institutional opening up still comes from the administrative system. There are not much problems for enterprises, let alone the common people. The main reason is that administrative resistance makes it difficult to realize our institutional opening up. Therefore, institutional opening up needs the reform of the administrative system in the next step. In fact, institutional opening up is not only applicable to opening up to the outside world, but also applicable to opening up to the inside world. The fundamental reason that a unified national market discussed above has not yet been formed lies in the mutual exclusion between all localities and between all enterprises.

Seventh, it is necessary to encourage private enterprises to go global. When we talk about the economy of level and stability, we must also involve international and domestic level and stability. In this regard, Zhejiang is particularly obvious. Zhejiang economy consists of two economies. One is the economy in Zhejiang province and the other is the economy for Zhejiang people. Zhejiang people go everywhere all over the world and all over the country. It is necessary to have a balanced development between domestic markets and international markets. The West also developed like this in its early days. When the domestic markets are saturated, it is necessary to open up overseas markets. However, Western countries went global through colonialism and imperialism, which is a kind of plunder, while we go global through the formation of a kind of division of labor. The next stage for China's going global is very important, especially for the "Belt and Road Initiative". And private enterprises still need to be encouraged to go global. Going global with state-owned enterprises and state-owned capital as the guide has almost completed its phased tasks. State-owned enterprises and state-owned capital are mainly concentrated in the field of infrastructure construction. So, who will engage in the people's livelihood economy? Engaging in the people's livelihood economy is not the advantage of state-owned enterprises, and only by letting private enterprises engaging in the people's livelihood economy will it be effective. When private enterprises go global and engage in the people's livelihood economy, they can also cooperate with local people. This is a win–win situation.

Eighth, it is necessary to set up a professional and neutral decision-making body for economic policy. This institution is very important. Level-stability economics must be embodied at the level of economic policy. So, who will make decisions? Our current decision-making mechanism still need to be improved and reformed. We should not make decisions by just a few economists or a few political figures, but rather include political figures, entrepreneurs and economists in various areas. After discussion, a scientific economic policy will be formed. At the end of 2021, it is necessary to make the three major rectifications of private enterprises (education and training, the real estate and the Internet) in order to lay a foundation for the development of private enterprises. However, whether it is in the scientific or feasible aspect of decision-making, we still made many mistakes. The mistakes develop mainly because we do not have a neutral policy institution to evaluate the consequences of these policies and to envision how these policies will be implemented.

In any case, in order to define China's economic problems and solve China's economic problems, we need a kind of Chinese economics that is built upon Chinese experience and practice. As discussed above, Chinese classical text in economics *Guanzi*, contains a wealth of contents. From this classic, we can deduce many methods to diagnose China's realistic economic problems and solve China's realistic economic problems. We need to make great efforts to carefully sort out traditional Chinese economics and think how to find out China's economic thoughts from traditional economics, so as to promote Chinese modernization in a more effective way. We do not refuse Western economic thoughts, but we need to make Western economic thoughts adapting to the Chinese context, and further merge and integrate Western economics with traditional Chinese economics. Although, as mentioned above, there are many similarities between Western economics and traditional Chinese economics, yet in comparison with Western economics, traditional Chinese economics is rooted on Chinese practical experience, and thus it can better explain and solve China's economic problems.

Index

Z. Yongnian, *The Great Convergence VS. The Great Divergence*, https://doi.org/10.1007/978-981-96-7846-4

D

E

G

Q

R

GPSR Compliance

The European Union's (EU) General Product Safety Regulation (GPSR) is a set of rules that requires consumer products to be safe and our obligations to ensure this.

If you have any concerns about our products, you can contact us on ProductSafety@springernature.com

In case Publisher is established outside the EU, the EU authorized representative is:

Springer Nature Customer Service Center GmbH
Europaplatz 3
69115 Heidelberg, Germany

Batch number: 10725851

Printed by Printforce, the Netherlands